FEUDAL
SOCIETY

MARC BLOCH

FEUDAL
SOCIETY

Translated by
L. A. MANYON

VOLUME
2
SOCIAL CLASSES AND POLITICAL
ORGANIZATION

THE UNIVERSITY OF CHICAGO PRESS

THE UNIVERSITY OF CHICAGO PRESS, CHICAGO 60637
Routledge & Kegan Paul Ltd., London E.C.4, England

Translated from the French LA SOCIÉTÉ FÉODALE. *English
translation* ©*Routledge & Kegan Paul, Ltd. 1961. All rights
reserved. Published 1961. Printed in the United States of
America.*

93 92 91   17
International Standard Book Number: 0–226–05979–0
Library of Congress Catalog Card Number: 61–4322

CONTENTS

v

CONTENTS

CONTENTS

Part V—Ties of Dependence among the Lower Orders of Society

VOLUME 2

SOCIAL CLASSES AND POLITICAL ORGANIZATION

Part VI—Social Classes

Part VII—Political Organization

CONTENTS

PLATES

VOLUME 1

VOLUME 2

PLATES

VOLUME 2
SOCIAL CLASSES AND POLITICAL ORGANIZATION

PART VI
Social Classes

INTRODUCTORY NOTE

THE most characteristic feature of the civilization of feudal Europe was the network of ties of dependence, extending from top to bottom of the social scale. (How such a distinctive structure arose and developed, what were the events and the mental climate that influenced its growth, what it owed to borrowings from a remoter past, we have endeavoured to show in Book I.) In the societies to which the epithet 'feudal' is traditionally applied, however, the lives of individuals were never regulated exclusively by these relationships of strict subjection or direct authority. Men were also divided into groups, ranged one above the other, according to occupation, degree of power or prestige. Moreover, above the confused mass of petty chiefdoms of every kind, there always existed authorities of more far-reaching influence and of a different character. From the second feudal age onwards, not only were the orders of society more and more strictly differentiated; there was also an increasing concentration of forces round a few great authorities and a few great causes. We must now direct our attention to the study of this second aspect of social organization; then we shall at last be in a position to attempt to answer the question which it has been the main purpose of our inquiry to elucidate, namely: by what fundamental characteristics, whether or not peculiar to one phase of Western evolution, have these few centuries deserved the name which thus sets them apart from the rest of European history? What portion of their heritage has been transmitted to later times?

XXI

THE NOBLES AS A *DE FACTO* CLASS

1 THE DISAPPEARANCE OF THE ANCIENT ARISTOCRACIES OF BIRTH

FOR the writers who first gave feudalism its name, for the men of the French Revolution, who worked to destroy it, the idea of nobility seemed inseparably linked with it. It would scarcely be possible, however, to find an association of ideas more palpably false—at least if we set any store by the exact use of historical terms. Certainly there was nothing egalitarian about the societies of the feudal era; but not every dominant class is a nobility. To deserve this name such a class must evidently combine two characteristics. First, it must have a legal status of its own, which confirms and makes effectual the superiority to which it lays claim. In the second place, this status must be hereditary—with the qualification, however, that a limited number of new families may be admitted to it, in accordance with formally established rules. In other words, actual power is not enough, nor is even that form of inheritance (effective though it is in practice) which consists as much in the advantages children enjoy through having parents of high status as in the wealth they may inherit; it is necessary, in addition, that social privileges as well as hereditary succession should be recognized by law. If in France we speak today of the upper middle classes as a capitalist aristocracy, it is only in irony. Even where, as in our modern democratic societies, the legal privileges of the nobility have disappeared, the memory of them keeps class consciousness alive; no one is accepted as a genuine nobleman unless he can prove that they were exercised by his ancestors. In this sense—and it is the only legitimate one—nobility made its appearance relatively late in western Europe. The first lineaments of the institution did not begin to emerge before the twelfth century, and it took definite shape only in the following century when the fief and vassalage were already in decline. Throughout the first feudal age, and in the period immediately preceding it, it was unknown.

In this respect the first feudal age differed from the earlier civilizations whose legacy it had received. The Later Empire had had the senatorial order, from which, under the first Merovingians, despite the disappearance of the legal privileges of former days, the leading Roman subjects of the Frankish king still proudly claimed descent. Among many German peoples

283

there had existed certain families officially described as 'noble'—in the vulgar tongue *edelinge*, which term the Latin texts render as *nobiles* and which, in Franco-Burgundian, long survived in the form *adelenc*. Their status allowed them specific advantages, notably a higher *wergild*; their members, as the Anglo-Saxon documents put it, were 'born dearer' than other men. Descended, so far as we know, from ancient dynasties of local chiefs—the 'chiefs of cantons' mentioned by Tacitus—the majority of them, where the monarchic form of government prevailed, had been gradually dispossessed of their political power in favour of the royal house, which itself was sprung originally from their ranks. They none the less retained some of their original prestige as sacred families.

But these distinctions did not survive the age of the barbarian kingdoms. Many of the *edeling* dynasties no doubt became extinct at an early date. Their very greatness made them the favourite target of private vengeance, proscriptions, and wars. Save in Saxony, very few outlasted the period immediately following the invasions—there were only four, for example, among the Bavarians in the seventh century. Among the Franks, assuming —and this is something that cannot be proved—that they also had known a hereditary aristocracy in former times, it had disappeared before the earliest written records. Similarly, the senatorial order constituted only an unstable and scattered oligarchy. Those families whose pride was founded on ancient memories naturally disappeared in the new kingdoms, where the effective bases of superiority among free men were of quite another type: wealth, with its corollary, power; and the king's service. Both these qualifications, though in practice they often passed from father to son, none the less left the way open for sudden rises and equally sudden falls. By a highly significant restriction of meaning, in England from the ninth or tenth century onwards only the relatives of the king retained the right to the name of *aetheling*.

The most striking feature of the history of the dominant families in the first feudal age is the shortness of their pedigrees—at least if we agree to reject not only the fables invented by the Middle Ages themselves, but also the ingenious though improbable conjectures which in our own day various scholars have founded on very hypothetical principles for the transmission of proper names. The earliest known ancestor of the Welfs, a family who after playing a considerable rôle in West Francia wore the crown of Burgundy from 888 to 1032, was a Bavarian count whose daughter married Louis the Pious. The line of the counts of Toulouse arose under Louis the Pious; that of the marquises of Ivrea, who were later kings of Italy, under Charles the Bald; and that of the Ludolfings, dukes of Saxony, then kings of East Francia and emperors, under Lewis the German. The Bourbons, descended from the Capetians, are probably today the oldest dynasty in Europe. Yet what do we know of the origins of their ancestor, Robert the Strong, who was killed in 866 and who already counted among the magnates of Gaul? Simply the name of his father and the possibility that he may have had Saxon blood.[1] It seems as if inevitably, once this crucial turning-point of the year 800 is reached, obscurity prevails. Moreover, these were particularly ancient houses more or less closely connected with those dynasties—sprung for the most part from Austrasia or the regions beyond the Rhine—to whom the first Carolingians had entrusted the chief positions of authority throughout the Empire. In northern Italy, in the eleventh century, the Attoni were masters of hill and plain over a large area; they were descended from a certain Siegfried, the owner of large estates in the county of Lucca, who died shortly before 950; beyond that date, nothing more can be ascertained. The middle of the tenth century also saw the sudden emergence of the Swabian Zähringen, the Babenbergs (the real founders of Austria), the lords of Amboise. . . . If we turn to feudal lineages of lower rank we lose the trail at a much more recent date.

Now, it is not enough in this case to lay the blame on the poverty of our sources. Undoubtedly, if the charters of the ninth and tenth centuries were less scarce we should discover a few more ancestral links. But the surprising thing is that we should need such chance records at all. In the days of their greatness the Ludolfings, the Attoni, the lords of Amboise, among others, all had their historians. How did it happen that those learned men were unable or unwilling to tell us anything about the ancestors of their masters? It is a fact that the genealogies of Icelandic peasants, transmitted for centuries by a purely oral tradition, are much better known to us than those of our medieval barons. So far as the latter were concerned, it seems evident that no interest was taken in their ancestry till the moment— relatively recent, as a rule—when for the first time one of them attained a really exalted rank. No doubt there were good reasons for thinking that before the chosen date the family history would have offered nothing of special interest; either because in fact it began at a rather humble social level—the celebrated Norman house of Bellême seems to have been descended from an ordinary cross-bowman of Louis d'Outre-Mer[2]—or (a more frequent case) because it had long remained half-concealed in the mass of those petty manorial lords whose origin as a group raises, as we shall see later, such difficult problems. But the chief reason for what appears to be so strange a silence was that these powerful individuals did not constitute a noble class, in the full sense of the word. To speak of nobility is to speak of pedigrees: in the case in point, pedigrees did not matter because there was no nobility.

[1] See the latest account of the problem by J. Calmette, in *Annales du Midi*, 1928.
[2] H. Prentout, 'Les origines de la maison de Bellême' in *Études sur quelques points d'histoire de Normandie*, 1926.

2 DIFFERENT MEANINGS OF THE WORD 'NOBLE'
IN THE FIRST FEUDAL AGE

This is not to say, however, that from the ninth to the eleventh century the word 'noble' (in Latin *nobilis*) was not to be found fairly frequently in the documents. But it had no precise legal meaning and simply indicated an actual or an accepted pre-eminence, in accordance with a variety of different criteria. Almost invariably it involved the idea of a certain distinction of birth; but it also implied a measure of wealth. Thus we find Paul the Deacon (an eighth-century writer who is usually more lucid than in this case), in a commentary on a passage of the *Rule* of St. Benedict, hesitating between, and confusing, these two interpretations.[1] From the beginning of the feudal era these uses of the word 'noble', though too fluctuating to admit of precise definition, at least reflected some major trends, and their very vicissitudes are instructive.

In days when so many men had to agree to hold their lands of a lord, the mere fact of escaping such subjection was a sign of superiority. It is not surprising therefore that the possession of an allod (even if this was no more than a peasant property) should have been sometimes considered a sufficient title to the name 'noble' or *edel*. It is also worth noticing that in the majority of the texts in which petty allodialists appear with this designation, we see them parading it only to surrender it immediately by becoming the tenants or serfs of a more powerful man.

If from the end of the eleventh century onwards we come across scarcely any more 'nobles' of this sort—in reality rather humble folk—the crystallization of the idea of nobility which was then taking place on altogether different lines was not the only reason. In a great part of the West practically the whole social class had disappeared; it had become extinct.

In the Frankish period a great number of slaves had received their freedom. Naturally these intruders were not readily accepted as equals by families which had never been sullied by the servile taint. With the 'free man' (*liber*), who might be a former slave set free or the recent descendant of a freedman, the Romans had not so long before contrasted the pure *ingenuus*; but in the Latin of the decadence the two words had become almost synonymous. An unblemished line was nevertheless genuine nobility in the vague sense in which that word was ordinarily employed. 'To be noble is to count among one's ancestors no one who has been subjected to slavery.' Such was the definition still given, towards the beginning of the eleventh century, by an Italian gloss, systematizing a usage of which we find more than one trace elsewhere.[2] But this use of the term did not survive the changes in social classifications either; as we have seen,

[1] *Bibliotheca Casinensis*, vol. IV, p. 151.
[2] *M.G.H., LL*, vol. IV, p. 557, col. 2, l. 6.

it was not long before the descendants of the former freedmen became for the most part quite simply serfs.

Nevertheless, even among the humble folk there were individuals who, while subjects of a lord as to their land, had none the less managed to retain their personal 'freedom'. Naturally a condition which had become so rare was invested with a particularly honourable character, which it was not contrary to the practices of the time to call 'nobility'. Even a few texts here and there seem to favour this equivalence; but freedom and nobility could never really be regarded as identical. To describe as nobles the mass of so-called free men, many of whom, as tenants, were subject to heavy and humiliating labour services—this idea was too repugnant to the common conception of social values to find general acceptance, and the temporary identification of the words 'noble' and 'free' was destined to leave no enduring traces save in the vocabulary of a special form of subordination —military vassalage.

Unlike the ties of many dependants, rural or domestic, the fealty of vassals was not heritable and their services were in a high degree compatible with the most exacting definition of freedom. Among all the lord's 'men' they were in a special sense his 'free men' (*francs hommes*); more than other fiefs, their tenements had, as we know, a claim to be called *francs-fiefs*. And since, in the motley crowd of the lord's dependants, their rôle as armed retainers and counsellors gave them the semblance of aristocracy, they were also distinguished from that crowd by the fine-sounding name of nobility. The little church which the monks of Saint-Riquier, about the middle of the ninth century, reserved for the devotions of the vassals maintained at the abbot's court bore the name of 'the nobles' chapel', in contrast with that of the 'common people', where the artisans and minor officials of the monastery heard mass. When Louis the Pious exempted the tenants of the monks of Kempten from military service, he specified that this exemption did not apply to the 'more noble persons' provided with 'benefits' by the abbey.[1] Of all the senses of the word, this one, which tended to confound the two ideas of vassalage and nobility, was destined to enjoy the longest life.

Finally, at a higher level, among those men who were neither of servile birth nor in a condition of humble dependence, this magic word might serve to segregate the most powerful, the oldest, and the most highly regarded families. 'Are there no more nobles in the kingdom?' asked the 'magnates' of West Francia, according to the chronicler, when they saw Charles the Simple relying wholly on the counsels of his favourite Hagano.[2] Now this upstart, humble as was his origin in comparison with the great dynasties of counts, was certainly not of lower social rank than the

[1] Hariulf, *Chronique*, ed. Lot, p. 308; cf. p. 300; *Monumenta boica*, vol. XXVIII, 2, p. 27, no. XVII.
[2] Richer, *Histoires*, I, c. 15.

household warriors to whom Saint-Riquier opened its *capella nobilium*. But did the epithet at that time ever suggest anything other than a relative superiority? It is significant that it is frequently to be found employed in the comparative: *nobilior*, 'more noble' than one's neighbour.

Nevertheless, in the course of the first feudal age, the word gradually lost its humbler uses and tended more and more to be reserved for those groups of powerful men who had been able to acquire a growing dominance in society as a result of the breakdown of government and the general extension of protective ties. In this sense the word was still loosely used, without any precise definition of status or caste; but not without a very strong sense of the supremacy of the rank so described. Certainly the strong sense of a hierarchic order was present in the minds of those parties to a peace pact in 1023 who swore to refrain from attacking 'noble-women' —no others were mentioned.[1] In short, if the concept of nobility as a legal class remained unknown, it is quite permissible from this period, by a slight simplification of terminology, to speak of a social class of nobles and especially, perhaps, of a noble way of life. For it was principally by the nature of its wealth, by its exercise of authority, and by its social habits that this group was defined.

3 THE NOBLE CLASS A CLASS OF LORDS

This dominant class has sometimes been described as a landed class, and if by that is meant that fundamentally its members derived their revenues from their control of the soil, we may agree. From what other source could they have looked for them? Yet it must be added that, when available, tolls, market fees, and fines levied on a local trade were not the least coveted of properties. The characteristic feature was some form of exploitation. Whatever the sources of the noble's income—agricultural land or, as was much more rarely the case, shops or workshops—he always lived on the labour of other men. In other words, he was above all a manorial lord; or to put it in another way, if not every man whose way of life could be described as noble was lucky enough to possess manors—he might be a vassal maintained in the chief's household or a younger son who had adopted the wandering life of a soldier of fortune—at least all who did belonged *ipso facto* to the upper ranks of society.

Now a problem arises here—among the most difficult of all those presented by the genesis of our civilization. A certain number of seignorial families were doubtless descended from adventurers who had risen from nothing; men-at-arms who, having received a share of the chief's property, had become his enfeoffed vassals. The ancestors of others, perhaps, were among those rich peasants of whose transformation into landlords, each

---

[1] Peace oath of Beauvais in C. Pfister, *Études sur le règne de Robert le Pieux*, 1885, p. lxi.

with a group of tenements, we catch a glimpse in certain documents of the tenth century. But such assuredly was not the most common case. Over a large part of the West the manor, in forms originally more or less rudimentary, was very ancient, and the class of lords, however much mixed and intermixed, cannot well have been less so. Certainly we shall never know how many of the persons to whom the villeins of feudal times owed rents and labour services would have been entitled, had they been aware of it, to include in their pedigrees the shadowy figures from whom so many European villages derive their names—the Brennos of Bernay, the Cornelius of Cornigliano, the Gundolf of Gundolfsheim, the Aelfred of Alversham—or else some of those local chiefs of Germania whom Tacitus depicts as grown rich through the 'gifts' of the peasants. The link is completely missing. But it is not impossible that with the fundamental contrast between the lords of manors and the immense multitude of tenants we are in the presence of one of the most ancient lines of cleavage in Western society.

4 THE PROFESSION OF ARMS

If the possession of manors was the mark of a genuinely noble status and, along with treasure in money or jewels, the only form of wealth which seemed compatible with high rank, this was due in the first place to the authority over other men which it implied. (Could there ever be a surer basis of prestige than to be able to say: 'It is my will'?) But another reason was that the very vocation of the noble prevented him from engaging in any direct economic activity. He was committed body and soul to his particular function—that of the warrior. This fact, which is of fundamental importance, explains the rôle of the military vassals in the formation of medieval aristocracy. They did not constitute the whole of it; the owners of allodial manors, quickly assimilated by social habits to the enfeoffed vassals and sometimes more powerful than they, could hardly have been excluded. The vassal groups, nevertheless, formed the basic element in it. Here again the evolution of the Anglo-Saxon vocabulary illustrates admirably the transition from the old conception of nobility as a sacred race to the new conception of it as consisting in a mode of life. Whereas the ancient laws contrasted *eorl* and *ceorl*—the noble, in the Germanic sense of the word, and the ordinary free man—the later laws, while retaining the second of these contrasted terms, replaced the first by words such as *thegn, thegnborn, gesithcund*, meaning a companion or vassal (especially a royal vassal) or else a descendant of vassals.

It was not only vassals, of course, who had the capacity or the duty to fight; nor were they the only ones with a love of fighting in that first feudal age, when society from top to bottom was imbued with the taste for violence or the fear of it. The laws which attempted to restrict or prohibit the bearing of arms by members of the lower classes did not make their appearance before the second half of the twelfth century, and they coincided both with the progress of legal differentiation between classes and with a relative abatement of disorder. The merchant—as he appears in an ordinance of Frederick Barbarossa—was a traveller who journeyed 'with sword on saddle'; and once back at his counter he retained the habits contracted in the course of the life of adventure that was inseparable from trading in that age. At the time of the turbulent revival of urban life it could be said of many burghers, as Gilbert of Mons said of those of Saint-Trond, that they were 'right puissant in arms'. (In so far as he is not purely legendary, the traditional type of shopkeeper with his aversion to fighting belongs to the period of settled commerce, as opposed to the old nomadism of the 'dusty-footed' merchants; he dates from the thirteenth century, at the earliest.) Furthermore, small as medieval armies were, they were never recruited from the nobility alone. The lord raised his foot-soldiers among his villeins. And though from the twelfth century onwards the military obligations of the latter were increasingly curtailed, and though, in particular, the very common limitation of the duration of service to one day had the effect of restricting the employment of the rural contingents to ordinary police operations, these changes were exactly contemporaneous with the attenuation of feudal service itself. The peasant pikemen or archers were not superseded by vassals; they were rendered superfluous by the introduction of mercenaries who served at the same time to make good the deficiency of enfeoffed knights. But whether he was a vassal or even—where such still existed—an allodial lord, the 'noble' of early feudal times, in contrast with all the temporary soldiers, had the special characteristic of being a better armed warrior and a professional warrior.

He fought on horseback; and though he might on occasion dismount during the battle, he always moved about on horseback. Moreover, he fought fully equipped; his offensive weapons were the lance and the sword, occasionally the mace, while for defence he wore a helmet and a garment made wholly or partly of metal, and he carried a round or triangular shield. Strictly speaking, it was not the horse alone which made the knight; his humbler companion, the squire, whose duty it was to look after the horses and arrange the change of mounts along the road, was also mounted. Sometimes in addition to the heavy cavalry of the knights, armies included the more lightly equipped horsemen usually known as 'serjeants'. The distinguishing mark of the highest class of fighting-man was the combination of horse and complete equipment.

The improvements introduced in the warrior's equipment from the Frankish period onwards had made it more costly (and also more difficult to handle), with the result that it became less and less possible for anyone who was not a rich man—or the vassal of a rich man—to take part in this form of warfare. As the logical consequence of the adoption, about the tenth century, of the stirrup, the short spear of former days, brandished at arm's length like a javelin, was abandoned and replaced by the long and heavy lance which the warrior, in close combat, held under his armpit and, when at rest, supported on the stirrup itself.[1] To the helmet was added the nasal and later the visor. Finally, the *broigne*, a sort of garment of leather or cloth, on which were sewn iron rings or plates, gave place to the hauberk, perhaps copied from the Arabs; completely woven of metal rings, it was of much more delicate workmanship, and might have to be imported. By degrees moreover, the class monopoly, which had at first been imposed by mere practical necessity, began to pass into law. In their effort to keep their manorial officials in a state of relative inferiority, the monks of Beaulieu, shortly after 970, forbade them to carry the shield and sword; those of St. Gall, at about the same time, reproached the stewards of their estates with possessing arms of excessively fine quality.[2]

Imagine a military force of the period. It presents a dual aspect. On the one hand there is a body of infantry as ill-equipped for attack as for defence, slow in advancing to the assault and slow in flight, and quickly exhausted by long marches on wretched tracks or across-country. On the other hand, looking down from their chargers on the poor wretches who, 'shamefully' as one court romance puts it, drag their feet in the dust and mire, are stalwart soldiers, proud of being able to fight and manoeuvre swiftly, skilfully, effectively—the only force, indeed, in the opinion of the Cid's biographer, which it is worth the trouble of counting when assessing the numerical strength of an army.[3] In a civilization where war was an everyday matter, there was no more vital contrast than this. The word 'knight', which had become almost synonymous with vassal, became also the equivalent of 'noble'. Conversely, more than one text in applying to the lower orders the contemptuous designation of *pedones*, 'foot-soldiers'—or rather perhaps 'foot-sloggers'—raised it almost to the status of a legal term. Among the Franks, said the Arab emir Ousâma, 'all pre-eminence belongs to the horsemen. They are in truth the only men who count. Theirs it is to give counsel; theirs to render justice.'[4]

Now is it surprising that in the eyes of generations which had good reasons for exalting force in its crudest form the fighting-man *par excellence* should have been the most feared, the most sought-after and the most respected of men? A theory at that time very widely current represented the human community as being divided into three 'orders': those who prayed, those who fought, and those who worked. It was unanimously

---

[1] See Plates VI and VII.

[2] Deloche, *Cartulaire de l'abbaye de Beaulieu*, no. L; *Casus S. Galli*, c. 48.

[3] Fritz Meyer, *Die Stände . . . dargestellt nach der altfr. Artus- und Abenteurromanen*, 1892, p. 115; *Poema del mio Cid*, ed. Menendez Pidal, v. 918.

[4] H. Derenbourg, *Ousâma Ibn Mounkidh*, I (*Publications École Langues Orientales*, 2e série, T. XII, 1), p. 476.

agreed that the second should be placed much higher than the third. But the evidence of the epic goes farther still, showing that the soldier had little hesitation in rating his mission even higher than that of the specialist in prayer. Pride is one of the essential ingredients of all class-consciousness. That of the 'nobles' of the feudal era was, above all, the pride of the warrior.

Moreover, fighting was for them not merely an occasional duty to be performed for the sake of their lord, or king, or family. It represented much more—their whole purpose in life.

XXII

THE LIFE OF THE NOBILITY

1 WAR

'I LOVE the gay Eastertide, which brings forth leaves and flowers; and I love the joyous songs of the birds, re-echoing through the copse. But also I love to see, amidst the meadows, tents and pavilions spread; and it gives me great joy to see, drawn up on the field, knights and horses in battle array; and it delights me when the scouts scatter people and herds in their path; and I love to see them followed by a great body of men-at-arms; and my heart is filled with gladness when I see strong castles besieged, and the stockades broken and overwhelmed, and the warriors on the bank, girt about by fosses, with a line of strong stakes, interlaced. . . . Maces, swords, helms of different hues, shields that will be riven and shattered as soon as the fight begins; and many vassals struck down together; and the horses of the dead and the wounded roving at random. And when battle is joined, let all men of good lineage think of naught but the breaking of heads and arms; for it is better to die than to be vanquished and live. I tell you, I find no such savour in food, or in wine, or in sleep, as in hearing the shout "On! On!" from both sides, and the neighing of steeds that have lost their riders, and the cries of "Help! Help!"; in seeing men great and small go down on the grass beyond the fosses; in seeing at last the dead, with the pennoned stumps of lances still in their sides.'

Thus sang, in the second half of the twelfth century, a troubadour who is probably to be identified with the petty nobleman from Périgord, Bertrand de Born.[1] The accurate observation and the fine verve, in contrast with the insipidity of what is usually a more conventional type of poetry, are the marks of an uncommon talent. The sentiment, on the other hand, is in no way extraordinary; as is shown in many another piece from the same social world, in which it is expressed, no doubt with less gusto, but with equal spontaneity. In war—'fresh and joyful war', as it has been called in our own day by someone who was not destined to see it at such close quarters—the noble loved first and foremost the display of physical strength, the strength of a splendid animal, deliberately maintained by constant exercises, begun in childhood. 'He who has stayed at school till the age of

---

[1] Ed. Appel, no. 40; compare, for example, *Girart de Vienne*, ed. Yeandle, v. 2108 *et seq.*

twelve,' says a German poet, repeating the old Carolingian proverb, 'and never ridden a horse, is only fit to be a priest.'[1] The interminable accounts of single combats which fill the epics are eloquent psychological documents. The reader of today, bored by their monotony, finds it difficult to believe that they could have afforded so much pleasure—as clearly they did—to those who listened to them in days of old; theirs was the attitude of the sedentary enthusiast to reports of sporting events. In works of imagination as well as in the chronicles, the portrait of the good knight emphasizes above all his athletic build: he is 'big-boned', 'large of limb', the body 'well-proportioned' and pitted with honourable scars; the shoulders are broad, and so is the 'fork'—as becomes a horseman. And since this strength must be sustained, the valiant knight is known for his mighty appetite. In the old *Chanson de Guillaume*, so barbarous in its tone, listen to Dame Guibourc who, after having served at the great table of the castle the young Girart, her husband's nephew, remarks to her spouse:

> *Par Deu, bel sire, cist est de de vostre lin,*
> *Et si mangue un grant braun porcin,*
> *Et a dous traitz beit un cester de vin.*
> *Ben dure guere deit il rendre a sun veisin.*[2]

> By God! fair sire! he's of your line indeed,
> Who thus devours a mighty haunch of boar
> And drinks of wine a gallon at two gulps;
> Pity the man on whom he wages war!

A supple and muscular body, however, it is almost superfluous to say, was not enough to make the ideal knight. To these qualities he must add courage as well. And it was also because it gave scope for the exercise of this virtue that war created such joy in the hearts of men for whom daring and the contempt for death were, in a sense, professional assets. It is true that this valour did not always prevent mad panics (we have seen examples of them in face of the Vikings), nor was it above resorting to crude stratagems. Nevertheless the knightly class knew how to fight—on this point, history agrees with legend. Its unquestionable heroism was nurtured by many elements: the simple physical reaction of a healthy human being; the rage of despair—it is when he feels himself 'wounded unto death' that the 'cautious' Oliver strikes such terrible blows, in order 'to avenge himself all he could'; the devotion to a chief or, in the case of the holy war, to a cause; the passionate desire for glory, personal or collective; the fatalistic acquiescence in face of ineluctable destiny, of which literature offers no more

---

[1] Hartmann von Aue, *Gregorius*, v, 1547–53.
[2] *La Chanson de Guillaume*, ed. D. McMillan (*Soc. des Anc. Textes Francais*), V. 1054 *et seq.*

poignant examples than some of the last cantos of the *Nibelungenlied*; finally, the hope of reward in another world, promised not only to him who died for his God, but also to him who died for his master.

Accustomed to danger, the knight found in war yet another attraction: if offered a remedy for boredom. For these men whose culture long remained rudimentary and who—apart from a few great barons and their counsellors—were seldom occupied by very heavy administrative cares, everyday life easily slipped into a grey monotony. Thus was born an appetite for diversions which, when one's native soil failed to afford the means to gratify it, sought satisfaction in distant lands. William the Conqueror, bent on exacting due service from his vassals, said of one of them, whose fiefs he had just confiscated as a punishment for his having dared to depart for the crusade in Spain without permission: 'I do not believe it would be possible to find a better knight in arms; but he is unstable and extravagant, and he spends his time gadding about from place to place.'[1] Of how many others could the same have been said! The roving disposition was especially widespread among the French. The fact was that their own country did not offer them, as did half-Moslem Spain, or, to a less degree, Germany with its Slav frontier, an arena for conquests or swift forays; nor, like Germany again, the hardships and the pleasures of the great imperial expeditions. It is also probable that the knightly class was more numerous there than elsewhere, and therefore cramped for room. In France itself it has often been observed that Normandy was of all the provinces the richest in bold adventurers. Already the German Otto of Freising spoke of the 'very restless race of the Normans'. Could it have been the legacy of Viking blood? Possibly. But it was above all the effect of the state of relative peace which, in that remarkably centralized principality, the dukes established at an early date; so that those who craved the opportunity for fighting had to seek it abroad. Flanders, where political conditions were not very different, furnished an almost equally large contingent of roving warriors.

These knights-errant—the term is a contemporary one[2]—helped the native Christians in Spain to reconquer the northern part of the peninsula from Islam; they set up the Norman states in southern Italy; even before the First Crusade they enlisted as mercenaries in the service of Byzantium and fought against its eastern foes; finally, they found in the conquest and defence of the Tomb of Christ their chosen field of action. Whether in Spain or in Syria, the holy war offered the dual attraction of an adventure and a work of piety. 'No need is there now to endure the monk's hard life in the strictest of the orders . . .' sang one of the troubadours; 'to accomplish honourable deeds and thereby at the same time to save oneself from

---

[1] Ordericus Vitalis, *Histoire ecclésiastique*, ed. Le Prevost, III, p. 248.
[2] *Guillaume le Maréchal*, ed. P. Meyer, vv. 2777 and 2782 (it referred to knights who frequented tournaments).

hell—what more could one wish?'[1] These migrations helped to maintain relations between societies separated from each other by great distances and sharp contrasts; they disseminated Western and especially French culture beyond its own frontiers. A case to strike the imagination is that of one Hervé 'the Francopol' who was taken prisoner by an emir in 1057 when in command on the shores of Lake Van. At the same time the blood-letting thus practised abroad by the most turbulent groups in the West saved its civilization from being extinguished by guerilla warfare. The chroniclers were well aware that at the start of a crusade the people at home in the old countries always breathed more freely, because now they could once more enjoy a little peace.[2]

Fighting, which was sometimes a legal obligation and frequently a pleasure, might also be required of the knight as a matter of honour: in the twelfth century, Périgord ran with blood because a certain lord thought that one of his noble neighbours looked like a blacksmith and had the bad taste to say so.[3] But fighting was also, and perhaps above all, a source of profit—in fact, the nobleman's chief industry.

The lyrical effusions of Bertrand de Born have been mentioned above. He himself made no secret of the less creditable reasons which above all disposed him 'to find no pleasure in peace'. 'Why', he asks, 'do I want rich men to hate each other?' 'Because a rich man is much more noble, generous and affable in war than in peace.' And more crudely: 'We are going to have some fun. For the barons will make much of us . . . and if they want us to remain with them, they will give us *barbarins*' (i.e. coin of Limoges). And again: 'Trumpet, drums, flags and pennons, standards and horses white and black—that is what we shall shortly see. And it will be a happy day; for we shall seize the usurers' goods, and no more shall beasts of burden pass along the highways by day in complete safety; nor shall the burgess journey without fear, nor the merchant on his way to France; but the man who is full of courage shall be rich.' The poet belonged to that class of petty holders of fiefs, the 'vavasours'—he so described himself—for whom life in the ancestral manor-house lacked both gaiety and comforts. War made up for these deficiencies by stimulating the liberality of the great and providing prizes worth having.

The baron, of course, out of regard for his prestige as well as his interest, could not afford to be niggardly in the matter of presents, even towards vassals summoned to his side by the strictest conventions of feudal duty. If it was desired to retain them beyond the stipulated time, to take them farther or call on them more often than an increasingly rigorous custom appeared to permit, it was necessary to give them more. Finally, in face of

[1] Pons de Capdeuil, in Raynouard, *Choix*, IV, pp. 89 and 92.
[2] C. Erdmann, *Die Entstehung des Kreuzzugsgedankens*, Stuttgart, 1935 (*Forschungen zur Kirchen- und Geistesgeschichte*, VI), pp. 312–13.
[3] Geoffroi de Vigeois, I, 6, in Labbé, *Bibliotheca*, II, 281.

the growing inadequacy of the vassal contingents, there was soon no army which could dispense with the assistance of that wandering body of warriors to whom adventure made so strong an appeal, provided that there was a prospect of gain as well as of mighty combats. Thus cynically, our Bertrand offered his services to the count of Poitiers: 'I can help you. I have already a shield at my neck and a helm on my head. . . . Nevertheless, how can I put myself in the field without money?'[1]

But it was undoubtedly considered that the finest gift the chief could bestow was the right to a share of the plunder. This was also the principal profit which the knight who fought on his own account in little local wars expected from his efforts. It was a double prize, moreover: men and things. It is true that the Christian code no longer allowed captives to be reduced to slavery and at most permitted a few peasants or artisans to be forcibly removed from one place to another. But the ransoming of prisoners was a general practice. A ruler as firm and prudent as William the Conqueror might indeed never release alive the enemies who fell into his hands; but most warriors were not so far-sighted. The ransoming of prisoners occasionally had more dreadful consequences than the ancient practice of enslavement. The author of the *chanson* of Girart de Roussillon, who certainly wrote from personal observation, tells us that in the evening after a battle Girart and his followers put to the sword all the humble prisoners and wounded, sparing only the 'owners of castles', who alone were in a position to buy their freedom with hard cash.[2] As to plunder, it was traditionally so regular a source of profit that in the ages accustomed to written documents the legal texts treat it as a matter of course—on this point, the barbarian codes, at the beginning of the Middle Ages, and the thirteenth-century contracts of enlistment at the end, speak with the same voice. Heavy wagons followed the armies, for the purpose of collecting the spoils of war. Most serious of all, by a series of transitions almost unnoticed by the rather simple minds of the time, forms of violent action which were sometimes legitimate—requisitions indispensable to armies without commissariat, reprisals exacted against the enemy or his subjects —degenerated into pure brigandage, brutal and mean. Merchants were robbed on the highway; sheep, cheeses, chickens were stolen from pens and farmsteads—as was done, typically, by a small Catalan landowner of the early thirteenth century bent on annoying his neighbours of the abbey of Canigou. The best of men contracted strange habits. William Marshal was certainly a valiant knight. Nevertheless when, as a young and landless man travelling through France from tourney to tourney, he encountered on the road a monk who was running away with a girl of noble family and who candidly avowed his intention of putting out to usury the money he

[1] Bertrand de Born, ed. Appel, 10, 2; 35, 2; 37, 3; 28, 3.
[2] Guibert de Nogent, *De vita*, ed. Bourgin, I, c. 13, p. 43; *Girart de Roussillon*, translated by P. Meyer, p. 42.

was carrying, William did not scruple to rob the poor devil of his cash, under the pretext of punishing him for his evil designs. One of his companions even reproached him for not having seized the horse as well.[1] Such practices reveal a signal indifference to human life and suffering. War in the feudal age was in no sense war in kid gloves. It was accompanied by actions which seem to us today anything but chivalrous; as for instance—a frequent occurrence, sometimes even in disregard of a solemn oath—the massacre or mutilation of garrisons which had held out 'too long'. It involved, as a natural concomitant, the devastation of the enemy's estates. Here and there a poet, like the author of *Huon of Bordeaux*, and later a pious king like St. Louis protested in vain against this 'wasting' of the countryside which brought such appalling miseries upon the innocent. The epics, the German as well as the French, are faithful interpreters of real life, and they show us a whole succession of 'smoking' villages. 'There can be no real war without fire and blood,' said the plain-spoken Bertrand de Born.[2]

In two passages exhibiting striking parallels, the poet of *Girart de Roussillon* and the anonymous biographer of the Emperor Henry IV show us what the return of peace meant for the 'poor knights': the disdainful indifference of the great, who would have no more need of them; the importunities of money-lenders; the heavy plough-horse instead of the mettlesome charger; iron spurs instead of gold—in short an economic crisis as well as a disastrous loss of prestige.[3] For the merchant and the peasant, on the contrary, peace meant that it was possible once again to work, to gain a livelihood—in short, to live. Let us appeal once more to the evidence of the observant *trouvère* of *Girart de Roussillon*. Outlawed and repentant, Girart with his wife wanders through the countryside. They meet some merchants, and the duchess thinks it prudent to make them believe that the exile whose features they think they recognize is no more. 'Girart is dead; I saw him buried.' 'God be praised,' the merchants reply, 'for he was always making war and through him we have suffered many ills.' At these words, Girart's brow darkened; if he had had his sword 'he would have smitten one of them'. It is a story based on actual experience and illustrates the fundamental hostility which separated the classes. It cuts both ways. For the knight, proud of his courage and skill, despised the unwarlike (*imbellis*) people—the villeins who in face of the armies scampered away 'like deer', and later on the townsmen, whose economic power

---

[1] For booty, see for example *Codex Euricianus*, c. 323; Marlot, *Histoire de l'église de Reims*, III (documents), no. LXVII (1127); For the wagons, *Garin le Lorrain*, ed. P. Paris, I, pp. 195 and 197; For the complaints of the monks of Canigou, Luchaire, *La société française au temps de Philippe Auguste*, 1909, p. 265.

[2] *Huon de Bordeaux*, ed. F. Guessard, p. 41, vv. 1353–4; Louis IX, *Enseignemens*, c. 23, in C. V. Langlois, *La vie spirituelle*, p. 40; Bertrand de Born, 26, v. 15.

[3] *Girart de Roussillon*, translated P. Meyer, §§ 633 and 637; *Vita Heinrici*, ed. W. Eberhard, c. 8.

seemed to him so much the more hateful in that it was obtained by means which were at once mysterious and directly opposed to his own activities. If the propensity to bloody deeds was prevalent everywhere—more than one abbot indeed met his death as the victim of a cloister feud—it was the conception of the necessity of war, as a source of honour and as a means of livelihood, that set apart the little group of 'noble' folk from the rest of society.

2 THE NOBLE AT HOME

Favourite sport though it was, war had its dead seasons; but at these times the knightly class was distinguished from its neighbours by a manner of life which was essentially that of a nobility.

We should not think of this mode of existence as having invariably a rural setting. Italy, Provence and Languedoc still bore the age-old imprint of the Mediterranean civilizations whose structure had been systematized by Rome. In those regions, each small community was traditionally grouped round a town or large village which was at one and the same time an administrative centre, a market, and a place of refuge; and consequently the normal place of residence of the powerful. These people continued as much as ever to inhabit the old urban centres; and they took part in all their revolutions. In the thirteenth century, this civic character was regarded as one of the distinctive traits of the southern nobility. In contrast with Italy, said the Franciscan Salimbene, a native of Parma, who visited the kingdom of St. Louis, the towns of France are inhabited only by burgesses; the nobility live on their estates. But, though true in general of the period in which the good friar was writing, the contrast would not have been equally true of the first feudal age. Undoubtedly in the purely merchant cities which, especially in the Low Countries and trans-Rhenish Germany, came into being almost entirely from the tenth or the eleventh century onwards—Ghent, Bruges, Soest, Lübeck and so many others— the dominant caste was almost invariably composed of men grown rich through trade; though where there was a governor of princely rank a small body of vassals was sometimes maintained, consisting of unenfeoffed knights or those who came regularly to perform their turn of duty. In the old Roman cities such as Rheims or Tournai, on the other hand, groups of knights seem to have resided over a long period, many of them no doubt attached to the courts of bishops or abbots. It was only gradually and in consequence of a more pronounced differentiation of classes that knightly society, outside Italy and southern France, became almost entirely divorced from the urban populations properly so called. Although the noble certainly did not cease altogether to visit the town, he henceforth went there only occasionally, in pursuit of pleasure or for the exercise of certain functions.

Everything tended to induce him to live in the country. First, there was the habit, which was becoming more and more widespread, of remunerating vassals by means of fiefs, consisting in the vast majority of cases of rural manors; then there was the weakening of feudal obligations, which favoured the tendency among the retainers who had now been provided with fiefs to live each in his own home, far from the kings, the great barons, and the bishops, who controlled the towns; finally, a taste for the open air, natural to these sportsmen, played its part. There is a moving story, told by a German monk, of a count's son who had been dedicated by his family to the monastic life; on the day when he was first subjected to the harsh rule of claustration, he climbed up to the highest tower of the monastery, in order 'at least to feast his vagrant soul on the spectacle of the hills and fields where he might no longer roam'.[1] The pressure of the burghers, who had very little desire to admit into their communities elements indifferent to their activities and their interests, accelerated the movement.

Thus whatever modifications it may be necessary to introduce into the picture of a nobility exclusively rural from the outset, it remains true that, ever since knights existed, a growing majority of them in the North and many even in the coastal regions of the Mediterranean ordinarily resided in a country mansion.

The manor-house usually stood in the midst of a cluster of dwellings, or nearby; sometimes there were several in the same village. The manor-house was sharply distinguished from the surrounding cottages, just as it was in the towns from the habitations of the poor—not only because it was better built, but above all because it was almost invariably designed for defence. The desire of the rich to protect their dwellings from attack was naturally as old as the social disorders themselves; witness those fortified *villae* whose appearance about the fourth century bears witness to the decline of the Roman peace. The tradition may have continued here and there in the Frankish period, but most of the 'courts' inhabited by rich proprietors and even royal palaces themselves long remained almost without permanent means of defence. It was the invasions of the Northmen or the Hungarians which, from the Adriatic to the plains of northern England, led not only to the repair or rebuilding of town ramparts, but also to the erection on every hand of the rural strongholds (*fertés*) which were destined to cast a perpetual shadow over the fields of Europe. Internal wars soon added to their number. The rôle of the great potentates, kings or princes, in this prolific building of castles, and their efforts to control it, will be dealt with later; for the present they need not detain us. For the fortified houses of the petty lords, scattered over hill and dale, had almost always been constructed without any authorization from above. They answered elementary needs, spontaneously felt and satisfied. A hagiographer has given a very exact account of them, although in an unsympathetic spirit: 'their purpose was to enable these men, constantly occupied with quarrels

[1] *Casus S. Galli*, c. 43.

and massacres, to protect themselves from their enemies, to triumph over their equals, to oppress their inferiors';[1] in short, to defend themselves and dominate others.

These edifices were generally of a very simple type. For a long time the most common, at least outside the Mediterranean regions, was the wooden tower. A curious passage of the *Miracles of St. Benedict* describes, towards the end of the eleventh century, the extremely primitive arrangement of one of these castles. On the first floor there was a large room where the 'power-ful man . . . together with his household, lived, conversed, ate, slept'; on the ground floor there was a storeroom for provisions.[2] Normally, a ditch was dug at the foot. Sometimes, at a little distance from the tower, there was a stockade or a rampart of beaten earth, surrounded in its turn by another ditch. This enclosure provided a place of safety for various domestic buildings and for the cook-house, which it was considered wise to place away from the tower on account of the risk of fire; it served at need as a refuge for the dependants; it prevented an immediate assault on the main building and obstructed the most effective method of attack, which was to set fire to it.[3] Tower and stockade frequently stood on a mound (*motte*), sometimes natural, sometimes—at least in part—man-made. Its purpose was twofold: to confront the attackers with the obstacle of the slope and to gain a better view of the surrounding country. But to garrison even one of these primitive wooden castles required more armed retainers than the ordinary run of knights could maintain. It was the great men who first had recourse to stone as a building-material; those 'rich men that build in stone', whom Bertrand de Born depicts amusing themselves by making 'from lime, sand and freestone . . . gateways and turrets, vaults and spiral staircases'.[4] It was adopted only slowly, in the course of the twelfth century or even the thirteenth, for the houses of knights of lesser and middle rank. Before the completion of the great clearings, the forests seem to have been easier and less expensive to exploit than the quarries; and while masonry called for specialist workers, the tenants, a permanent source of compulsory labour, were almost all to some extent carpenters as well as wood-cutters.

There is no doubt that for the peasant his lord's little fortress sometimes provided a defence and a refuge. Contemporary opinion had nevertheless good reasons for regarding it as, above all, a dangerous haunt. For those concerned to keep the peace, for the townsmen, interested in preserving freedom of communications, for the kings or princes, there was to be no more urgent task than that of razing to the ground the countless castles with which so many petty local tyrants had covered the plains. And,

---

[1] *Vita Johannis ep. Teruanensis,* c. 12, in *M.G.H., Scriptores,* vol. XIV, 2, p. 1146.
[2] *Miracula S. Benedicti,* ed. Certain, VIII, c. 16.
[3] See Plate VIII.
[4] See Plate IX.

whatever may have been said on this subject, it was not only in the novels of Mrs. Radcliffe that castles, whether large or small, had their *oubliettes*. Lambert of Ardres, describing the fortress of Tournehem, rebuilt in the twelfth century, did not forget the deep dungeons 'where the prisoners, amidst darkness, vermin and ordure, ate the bread of sorrow'.

As is indicated by the very nature of his dwelling, the knight lived in a state of perpetual watchfulness. A lookout man, a familiar figure in the epic as well as in lyric poetry, kept his nightly watch on the summit of the tower. Lower down, in the two or three rooms of the cramped fortress, a whole little world of permanent residents, with an admixture of transient guests, lived together in conditions that admitted of no privacy. Partly, no doubt, this was due to lack of space, but it was also the result of habits which in that age seemed inseparable from the position of a chief. Day and night, the baron was surrounded by retainers—men-at-arms, menials, household vassals, young nobles committed to his care as 'nurslings'—who served him, guarded him, conversed with him and who, when the hour of sleep at last arrived, continued to keep faithful watch over him even when he was in bed with his wife. 'It is not seemly that a lord should eat alone' was an opinion still held in thirteenth-century England.[1] In the great hall the tables were long and most of the seats were benches on which the diners sat side by side. Poor persons took up their lodging under the staircase—where two illustrious penitents died: St. Alexis, in legend, and Count Simon de Crépy, in fact. This way of living, incompatible with any sort of private meditation, was general at this time; the monks themselves slept in dormitories, not in cells. It explains why some people chose to take refuge in the only ways of life which at that time were compatible with the enjoyment of solitude—those of the hermit, the recluse, and the wanderer. On the cultural side, it meant that among the nobles knowledge was transmitted much less by books and study than by reading aloud, the reciting of verse, and personal contacts.

3 OCCUPATIONS AND DISTRACTIONS

Though usually a countryman in the sense that his home was in the country, the noble was nevertheless no agriculturalist. To put his hand to the hoe or the plough would have been an indication that he had come down in the world—as happened to a poor knight whose history is known to us through a collection of anecdotes. And if he sometimes liked to contemplate the workers in the fields or the yellowing harvest on his estates, it does not appear that as a rule he took a very direct part in the management of the farm.[2] The manuals of estate management, when they came to be written, were intended not for the master, but for his stewards; the 'country

---

[1] Robert Grosseteste's *Rules* in Walter of Henley's *Husbandry*, ed. E. Lamond.
[2] Marc Bloch, *Les caractères originaux de l'histoire rurale française*, 1931, p. 148.

gentleman' belongs to quite another age—after the economic revolution in the sixteenth century. Although the rights of jurisdiction which he possessed over his tenants constituted one of the essential sources of his power, the lord of the village as a rule exercised them much less frequently in person than through the agency of bailiffs, themselves of peasant extraction. Nevertheless the exercise of judicial functions was certainly one of the few peaceful occupations of the knight. As a rule he only concerned himself with judicial duties within the framework of his class, which meant that he either settled the law-suits of his own vassals or sat as judge of his peers in the court to which he had been summoned by his feudal lord; but where public justice survived, as in England and Germany, he took his place in the court of the county or the hundred. There was enough of this activity to make the legal spirit one of the earliest cultural influences to be diffused in knightly circles.

The favourite amusements of the nobility bore the imprint of a warlike temper.

First, there was hunting. As has already been said, it was more than a sport. The people of western Europe were not yet living in surroundings from which the menace of wild beasts had been finally removed. Moreover, at a time when the flesh of cattle, inadequately fed and of poor stock, furnished only indifferent meat, much venison was eaten, especially in the homes of the rich. Since hunting thus remained an almost necessary activity, it was not altogether a class monopoly. The case of Bigorre, where it was forbidden to peasants as early as the beginning of the twelfth century, appears to be an exception.[1] Nevertheless kings, princes, and lords, each within the limits of his own authority, everywhere tended to monopolize the pursuit of game in certain reserved areas: large animals in the 'forests' (which term, originally, denoted every area thus reserved, whether wooded or not), rabbits and hares in the 'warrens'. The legal foundation of these claims is obscure; it seems as though they seldom had any save the decree of the master, and very naturally it was in a conquered country—the England of the Norman kings—that the creation of royal forests, too often at the expense of arable land, was most extensive, and their protection most stringent. Such abuses attest the strength of a taste which was very much a class characteristic; and so do the requisitions imposed on the tenants—the obligation to lodge and feed the lord's pack of hounds, and to construct hunting-boxes in the woods, at the season of the great meets. The monks of St. Gall made it a primary cause of complaint against their stewards, whom they accused of seeking to raise themselves to the ranks of nobles, that they bred dogs to pursue hares and, worse still, wolves, bears, and boars. Moreover, in order to practise the favourite sports of coursing with greyhounds and hawking, which—among other contributions—had been transmitted to the West by the equestrian societies of the Asiatic plains,

[1] *Fors de Bigorre*, c. XIII.

wealth, leisure and dependants were necessary. Of more than one knight it could have been said, as was said of a count of Guines by the biographer of his house, that 'he set greater store by a goshawk beating the air with its wings than by a preaching priest', or, in the naive and charming words which a minstrel puts into the mouth of one of his characters, as he sees the murdered hero surrounded by the howling pack: 'A nobleman he was; greatly did his hounds love him.'[1] By bringing these warriors closer to nature, the chase awakened in them a form of sensibility which otherwise they would doubtless have lacked. If they had not been brought up by the tradition of their class 'to know the wood and the river's edge', would the poets of knightly rank, who were to contribute so much to the French lyric and the German *Minnesang*, have found notes so true to sing the dawn or the joys of the month of May?

Then there were the tournaments. In the Middle Ages the tournament was generally thought to be of relatively recent origin, and the name of its supposed inventor was even mentioned—a certain Geoffroy de Preuilly, said to have died in 1066. In reality the practice of these make-believe combats undoubtedly dates back to the remotest times: witness the 'pagan games', sometimes fatal, mentioned in 895 by the council of Tribur. The custom was continued, among the people, at certain feasts—Christianized rather than Christian—as for example those other 'pagan games' (the recurrence of the word is significant) in 1077, during which the son of a cobbler of Vendôme, who was taking part in them with other young people, was mortally wounded.[2] The contests of young men are an almost universal feature of folklore. In the armies, moreover, the imitation of war at all times provided a training for troops as well as a pastime. During the celebrated interview which the 'Oaths of Strasbourg' made famous, Charles the Bald and Lewis the German diverted themselves with a spectacle of this kind, and did not disdain to participate actively. The distinctive contribution of the feudal age was to evolve from these contests, whether military or popular, a type of mock battle at which prizes were generally offered, confined to mounted combatants equipped with knightly arms; and hence to create a distinctive class amusement, which the nobility found more exciting than any other.

Since these meetings, which could not be organized without considerable expense, usually took place on the occasion of the great 'courts' held from time to time by kings or barons, enthusiasts roamed the world from tournament to tournament. These were not only poor knights, sometimes grouped in 'companies', but also very great lords, such as the count of Hainault, Baldwin IV, or among the English princes, Henry, the 'Young King', who however scarcely distinguished himself in the lists. As in our

---

[1] Lambert of Ardres, *Chronique*, c. LXXXVIII; *Garin le Lorrain*, ed. P. Paris, II, p. 244.

[2] C. Métais, *Cartulaire de l'abbaye . . . de la Trinité de Vendôme*, I, no. CCLXI.

present-day sporting events, the opponents were normally grouped by regions; a great scandal arose one day at a tournament near Gournay when the men of Hainault took the side of the men of France proper, instead of joining the Flemings and the men of Vermandois, who were, in this sphere at least, their normal allies. There can be no doubt that these games helped to establish provincial solidarities. So much was this the case that it was not always a question of make-believe battle: far from it. Wounds were not uncommon, nor even mortal blows when—to borrow the words of the poet of *Raoul de Cambrai*—the jousting 'took an ill turn'. This explains why the wisest sovereigns frowned upon these frolics, in which the blood of vassals was drained away. The Plantagenet Henry II formally prohibited them in England. For the same reason—and also on account of their connection with the revels at popular feasts, which savoured of 'paganism' —the Church rigorously forbade them, going to the length of refusing burial in consecrated ground to the knight who had met his death in this way, even if he had repented. The fact that, in spite of legislation by lay and ecclesiastical authorities, the practice could not be eradicated shows how deep was the need that it satisfied.

Nevertheless, the passion for tournaments, as for genuine warfare, was not always disinterested. Since the victor frequently took possession of the equipment and horses of the vanquished and sometimes even of his person, releasing him only on payment of a ransom, skill and strength were profitable assets. More than one jousting knight made a profession, and a very lucrative one, out of his skill in combat. Thus the love of arms inextricably combined the ingredients of 'joy' and the appetite for gain.[1]

4 RULES OF CONDUCT

It was natural that a class so clearly defined by its mode of life and its social supremacy should eventually devise a code of conduct peculiar to itself. But it was only during the second feudal age, which was in every sense the age of awakening self-consciousness, that these rules assumed a precise form and, along with it, a more refined character.

The term which, from about the year 1100, commonly served to describe the sum of noble qualities was the characteristic word 'courtesy' (*courtoisie*), which is derived from *cour* (at that time written and pronounced, as in English today, with a final 't'). It was in fact in the assemblies, temporary or permanent, which were formed round the principal barons and the kings, that these laws of conduct came to be evolved; the isolation of the knight in his 'tower' would not have permitted their development. Emulation and social contacts were necessary, and that is why this advance in moral

[1] On tournaments, in addition to the works listed in the Bibliography, see Waitz, *Deutsche Verfassungsgeschichte*, V, 2nd ed., p. 456; *Guillaume le Maréchal*, ed. P. Meyer, III, p. xxxvi *et seq*; Gislebert of Mons, *Chronique*, ed. Pertz, pp. 92–3; 96; 102; 109–10; 128–30; 144; *Raoul de Cambrai*, v. 547.

sensibility was bound up both with the consolidation of the great principalities or monarchies and with the restoration of a greater degree of intercommunication. Another term was *prudhomme*, and as 'courteous' (*courtois*) gradually acquired a more commonplace meaning, this word was used more and more frequently to denote something higher: a name so great and so good that merely to pronounce it 'fills the mouth', declared St. Louis, intending thereby to vindicate the secular virtues as against those of the monk. Here again the semantic evolution is extremely instructive. For *prudhomme* is in fact the same word as *preux* which, having departed from its first rather vague sense of 'useful' or 'excellent', was later applied above all to warlike valour. The two terms diverged—*preux* keeping its traditional meaning—when it began to be felt that strength and courage were not enough to make the perfect knight. 'There is a great difference between the *homme preux* and the *prudhomme*,' Philip Augustus is said to have remarked one day; he regarded the second as much the superior of the two.[1] This might seem like hair-splitting; but if we go to the root of the matter it is a precious piece of evidence on the evolution of the knightly ideal.

Whether it was a question of ordinary usages of decorum or of moral precepts properly so called, of *courtoisie* in the strict sense, or of *prudhommie*, the new code was unquestionably born in the courts of France and in those of the Meuse region, which were completely French in language and manners. As early as the eleventh century French manners were being imitated in Italy.[2] In the next two centuries, these influences became still more pronounced; witness the vocabulary of the German knightly class, full of 'alien' words, which had come in as a rule via Hainault, Brabant or Flanders. *Höflich* itself is only an imitation of *courtois*, courteous. More than one young German-speaking noble came to learn the rules, as well as the language, of good taste at the courts of the French princes. Does not the poet Wolfram von Eschenbach call France 'the land of well-conducted chivalry'? This dissemination of an aristocratic form of culture was only one feature of the influence exercised at that time throughout Europe—chiefly, it goes without saying, among the upper classes—by French culture as a whole; others were the propagation of artistic and literary ideals; the prestige of the schools of Chartres, and later of Paris; and the virtually international use of the French language. And doubtless it is not impossible to find reasons for this: the long expeditions through the West carried out by the most adventurous chivalry in Europe; the relative prosperity of a country affected much earlier than Germany (though not, indeed, than Italy) by the development of trade; the distinction, emphasized at a very early date, between the knightly class and the unwarlike rabble; the absence, despite so many local wars, of any internal conflicts com-

---

[1] Joinville, c. CIX.
[2] Rangerius, *Vita Anselmi* in *M.G.H., Scriptores*, XXX, 2, p. 1252, v. 1451.

VI. FIGHTING WITH THE LANCE: THE OLD STYLE AND THE NEW

The Battle of Hastings: the Norman knights advance to the attack, some using the lance as a javelin, others handling it in the new manner. Bayeux Tapestry, end of the 11th century.

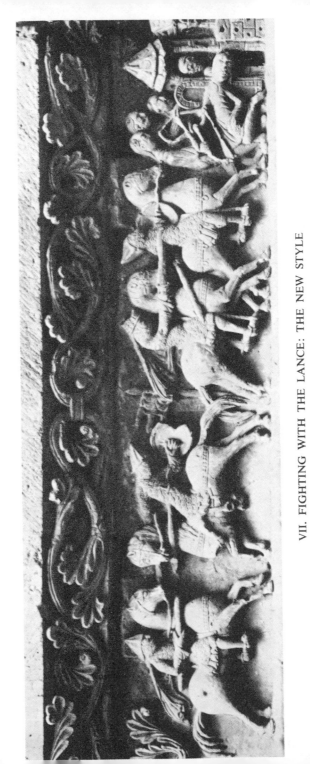

VII. FIGHTING WITH THE LANCE: THE NEW STYLE

Frieze of west façade of Angoulême Cathedral, first third of the 12th century.

parable with those which resulted within the Empire from the great quarrels of emperors and popes. But this having been said, we may well ask ourselves if it is not futile to attempt to explain something which, in the present state of our knowledge of man, seems to be beyond our understanding—the ethos of a civilization and its power of attraction.

'We shall yet talk of this day in ladies' chambers,' said the count of Soissons, at the battle of Mansurah.[1] This remark, the equivalent of which it would be impossible to find in the *chansons de geste*, but which might have been heard on the lips of more than one hero of courtly romance as early as the twelfth century, is characteristic of a society in which sophistication has made its appearance and, with it, the influence of women. The noblewoman had never been confined within her own secluded quarters. Surrounded with servants, she ruled her household, and she might also rule the fief—perhaps with a rod of iron. It was nevertheless reserved for the twelfth century to create the type of the cultivated great lady who holds a salon. This marks a profound change, when we consider the extraordinary coarseness of the attitude usually ascribed by the old epic poets to their heroes in their relations with women, even with queens —not stopping at the grossest insults, which the lady requites with blows. One can hear the guffaws of the audience. The courtly public had not lost their taste for this heavy humour; but they now allowed it only—as in the *fabliaux*—at the expense of the peasants or the bourgeoisie. For courtesy was essentially an affair of class. The boudoir of the high-born lady and, more generally, the court, was henceforth the place where the knight sought to outshine and to eclipse his rivals not only by his reputation for great deeds of valour, but also by his regard for good manners and by his literary talents.

As we have seen, the nobility had never been completely illiterate; still less had it been impervious to the influence of literature, though this was listened to rather than read. But a great step forward was taken when knights themselves became literary men. It is significant that the *genre* to which they devoted themselves almost exclusively up to the thirteenth century was lyric poetry. The earliest of the troubadours known to us—it should be added that he was certainly not the first—ranked among the most powerful princes in France. This was William IX of Aquitaine (d. 1127). In the list of Provençal singers who followed him, as also a little later among their rivals, the lyric poets of the North, all ranks of the knighthood were abundantly represented—leaving aside, of course, the professional minstrels kept by the great. These short pieces, which were generally characterized by an intricate technique—sometimes amounting to deliberate hermeticism, the famous 'close' style (*trobar clus*)—were admirably suited for recital in aristocratic gatherings. The fact that the nobility was thus able to savour and to find genuine enjoyment in pleasures

[1] Joinville, c. XLIX.

too refined to be appreciated by villeins naturally reinforced its sense of superiority. As the poems were usually set off by singing and instrumental accompaniment the charm of music was wedded to the charm of words, and exercised an equally potent influence. William Marshal, who had been so tough a fighter, on his deathbed, longing, but not daring, to sing himself, would not say farewell to his daughters till they had allowed him to hear for the last time the 'sweet sound' of some *rotrouenges*.[1] And it was while listening to Volker's fiddle in the calm night, that the Burgundian heroes of the *Nibelungenlied* fell into what was to be their last sleep.

Towards the pleasures of the flesh the attitude of the knightly class appears to have been frankly realistic. It was the attitude of the age as a whole. The Church imposed ascetic standards on its members and required laymen to restrict sexual intercourse to marriage and the purpose of procreation. But it did not practise its own precepts very effectively, and this was especially true of the secular clergy, among whom even the Gregorian reform purified the lives of few but the episcopate. Significantly, we are told with admiration of pious persons, parish priests, nay even abbots, of whom 'it is said' that they died virgins. The example of the clergy proves how repugnant continence was to the majority of men: it was certainly not calculated to inspire it in the faithful. As a matter of fact—if we exclude such intentionally comic episodes as Oliver's boasting about his virility in the *Pèlerinage de Charlemagne*—the tone of the epics is fairly chaste. This was because their authors did not attach great importance to describing goings-on which had in fact no epic quality. Even in the less reticent narratives of the age of 'courtesy', libertinism is commonly represented as something for which the womenfolk rather than the heroes are responsible. Here and there nevertheless a characteristic touch gives a hint of the truth —as in the old poem of *Girart de Roussillon* where we find a vassal, who is required to give hospitality to a messenger, providing him with a beautiful girl for the night. And doubtless those 'delightsome' encounters were not wholly fictitious which, according to the romances, the castles so happily facilitated.[2]

The evidence of history is clearer still. The noble's marriage, as we know, was often an ordinary business transaction, and the houses of the nobility swarmed with bastards. At first sight, the advent of 'courtesy' does not seem to have effected any great change in these morals. Certain of the songs of William of Aquitaine sing the praises of sensual pleasure in barrack-room style and this attitude was to find more than one imitator among the poets who succeeded him. Nevertheless, with William, who was apparently the heir of a tradition whose origins elude us, another conception of love

---

[1] [A *rotrouenge* was a type of song with a refrain, composed by the *trouvères*.]

[2] *Girart de Roussillon*, translated P. Meyer, S. 257 and 299. Cf. *La Mort de Garin*, ed. E. du Méril, p. xl. And see, among others, the delicately voluptuous scene in *Lancelot*, ed. Sommer, *The Vulgate Version of the Arthurian Romances*, III, p. 383.

was already emerging—that 'courtly' love, which was certainly one of the most curious products of the moral code of chivalry. Can we conceive of Don Quixote without Dulcinea?

The characteristic features of courtly love can be summarized fairly simply. It had nothing to do with marriage, or rather it was directly opposed to the legal state of marriage, since the beloved was as a rule a married woman and the lover was never her husband. This love was often bestowed upon a lady of higher rank, but in any case it always involved a strong emphasis on the man's adoration of the woman. It professed to be an all-engrossing passion, constantly frustrated, easily jealous, and nourished by its own difficulties; but its stereotyped development early acquired something of a ritual character. It was not averse to casuistry. Finally, as the troubadour Geoffrey Rudel said, in a poem which, wrongly interpreted, gave rise to the famous legend of Princess Far-away, it was, ideally, a 'distant' love. It did not indeed reject carnal intercourse on principle, nor according to Andrew the Chaplain, who discoursed on the subject, did it despise minor physical gratifications if obliged to renounce 'the ultimate solace'. But absence or obstacles, instead of destroying it, only enriched it with a poetic melancholy. If possession, always to be desired, was seen to be quite out of the question, the sentiment none the less endured as an exciting emotion and a poignant joy.

Such is the picture drawn for us by the poets. For courtly love is only known to us through literature and for that reason it is very difficult to determine to what extent it was merely a fashionable fiction. It is certain that, though tending in some measure to dissociate sentiment from sensuality, it by no means prevented the flesh from seeking satisfaction in a more direct way; for we know that with the majority of men emotional sincerity exists on several planes. In any case we may be sure that such an idea of amorous relationships, in which today we recognize many elements with which we have now become familiar, was at first a strikingly original conception. It owed little to the ancient arts of love, or even—although they were perhaps nearer to it—to the always rather equivocal treatises which Graeco-Roman civilization devoted to the analysis of masculine friendship. In particular the humble attitude of the lover was a new thing. We have seen that it was apt to express itself in terms borrowed from the vocabulary of vassal homage; and this was not merely a matter of words. The identification of the loved one and the lord corresponded to an aspect of social morality entirely characteristic of feudal society.

Still less, in spite of what has sometimes been said, was this code dependent on religious ideas.[1] If we leave out of account a few superficial

[1] In connection with courtly love and the lyric poetry which served as its expression, the question of Arab influence has also been raised by some scholars. No conclusive proof seems so far to have been adduced. Cf. in addition to A. Jeanroy, *La poésie lyrique des troubadours*, 1934, II, p. 366, a review by G. Appel in *Zeitschrift für romanische Philologie*, LII, 1932, p. 770 (on A. R. Nykl).

analogies, which are at the most only the result of environment, we must in fact recognize that it was directly opposed to them, although its adherents had no clear consciousness of this antithesis. It made the love of man and woman almost one of the cardinal virtues, and certainly the supreme form of pleasure. Above all, even when it renounced physical satisfaction, it sublimated—to the point of making it the be-all and end-all of existence—an emotional impulse derived essentially from those carnal appetites whose legitimacy Christianity only admits in order to curb them by marriage (profoundly despised by courtly love), in order to justify them by the propagation of the species (to which courtly love gave but little thought), and in order, finally, to confine them to a secondary plane of moral experience. It is not in the knightly lyrics that we can hope to find the authentic echo of the attitude of contemporary Christianity towards sexual relations. This is expressed, quite uncompromisingly, in that passage of the pious and clerical *Queste du Saint-Graal* where Adam and Eve, before they lie together under the Tree to beget 'Abel the Just', beg the Lord to bring down upon them a great darkness to 'comfort' their shame.

The contrast between the two moralities in their treatment of this subject perhaps provides us with the key to the problem of social geography presented by these new preoccupations with romantic love. Like the lyrical poetry which has preserved them for us, they arose as early as the end of the eleventh century in the courtly circles of southern France. It was only a reflection of them which appeared a little later in the North—still in the lyrical form or through the medium of the romances—and which subsequently passed into the German *Minnesang*.

Now, it would be absurd to attempt to explain this fact by attributing some indefinable superiority to the civilization of Languedoc. Whether relating to the artistic, the intellectual or the economic sphere, the claim would be equally untenable. It would mean ignoring the French epic, Gothic art, the first efforts of philosophy in the schools between Loire and Meuse, the fairs of Champagne, and the teeming cities of Flanders. It is beyond dispute, on the other hand, that in the South the Church, especially during the first feudal age, was less rich, less cultivated, less active than in the northern provinces. No great works of clerical literature, no great movements of monastic reform emanated from that region. This relative weakness of the religious centres alone can explain the extraordinary successes achieved, from Provence to the region of Toulouse, by heresies fundamentally international; and it was also no doubt the reason why the higher ranks of the laity, being less subject to clerical influence, were relatively free to develop their own secular morality. Moreover, the fact that these precepts of courtly love were subsequently so easily propagated shows how well they served the new requirements of a class. They helped it to become aware of itself. To love in a different way from the generality of men must inevitably make one feel different from them.

That a knight should carefully calculate his booty or his ransoms and, on returning home, impose a heavy 'tallage' on his peasants provoked little or no criticism. Gain was legitimate; but on one condition—that it should be promptly and liberally expended. 'I can assure you,' said a troubadour when he was reproached for his brigandage, 'if I robbed, it was to give, not to hoard.'[1] No doubt we are entitled to regard as a little suspect the insistence with which the minstrels, those professional parasites, extolled above all other duties that of generosity, *largesse*, 'lady and queen in whose light all virtues shine'. No doubt also, among the nobles of middle or lesser rank and still more perhaps among the great barons, there were always miserly or merely prudent individuals, more inclined to amass scarce coin or jewels in their coffers than to distribute them. It is none the less true that, in squandering a fortune that was easily gained and easily lost, the noble thought to affirm his superiority over classes less confident in the future or more careful in providing for it. This praiseworthy prodigality might not always stop at generosity or even luxury. A chronicler has preserved for us the record of the remarkable competition in wasteful expenditure witnessed one day at a great 'court' held in Limousin. One knight had a plot of ground ploughed up and sown with small pieces of silver; another burned wax candles for his cooking; a third, 'through boastfulness', ordered thirty of his horses to be burnt alive.[2] What must a merchant have thought of this struggle for prestige through extravagance— which reminds us of the practices of certain primitive races? Here again different notions of honour marked the line of separation between the social groups.

Thus set apart by its power, by the nature of its wealth and its mode of life, by its very morals, the social class of nobles was toward the middle of the twelfth century quite ready to solidify into a legal and hereditary class. The ever more frequent use which from that time onwards seems to have been made of the word *gentilhomme*—man of good *gent* or lineage—to describe the members of this class is an indication of the growing importance attributed to qualities of birth. With the wide adoption of the ceremony of 'dubbing' or formal arming of the knight the legal class of nobility took definite shape.

[1] Albert de Malaspina, in C. Appel, *Provenzalische Chrestomathie*, 3rd ed., no. 90, v 19 *et seq.*

[2] Geoffroi de Vigeois, I, 69 in Labbe, *Bibliotheca*, II, p. 322.

XXIII

CHIVALRY

1 DUBBING TO KNIGHTHOOD

FROM the second half of the eleventh century, various texts, soon to become more numerous, begin to mention that here and there a ceremony has taken place for the purpose of 'making a knight'. The ritual consisted of several acts. To the candidate, who as a rule was scarcely more than a boy, an older knight first of all handed over the arms symbolic of his future status; in particular, he girded on his sword.[1] Then, almost invariably, this sponsor administered a heavy blow with the flat of his hand on the young man's neck or cheek—the *paumée* or *colée*, as the French documents term it. Was it a test of strength? Or was it—as was held by some rather late medieval interpreters—a method of making an impression on the memory, so that, in the words of Ramon Lull, the young man would remember his 'promise' for the rest of his life? The poems do indeed often show the hero trying not to give way under this rude buffet—the only one, as a chronicler remarks, which a knight must always receive and not return;[2] on the other hand, as we have seen, a box on the ear was one of the commonest methods, sanctioned by the legal customs of the time, of ensuring the recollection of certain legal acts—though it is true that it was inflicted on the witnesses and not on the parties themselves. But a very different and much less purely rational meaning seems at first to have attached to the gesture of 'dubbing' (the word was derived from an old Germanic verb meaning 'to strike'), originally considered so essential to the making of a knight that the term came to be used habitually to describe the whole ceremony. The contact thus established between the hand of the one who struck the blow and the body of the one who received it transmitted a sort of impulse—in exactly the same way as the blow bestowed by the bishop on the clerk whom he is ordaining priest. The ceremony often ended with an athletic display. The new knight leapt on his horse and proceeded to transfix or demolish with a stroke of his lance a suit of armour attached to a post; this was known as the *quintaine*.

---

[1] See Plate X.

[2] Raimon Lull, *Libro de la orden de Caballeria*, ed. J. R. de Luanco, Barcelona, R. Academia de Buenos Letras, 1901, **IV**, 11. English translation: *The Book of the Ordre of Chivalry trans. and printed by W. Caxton*, ed. Byles, 1926 (Early English Text Society).

By its origins and by its nature dubbing to knighthood is clearly connected with those initiation ceremonies of which primitive societies, as well as those of the ancient world, furnish many examples—practices which, under different forms, all had the common object of admitting the young man to full membership of the group, from which his youth had hitherto excluded him. Among the Germans they reflected a warlike society. Without prejudice to certain other features—such as the cutting of the hair, which was sometimes found later, in England, in association with dubbing—they consisted essentially in a delivery of arms. This is described by Tacitus and its persistence at the period of the invasion is attested by many texts. There can be no doubt as to the continuity between the Germanic ritual and the ritual of chivalry. But in changing its setting the act had also changed its social significance.

Among the Germans all free men were warriors. All had therefore the right to initiation by arms wherever this practice was an essential part of the tradition of the folk (we do not know if it was universal). On the other hand, one of the characteristics of feudal society was, as we know, the formation of a group of professional fighting-men, consisting primarily of the military vassals and their chiefs. The performance of the ancient ceremony naturally became restricted to this military class; and in consequence it came near to losing any kind of permanent social foundation. It had been the rite which admitted a man to membership of the people. But the people in the ancient sense—the small *civitas* of free men—no longer existed; and the ceremony began to be used as the rite which admitted a man to membership of a class, although this class still lacked any clear outline. In some places the usage simply disappeared; such seems to have been the case among the Anglo-Saxons. But in the countries where Frankish custom prevailed it survived, though for a long time it was not in general use or in any way obligatory.

Later, as knightly society became more clearly aware of what separated it from the unwarlike multitude and raised it above them, there developed a more urgent sense of the need for a formal act to mark the individual's entry into the society so defined, whether the new member was a young man of 'noble' birth who was being admitted into adult society, or—as happened much more rarely—some fortunate upstart placed on a level with men of ancient lineage by recently acquired power, or merely by his own strength or skill. In Normandy, as early as the end of the eleventh century, to say of the son of a great vassal: 'He is not a knight', was tantamount to implying that he was still a child or an adolescent.[1]

Undoubtedly the concern thus to symbolize every change of legal status as well as every contract by a visible gesture conformed to characteristic tendencies in medieval society—as witness the frequently picturesque ritual of entry into the craft gilds. It was necessary, however, that the change of

[1] Haskins, *Norman Institutions*, 1918, p. 282, c. 5.

status thus symbolized should be clearly recognized as such, which is why the general adoption of the ceremony of dubbing really reflected a profound modification in the idea of knighthood.

During the first feudal age, what was implied by the term *chevalier*, knight, was primarily a status determined either by a *de facto* situation or by a legal tie, the criterion being purely personal. A man was called *chevalier* because he fought *à cheval*, on horseback, with full equipment; he was called the *chevalier* of someone when he held a fief of that person, on condition of serving him armed in this fashion. The time came, however, when neither the possession of a fief nor the criterion—necessarily a somewhat vague one—of mode of life was any longer sufficient to earn the title; a sort of consecration was necessary as well. The transformation was completed towards the middle of the twelfth century. A turn of phrase in use even before 1100 will help us to grasp its significance. A knight was not merely 'made'; he was 'ordained'. This was how it was put, for example, in 1098 by the count of Ponthieu as he was about to arm the future Louis VI.[1] The whole body of dubbed knights constituted an 'order', *ordo*. These are learned words, ecclesiastical words, but we find them from the beginning on the lips of laymen. They were by no means intended—at least when they were first used—to suggest an assimilation with holy orders. In the vocabulary which Christian writers had borrowed from Roman antiquity, an *ordo* was a division of society, temporal as well as ecclesiastical. But it was a regular, clearly defined division, conformable to the divine plan—an institution, really, and not merely a plain fact.

Nevertheless, in a society accustomed to live under the sign of the supernatural, the rite of the delivery of arms, at first purely secular, could scarcely have failed to acquire a sacred character and two usages, both of them very old, gave openings for the intervention of the Church.

In the first place there was the blessing of the sword. Originally it had had no specific connection with the dubbing. Everything in the service of man seemed in that age to call for this protection from the snares of the Devil. The peasant obtained a blessing for his crops, his herd, his well; the bridegroom, for the marriage bed; the pilgrim, for his staff. The warrior naturally did the same for the tools of his profession. The oath 'on consecrated arms' was already known to the old Lombard law.[2] But most of all the arms with which the young warrior was equipped for the first time seemed to call for such sanctification. The essential feature was a rite of contact. The future knight laid his sword for a moment on the altar. This gesture was accompanied or followed by prayers, and though these were inspired

---

[1] *Rec. des Histor. de France*, XV, p. 187.

[2] *Ed. Rothari*, c. 359. Insufficient research has hitherto been devoted to the liturgy of dubbing to knighthood. In the bibliography will be found an indication of the works and collections which I have consulted. This first attempt at classification, rudimentary though it is, was only made possible for me by the kind assistance of my Strasbourg colleague, Abbé Michel Andrieu.

by the general form of benediction, they early took on a form specially appropriate to an investiture. In this form they appeared already, shortly after 950, in a pontifical compiled in the abbey of St. Alban of Mainz. This compilation, a substantial part of which was doubtless based on borrowings from older sources, was soon in use throughout Germany, as well as in northern France, England, and even Rome itself, where it was imposed by the influence of the Ottonian court. It diffused far and wide the model of benediction for the 'newly-girt' sword. It should be understood, however, that this consecration at first constituted only a sort of preface to the ceremony. The dubbing proceeded afterwards according to its peculiar forms.

Here again, however, the Church was able to play its part. Originally the task of arming the adolescent could as a rule be performed only by a knight already confirmed in that status—his father, for example, or his lord; but it might also be entrusted to a prelate. As early as 846, Pope Sergius had girded the baldric on the Carolingian Louis II. Similarly, William the Conqueror later had one of his sons dubbed by the archbishop of Canterbury. No doubt this compliment was paid less to the priest as such than to the prince of the Church, chief of many vassals. Nevertheless, a pope or a bishop could scarcely dispense with religious ceremonial. In this way, the liturgy was enabled to permeate the whole ceremony of dubbing.

This process was completed by the eleventh century. It is true that a pontifical of Besançon composed at this time contains only two benedictions of the sword, both of them very simple. But from the second of these it emerges very clearly that the officiating priest was supposed to do the arming himself. Nevertheless, to find a genuine religious ritual of dubbing, we must look farther north, towards the region between Seine and Meuse which was the true cradle of most authentic feudal institutions. Our oldest piece of evidence here is a pontifical of the province of Rheims, compiled towards the beginning of the century by a cleric who, while taking the Mainz collection as his model, none the less drew abundantly on local usages. Together with a benediction of the sword, which reproduces that in the Rhenish original, the liturgy comprises similar prayers for the other arms or insignia—banner, lance, shield, with the single exception of the spurs, the delivery of which was to the end reserved for laymen. Next follows a benediction upon the future knight himself, and finally it is expressly mentioned that the sword will be girded on by the bishop. After an interval of nearly two centuries, the ceremonial appears in a fully developed form, once again in France, in the pontifical of the bishop of Mende, William Durand, which was compiled about 1295, though its essential elements apparently date from the reign of St. Louis. Here the consecratory rôle of the prelate is carried to the ultimate limit. He now not only girds on the sword; he also gives the *paumée*; in the words of the text, he 'marks' the aspirant 'with the character of knighthood'. Adopted in the fourteenth century by the Roman pontifical, this form was destined to become the official rite of Christendom. As to the accessory practices—the purifying bath, imitated from that taken by catechumens, and the vigil of arms—these do not appear to have been introduced before the twelfth century or ever to have been anything but exceptional. Moreover, the vigil was not always devoted entirely to pious meditations. If we are to believe a poem of Beaumanoir, it was not unknown for it to be whiled away to the sound of fiddles.[1]

Nevertheless, it would be a mistake to suppose that any of this religious symbolism was ever indispensable to the making of a knight, if only because circumstances would often have prevented it from being carried out. At all times knights might be made on the field, before or after the battle; witness the accolade (*colée*)—performed with the sword, according to late medieval practice—which Bayard bestowed on his king after Marignano. In 1213, Simon de Montfort had surrounded with a religious pomp worthy of a crusading hero the dubbing of his son, whom two bishops, to the strains of *Veni Creator*, armed as a knight for the service of Christ. From the monk Pierre des Vaux-de-Cernay, who took part in it, this ceremony drew a characteristic exclamation: 'O new fashion of chivalry! Fashion unheard of till then!' The less ostentatious blessing of the sword itself, according to the evidence of John of Salisbury,[2] was not general before the middle of the twelfth century. It seems, however, to have been very widely adopted at that time. The Church, in short, had tried to transform the ancient delivery of arms into a 'sacrament'—the word, which is found in the writings of clerics, gave no offence in an age when theology was still far from having assumed a scholastic rigidity and people continued freely to lump together under the name of sacrament every kind of act of consecration. It had not been wholly successful in this; but it had carved out a share for itself, larger in some places, more restricted in others. Its efforts, by emphasizing the importance of the rite of ordination, did much to kindle the feeling that the order of chivalry was a society of initiates. And since every Christian institution needed the sanction of a legendary calendar, hagiography came to its aid. 'When at mass the epistles of St. Paul are read,' says one liturgist, 'the knights remain standing, to do him honour, for he was a knight.'[3]

2 THE CODE OF CHIVALRY

Once the religious element had been introduced, its effects were not confined to strengthening the *esprit de corps* of the knightly world. It also exercised a potent influence on the moral law of the group. Before the

---

[1] *Jehan et Blonde*, ed. H. Suchier (*Oeuvres poétiques de Ph. de Rémi*, II, v. 5916 *et seq.*).
[2] *Polycraticus*, VI, 10 (ed. Webb, II, p. 25).   [3] Guillaume Durand, *Rationale*, IV, 16.

future knight took back his sword from the altar he was generally required to take an oath defining his obligations.[1] It was not taken by all dubbed knights, since not all of them had their arms blessed; but, many ecclesiastical writers considered, with John of Salisbury, that by a sort of quasi-contract even those who had not pronounced it with their lips were 'tacitly' bound by the oath through the mere fact of having accepted knighthood. Little by little the rules thus formulated found their way into other texts: first into the prayers, often very beautiful ones, which punctuated the course of the ceremony; later, with inevitable variations, into various writings in the vulgar tongue. One of these, composed shortly after 1180, was a celebrated passage from the *Perceval* of Chrétien de Troyes. In the following century these rules were set forth in some pages of the prose romance of *Lancelot*; in the German *Minnesang*, in a fragment of the 'Meissner'; finally and above all, in the short French didactic poem entitled *L'Ordene de Chevalerie*. This little work had a great success. Paraphrased before long in a cycle of Italian sonnets, imitated in Catalonia by Ramon Lull, it opened the way to the abounding literature which, during the last centuries of the Middle Ages, drained to the lees the symbolic significance of the dubbing ceremony and, by its final extravagances, proclaimed the decadence of an institution which had become more a matter of etiquette than of law, and the impoverishment of the very ideal which men professed to rate so high.

Originally this ideal had not lacked genuine vitality. It was super-imposed on rules of conduct evolved at an earlier date as the spontaneous expression of class consciousness; rules that pertained to the fealty of vassals (the transition appears clearly, towards the end of the eleventh century, in the *Book of the Christian Life* by Bishop Bonizo of Sutri, for whom the knight is, first and foremost, an enfeoffed vassal) and constituted above all a class code of noble and 'courteous' people. From these secular moral precepts the new decalogue borrowed the principles most acceptable to the religious mind: generosity; the pursuit of glory or 'praise' (*los*); contempt for fatigue, pain and death—'he has no desire to embrace the knight's profession,' says the German poet Thomasin, 'whose sole desire is to live in comfort'.[2] But this reorientation was effected by imparting to these same rules a Christian colouring; and, still more, by cleansing the knightly tradition of those profane elements which had occupied, and in practice continued to occupy, so large a place in it—that dross which had brought to the lips of so many rigorists, from St. Anselm to St. Bernard, the old play on words so charged with the cleric's contempt for the world: *non militia, sed malitia*:[3] 'Chivalry is tantamount to wickedness.' But after the Church had finally appropriated the feudal virtues, what writer would

---

[1] Peter of Blois, ep. XCIV.   [2] *Der Wälsche Gast*, ed. Rückert, vv. 7791-2.
[3] Anselm, *Ep.*, I (*P.L.*, CLVIII, col. 1147); St. Bernard, *De laude novae militiae*, 77, c. 2.

thenceforth have dared to repeat this equation? Lastly, to the old precepts which had undergone this process of refinement, others were added of an exclusively spiritual character.

The clergy and the laity were therefore united in demanding of the knight that piety without which Philip Augustus himself considered that he was no true *prudhomme*. He must go to mass 'every day' or at least 'frequently'; he must fast on Friday. Nevertheless this Christian hero remained by nature a warrior. What he looked for most from the benediction upon his arms was that it would make them effective, as is clearly shown in the wording of the prayers themselves. But the sword thus consecrated, though it might still as a matter of course be drawn at need against his personal enemies or those of his lord, had been given to the knight first of all that he might place it at the service of good causes. The old benedictions of the end of the tenth century already lay emphasis on this theme, which is greatly expanded in the later liturgies. Thus a modification of vital importance was introduced into the old ideal of war for war's sake, or for the sake of gain. With this sword, the dubbed knight will defend Holy Church, particularly against the infidel. He will protect the widow, the orphan, and the poor. He will pursue the malefactor. To these general precepts the lay texts frequently add a few more special recommendations concerning behaviour in battle (not to slay a vanquished and defenceless adversary); the practice of the courts of law and of public life (not to take part in a false judgment or an act of treason—if they cannot be prevented, the *Ordene de Chevalerie* modestly adds, one must withdraw); and lastly, the incidents of everyday life (not to give evil counsel to a lady; to give help, 'if possible', to a fellow-being in distress).

It is hardly surprising that the realities of knightly life, with its frequent trickery and deeds of violence, should have been far from conforming always to these aspirations. One might also be inclined to observe that, from the point of view either of a 'socially' inspired ethic or of a more purely Christian code, such a list of moral precepts seems a little short. But this would be to pass judgment, whereas the historian's sole duty is to understand. It is more important to note that in passing from the ecclesiastical theorists or liturgists to the lay popularizers the list of knightly virtues appears very often to have undergone a rather disturbing attenuation. 'The highest order that God has made and willed is the order of chivalry,' says Chrétien de Troyes, in his characteristically sweeping manner. But it must be confessed that after this high-sounding preamble the instructions which his *prudhomme* gives to the young man he is knighting seem disconcertingly meagre. It may well be that Chrétien represents the 'courtesy' of the great princely courts of the twelfth century rather than the *prudhommie*, inspired by religious sentiments, which was in vogue in the following century in the circle of Louis IX. It is doubtless no accident that the same epoch and the same environment in which this knightly saint lived should have given birth to the noble prayer (included in the *Pontifical* of William Durand) which may be regarded as a kind of liturgical commentary on the knights carved in stone on the porch of Chartres and the inner wall of the façade of Rheims: 'Most Holy Lord, Almighty Father . . . thou who hast permitted on earth the use of the sword to repress the malice of the wicked and defend justice; who for the protection of thy people hast thought fit to institute the order of chivalry . . . cause thy servant here before thee, by disposing his heart to goodness, never to use this sword or another to injure anyone unjustly; but let him use it always to defend the Just and the Right.'

Thus the Church, by assigning to it an ideal task, finally and formally approved the existence of this 'order' of warriors which, conceived as one of the necessary divisions of a well-ordered society, was increasingly identified with the whole body of dubbed knights. 'O God, who after the Fall, didst constitute in all nature three ranks among men,' we read in one of the prayers in the Besançon liturgy. At the same time it provided this class with a religious justification of a social supremacy which had long been a recognized fact. The very orthodox *Ordene de Chevalerie* says that knights should be honoured above all other men, save priests. More crudely, the romance of *Lancelot*, after having explained how they were instituted 'to protect the weak and the peaceful', proceeds—in conformity with the emphasis on symbols common to all this literature—to discover in the horses which they ride the peculiar symbol of the 'people' whom they hold 'in right subjection'. 'For above the people must sit the knight. And just as one controls a horse and he who sits above leads it where he will, so the knight must lead the people at his will.' Later, Ramon Lull did not think he offended Christian sentiment by saying that it was conformable to good order that the knight should 'draw his well-being' from the things that were provided for him 'by the weariness and toil' of his men.[1] This epitomizes the attitude of a dominant class: an attitude eminently favourable to the development of a nobility in the strictest sense of the term.

[1] *Libro de la orden de Caballeria*, I, 9. The whole passage has a remarkable flavour.

XXIV

TRANSFORMATION OF THE NOBILITY INTO A LEGAL CLASS

1 THE INHERITANCE OF KNIGHTHOOD AND NOBILITY

ABOUT 1119, the Order of the Temple was founded for the protection of the settlements in the Holy Land. It consisted of two categories of fighting-men, distinguished from each other by their dress, their arms and their rank. In the higher category were the 'knights'; in the lower, the ordinary 'serjeants'—white mantles contrasted with brown. There can be no doubt that from the first the contrast corresponded to a difference of social origin among the recruits. Nevertheless, the earliest *Rule*, drawn up in 1130, does not contain any precise provisions on this subject. What might be called the consensus of opinion evidently decided into which of the two grades a man was to be admitted. A little more than a century later (*c.* 1250) the second *Rule*, by contrast, displays an uncompromising legalism. To be entitled to wear the white mantle, it was first of all necessary that the candidate should have been knighted before his entry into the Order. But even that was not enough. He had to be in addition 'a knight's son or a descendant of knights on his father's side'; in other words, as it is expressed in another passage, he had to be a 'nobleman' (*gentilhomme*). For, as the *Rule* again prescribes, it is only on this condition that a man 'must and can' receive knighthood. This is not all. What happens if a newcomer chooses to conceal his knightly rank and slip in among the serjeants? Once the truth is known, he is to be put in irons.[1] Even among the soldier-monks in this mid-thirteenth century, pride of class, which regarded any voluntary forfeiture of rank as a crime, counted for more than Christian humility. Between 1130 and about 1250, therefore, an important development had taken place: the right to be made a knight had been transformed into a hereditary privilege.

In the countries where the legislative tradition had never been lost, or had lapsed and been revived, the new law was defined by various edicts.

---

[1] For the old rule, see G. Schnürer, *Die ursprüngliche Templerregel*, 1903. For a French text of the rule: H. de Curzon, *La règle du Temple* (Soc. de l'hist. de France), c. 431; 445; 446; 448. For similar provisions among the Hospitallers, in the general chapter of 19th September, 1262, Delaville Le Roulx, *Cartulaire général*, III, p. 47, c. 19.

In 1152, a peace ordinance of Frederick Barbarossa at one and the same time forbade 'peasants' to carry the lance and the sword—knightly weapons—and recognized as 'lawful knights' only men whose ancestors had been knights before them; another, in 1187, expressly forbade the sons of peasants to get themselves knighted. As early as 1140, Roger II of Sicily decreed that only the descendants of knights be admitted to knighthood; and in this he was followed in 1234 by King James I of Aragon and in 1294 by Count Charles II of Provence. In France there was at that time almost no statute law. But the judgments of the royal court under St. Louis were explicit on this point, and so were the customaries. Except by a special dispensation from the king, no knighthood could lawfully be conferred unless the father of the recipient or his grandfather, in the male line, had been a knight (perhaps as early as this period, in any case not much later, the provincial customs of at least a part of Champagne agreed that this 'nobility' could be transmitted through the mother). The same conception seems also to form the basis of a passage, admittedly less clear, in the great treatise on Castilian law, the *Siete Partidas*, compiled about 1260 on the orders of King Alfonso the Wise. It is a striking fact that these various texts were almost contemporaneous and in perfect accord not only with each other, but also with the rule of the Temple, an international Order. On the continent at least—the case in England, as we shall see, was otherwise—the evolution of the upper classes followed a fundamentally uniform pattern.[1]

It is true that when they expressly imposed the hereditary rule sovereigns and courts of law were hardly aware that they were doing anything new, since at all times the great majority of those who were knighted were descendants of knights. In the eyes of an increasingly exclusive group opinion, only high birth—'guarantee of the continuation of ancient honour', as it was called by Ramon Lull—enabled a man to observe the code of behaviour to which he was committed by the delivery of arms. 'Ah, God! how badly is the good warrior rewarded who makes the son of a villein a knight!' exclaims the poet of *Girart de Roussillon*, about 1160;[2] which, however, testifies to the fact that these intruders were by no means rare. No law, no custom, could altogether exclude them. Moreover, they appeared at times to be almost necessary for the recruitment of armies; for that same class prejudice produced a strong conviction that only knights had the right to fight on horseback fully armed. In 1302, on the eve of the battle of Courtrai, the Flemish princes, desiring to have a cavalry force,

---

[1] *M.G.H.*, *Constitutiones*, I, p. 197, c. 10; p. 451, c. 20; H. Niese, *Die Gesetzgebung der norm. Dynastie*, p. 67; P. de Marca, *Marca Hisp.*, col. 1430, c. 12; Papon, *Histoire Genérále de Provence*, III, p. 423; *Siete Partidas*, Part II., XXI, I, 2. Cf. for Portugal, E. Prestage, *Chivalry*, p. 143. For France, the references are too numerous to be listed here; cf. Petit-Dutaillis, *L'Essor des États d'Occident*, p. 22 *et seq.*

[2] Raimon Lull, *Libro de la orden de Caballeria*, ed. I, R. de Luanco, III, 8; *Girart de Roussillon*, trans. P. Meyer, p. 28 (cf. ed. Foerster, *Roman.Studien*, vol. V, v. 940 *et seq.*).

knighted a number of rich burghers whose wealth enabled them to provide themselves with the necessary horses and equipment.[1] The transformation of what had long been by mere convention a hereditary vocation, liable to many setbacks, into a legalized and jealously-guarded privilege was therefore of capital importance, even if contemporaries had no clear awareness of this development. The profound social changes which were in progress at that time on the fringes of the knightly world had certainly done much to inspire these Draconian measures.

In the twelfth century a new power was born—the urban patriciate. In these rich merchants who frequently acquired manors and many of whom had aspired to 'the baldric of knighthood', for themselves or their sons, the hereditary warriors could not fail to recognize elements much more foreign to their own mentality and way of life—much more disturbing also on account of their number—than the soldiers of fortune or the manorial officials who had hitherto provided most of the non-noble candidates for knighthood. We know, through Bishop Otto of Freising, the reactions of the German barons to the knighthoods which they considered were too freely distributed, in northern Italy, to 'men in trades and crafts'; Beaumanoir, in France, has very clearly explained how the pressure of the new social classes, eager to invest their capital in land, led the kings to take the precautions necessary to prevent the purchase of a fief from making every *nouveau riche* the equal of a descendant of knights. When a class feels itself threatened it tends to close its ranks.

It would be a mistake, however, to imagine that there was, in theory, any insuperable obstacle. A class of powerful individuals could not transform itself completely into a hereditary caste without being compelled to exclude from its ranks the new forces whose inevitable emergence is the very law of life, thereby condemning itself, as a social group, to permanent enfeeblement. Thus the evolution of legal opinion during the feudal period tended much less to impose a strict ban on new admissions than to subject them to rigorous control. Formerly every knight could make a knight. Such was still the opinion of three resourceful persons of whom Beaumanoir writes towards the end of the thirteenth century. All three were knights themselves, but they needed, as a mere lay-figure, a fourth person of the same rank whose presence was required by custom for a particular legal transaction. So on their way they laid hold of a peasant and gave him the accolade, saying: 'Be thou a knight!' By that date, however, such action had become illegal, and a heavy fine was the just punishment for this anachronism. For a member of the knightly order no longer had the right to confer membership on others unless the aspirant was already of knightly lineage. When such was not the case he might indeed be knighted, but only by special permission from the sole authority who, according to contemporary notions, was entitled to exercise the extraordinary power of

[1] P. Thomas, *Textes historiques sur Lille*, II, 1936, p. 237.

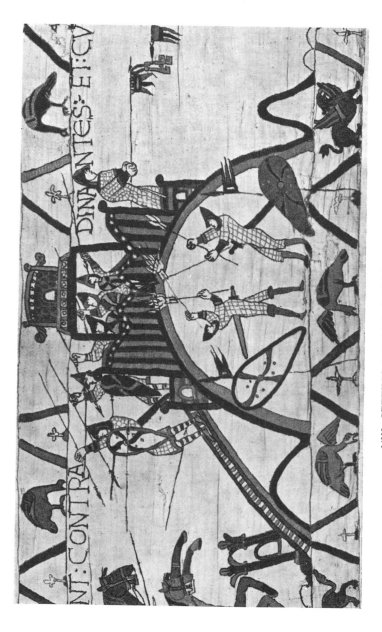

VIII. SETTING FIRE TO A WOODEN CASTLE

Capture of Dinan. Bayeux Tapestry, end of the 11th century.

IX. THE BARON BUILDS IN STONE

The keep of Langeais, built in 994-995 by Fulk Nerra, Count of Anjou.

dispensing from customary rules: namely the king, the sole bestower, as Beaumanoir says, of 'novelties'.

We have already seen that this was the ruling of the French royal judges as early as St. Louis. Soon, at the Capetian court, the practice arose of giving these authorizations the form of 'letters of chancery', described almost from the first as 'letters of nobility'—for to be qualified to receive knighthood was to succeed in being assimilated to the 'nobles' by birth. The first examples we possess of documents of this kind, which had a great future before them, date from Philip III or Philip IV. Occasionally the king, in accordance with ancient practice, made use of his prerogative to reward with the accolade some act of gallantry on the field of battle—as did Philip the Fair, who knighted a butcher after the battle of Mons-en-Pevèle.[1] Most frequently, however, it was received in recognition of long services or of a pre-eminent social position. 'Letters of nobility' not only permitted a new knight to be created: since the capacity to receive knighthood was transmitted from generation to generation, they in effect brought into being each time a whole new line of knights.

Sicilian legislation and practice were based on exactly the same principles as those just described; and this was also true of Spain. In the Empire—though the decrees of Barbarossa did not actually provide for this—we know that the Emperor considered that he had a right to confer knighthood on ordinary soldiers;[2] thus showing that he did not regard himself as being personally bound by the seemingly absolute prohibitions of his own laws. Moreover, from the following reign onwards the example of Sicily exercised an influence over sovereigns who, for more than half a century, were to unite both crowns. From the time of Conrad IV, who began to reign independently in 1250, we find the German monarchs granting, by letters, permission to receive the 'baldric of knighthood' to persons who had no claim to it by birth.

Certainly the monarchies did not succeed without difficulty in establishing this monopoly. Roger II of Sicily himself made an exception in favour of the abbot of La Cava. In France the nobles and prelates of the *séné-chaussée* of Beaucaire still claimed in 1298—with what success we do not know—the unrestricted right to create knights among the townsmen.[3] Resistance was strong, especially on the part of the great feudatories. Under Philip III, the king's court had to institute proceedings against the courts of Flanders and Nevers, who were guilty of illegally knighting 'villeins'. (The latter were in fact wealthy persons.) Later, in the disorders of the time of the Valois, the great princes of the royal houses had less difficulty in arrogating this privilege to themselves. It was. naturally in the Empire that the right to admit newcomers to knighthood in this way was most widely exercised: by territorial princes like the bishop of

---

[1] *Rec. des Hist. de France*, XXII, p. 18.   [2] Otto of Freising, *Gesta*, II, 23.
[3] *Hist. de Languedoc*, 2nd ed., VIII, col. 1747.

Strasbourg,[1] from 1281; and even occasionally, in Italy, by urban communes such as Florence, which possessed the right as early as 1260. But this represented simply the dismemberment of regalian rights: the principle that the sovereign alone had the right to remove the impediment was preserved. More serious was the case of the interlopers—and there were certainly a good many of them—who took advantage of the actual situation to insinuate themselves illicitly into the ranks of knighthood. Since the nobility remained in large measure a class distinguished by its power and its mode of life, common opinion, in spite of laws, seldom refused to the possessor of a military fief, to the lord of a manor, or to the veteran warrior whatever his origin, the name of noble and the right, accordingly, to receive knighthood. Since in most cases the title derived from long usage after some generations, no one dreamed of disputing the family's right to it; and in this situation the governments' usual course was merely to exact a little money from those concerned by ratifying the abuse. It is none the less true that the transformation of *de facto* inheritance into legal inheritance, in the course of a long process of spontaneous development, had been made possible only by the strengthening of the royal or princely authority which alone was capable both of instituting a stricter control of society and of regularizing the inevitable and salutary transitions from class to class by making them legal. If the Parlement of Paris had not existed or had lacked the strength needed to execute its judgments, there would not have been a petty lord in the kingdom who would not have contrived to make knights as he thought fit.

There was at that time scarcely an institution which, in the hands of perpetually needy governments, was not more or less transformed into a money-making machine. The authorizations to create knights were no exceptions to the rule. Like other documents issued by the chancelleries, royal letters, with very rare exceptions, were not granted free of charge. There were also cases where people paid in order not to have to prove their origin.[2] But Philip the Fair seems to have been the first sovereign openly to make knighthood a saleable commodity. In 1302, after the defeat of Courtrai, commissioners scoured the provinces in order to canvass people prepared to pay for ennoblement, and at the same time to sell the royal serfs their freedom. It does not appear, however, that this practice was very general at that time either in Europe or in France itself, or that the returns were large. At a later date the kings learned to make the *savonette à vilains*—'peasants' toilet soap'—one of their regular sources of revenue and for the rich taxpayers it afforded a means of escaping, by a single payment, the taxes from which the nobility were exempted. But until about the middle of the fourteenth century, the fiscal privilege of the nobles

---

[1] *Annal. Colmar.* in *M.G.H.* SS, XVII, p. 208, l. 15; cf. p. 244, l. 31.
[2] A. de Barthélemy, 'De la qualification de chevalier' in *Revue nobiliaire*, 1868, p. 123, and 'Études sur les lettres d'anoblissement' in *Revue nobiliaire*, 1869, p. 205.

remained as ill-defined as State taxation itself; and *esprit de corps*, very strong in knightly society—to which the princes themselves were conscious of belonging—would doubtless scarcely have permitted the multiplication of favours which were felt to be so many insults to men of noble birth.

If access to the circle of knights by birth was not absolutely closed, the door was nevertheless only very slightly ajar. It was certainly very much less easy to enter than it had been before or would be in the future; hence the violent reaction against the nobility which, in France at least, broke out in the fourteenth century. What more striking proof can be found of the solidarity and exclusive spirit of a class than the fierceness of the attacks to which it is subjected? 'Revolt of the non-nobles against the nobles'— the expression, which was virtually in official use at the time of the Jacquerie, is revealing; and not less so is the list of combatants. Étienne Marcel, a rich burgess and the first magistrate of the first of cities, deliberately set himself up as the enemy of the nobles. Under Louis XI or Louis XIV he would have been one of them himself. In truth, the period from about 1250 to about 1400 was, on the continent, the period which witnessed the most rigid stratification of social classes.

2 THE DESCENDANTS OF KNIGHTS BECOME A PRIVILEGED CLASS

By itself, however, the restriction of knighthood to members of families already confirmed in that status or to the recipients of exceptional favours would not have sufficed to form a genuine nobility. For this would have meant that the privileges which according to the conception of nobility were inseparable from noble birth would have been made dependent on a ceremony which might or might not be carried out. It was not just a question of prestige. Increasingly the pre-eminent position which it was agreed to accord to knights, both as 'ordained' warriors and as vassals charged with the highest responsibilities in war and counsel, tended to take concrete shape in a precise legal code. Now, from the end of the eleventh century to the first years of the thirteenth, the same rules were reproduced throughout feudal Europe. In order to enjoy these advantages it was necessary in the first place that a man should efficiently perform his duties as a vassal, 'that he have arms and horses, that, unless prevented by age, he take part in the host and in the expeditions, in the assemblies and in the courts', say the *Usages* of Catalonia. It was also necessary that he should have been knighted. The general weakening of vassal services had the result that gradually the first condition ceased to be insisted on; the later texts pass it over in silence. The second, on the other hand, remained for a long time very much in force. As late as 1238, a private family regulation, the statute of the parceners who possessed in common the castle of La Garde-Guérin in the Gévaudan, gives priority to a younger son over the eldest, if the former has received knighthood and the latter has not. Suppose it happened nevertheless—no matter where—that a knight's son failed to be knighted in his turn and remained a simple 'squire' (the traditional title of the noble youth in the service of his elders), then once he had passed the age after which such neglect was deemed no longer permissible—twenty-five in Flanders and Hainault, thirty in Catalonia—he was numbered among the 'clod-hoppers'.[1]

But pride of birth had become too potent for these requirements to be maintained for ever. Their disappearance was effected by stages. In Provence in 1235, and in Normandy about the same time, it was still only the son who was recognized as having a right to the benefits of the father's rank, without any obligation to get himself knighted, and if he in his turn had a son the latter, according to the conditions laid down in the Provençal text, must personally receive knighthood if he wished to share those privileges. More significant still is the series of charters granted by the German kings to the men of Oppenheim: the same rights are granted in 1226 to knights, from 1269 to 'knights and sons of knights', and in 1275 to 'knights, their sons and their grandsons'.[2] People must at times have grown weary of counting the generations. In any case the formal reception of arms continued to be regarded as a duty which the noble youth could not evade without in some degree losing caste. In the family of the counts of Provence, of the house of Barcelona, however, it was delayed as long as possible owing to an extraordinary superstition that it was a presage of approaching death.[3] Since to be knighted involved by convention the assembling of the complete equipment necessary to effective service in the field, the kings of France, from Philip Augustus to Philip the Fair, tried to make the ceremony obligatory for those of their subjects who belonged to knightly families. So little did they succeed in this, however, that the royal administration, powerless even to obtain a lucrative financial yield from the collection of fines or the sale of dispensations, had in the end to content itself merely with ordering this class, as soon as war threatened, to be in possession of arms.

In the last years of the thirteenth century, the evolution was almost everywhere complete. What henceforth made the noble was not the old rite of initiation, now reduced to the status of a polite formality and neglected by the majority because as a rule it involved great expense; it was the hereditary right to be knighted, whether or not that right was exercised. One calls a nobleman, writes Beaumanoir, whoever is 'of knightly lineage'. And shortly after 1284 the earliest authorization of knighthood granted by the chancellery of the kings of France to a person not of noble

[1] *Usatici Barcin.*, c. 9 and 8; C. Porrée, *Études historiques sur le Gévaudan*, 1919 (and *Bibl. Éc. Chartes*, 1907), p. 62, c. 1; Peace Charter of Hainault (1200), in *M.G.H.*, SS. XXI, p. 619.

[2] *Summa de legibus*, in Tardif, vol. II, XIV, 2; F. Benoit, *Recueil des actes des comtes de Provence*, II, no. 246, c; ixa, 275, c; va, 277; 278 (1235–1238). P. Guilhiermoz, *Essai sur les origines de la noblesse en France au moyen-âge*, 1902, p. 481.

[3] 'Annales Colonienses max.' in *M.G.H.*, SS. XVII, p. 845.

birth raised at one stroke, without imposing any conditions at all, the entire posterity of the recipient 'to the privileges, rights and franchises which the nobles are accustomed to enjoy by virtue of the two lines of descent'.[1]

3 THE LAW OF THE NOBLES

This body of private law (which with certain necessary modifications applied to women of noble birth as well as to men) varied considerably in its details from one region to another. Moreover it evolved only slowly, and in the course of time underwent important modifications. We shall confine ourselves here to noting the most general characteristics as they emerged in the course of the thirteenth century.

Traditionally, the ties of vassalage were the form of dependence peculiar to the upper classes. But here, as elsewhere, a *de facto* situation was replaced by a legal monopoly. Formerly a man had been regarded as noble because he was a vassal. Henceforth, by a veritable reversal of the order of the terms, it was impossible, in theory, to be a vassal—in other words to hold a military fief or 'free' fief—if one did not already rank among the nobles by birth. This was commonly admitted almost everywhere towards the middle of the thirteenth century. Nevertheless, the rise of burgher wealth as well as the need of money by which the old families were so often harassed did not allow the rule to be maintained in all its rigour. Not only was it in practice very far from being constantly observed—which opened the way to many usurpations of nobility—but even in law it was necessary to make provision for exemptions. Sometimes these were general in scope, as for example those in favour of persons born of a noble mother and a non-noble father;[2] more often, they were in favour of individuals. The latter sort, once again, redounded to the profit of the monarchs who alone were capable of legitimizing such anomalies in the social order, and were not in the habit of distributing these favours free. Since the fief was most frequently a manor, political authority over the common people tended as a result of these practices to be detached from noble rank. But what if the fief involved the submission of sub-vassals? If the latter were noblemen the right of the non-noble purchaser to require homage from them was not ordinarily recognized; he had to be content with taxes and services, without gestures of fealty. There was even reluctance to admit that he could himself, as a vassal, do homage to his superior lord. The ceremony was reduced to an oath of fealty or, at any rate, the kiss was omitted from it, as being too egalitarian. Even in the manner of soliciting or contracting obedience there were forms that were forbidden to the man of low birth.

Military vassals had for a long time been governed by a law which

[1] A. de Barthélemy, 'De la qualification de chevalier', in *Revue nobiliaire*, 1869, p. 198.
[2] Beaumanoir, II, § 1434.

differed from the common rules. They were not tried by the same courts as other dependants; their fiefs were not inherited in the same way as other properties. Their family status itself bore the marks of their rank. When the nobility arose from among the possessors of military fiefs, the customary law formerly attached to the exercise of a function tended to become the customary law of a group of families. On this point, a change in terminology is instructive: whereas formerly people had spoken of *bail féodal*, 'feudal wardship' (the institution has been defined in an earlier chapter),[1] henceforth they began to say in France *garde noble*, 'noble wardship'. As was natural for a class which derived its distinctive character from very ancient institutions, the private law of the nobles retained in many respects an archaic cast.

A number of other features underlined still more emphatically the social supremacy of the class as well as its character as a fighting order. If it was a question of maintaining purity of blood, there was obviously no more effective means than the complete prohibition of marriages with persons of inferior status. Only in the imported feudalism of Cyprus and the hierarchic society of Germany, however, did it come to that; and in the latter country, which was characterized, as we shall see, by a highly-developed system of gradations within the nobility itself, it was only the higher ranks and not the petty knights, sprung from former manorial officials, who were restricted in this way. Elsewhere the memory of the ancient equality of free men continued, so far as marriage was concerned, to be reflected in law, if not in practice. Everywhere, however, certain great religious communities, which hitherto had displayed their aristocratic spirit only in rejecting postulants of servile origin, decided now to admit them only if they were descended from the nobility.[2] Everywhere also— earlier in one place, later in another—we find evidence that the noble was specially protected in his person against the non-noble; that he was subject to an exceptional penal law, with heavier fines, as a rule, than those exacted from the common people; that recourse to private vengeance, regarded as inseparable from the bearing of arms, tended to be reserved for him; that the sumptuary laws assigned to him a place apart. The importance attached to birth as the source of privilege was expressed in the transformation of the old individual signs of 'recognition', painted on the knight's shield or engraved on his seal, into the armorial bearings, sometimes transmitted with the fief but more often handed down, even without the property,

---

[1] pp. 201–3.
[2] The works of A. Schulte, *Der Adel und die deutsche Kirche im Mittelalter*, 2nd ed., Stuttgart, and of Dom Ursmér Berlière, *Le recrutement dans les monastères bénédictins aux XIIIe et XIVe siècles* (*Mém. Acad. royale Belgique* in-8, 2e série, XVIII), provide a great deal of information on this subject, though with an insufficiency of exact chronological and critical data. Whatever Schulte thinks, it follows from the texts cited that —allowing for the very loose sense in which the words *nobiles* and *ignobiles* were used in early times—the monopoly of the nobles, in the exact sense of the term, was everywhere a relatively late phenomenon. The admission of the unfree sets quite another problem.

from generation to generation. The use of these symbols of continuity, first seen in the royal and princely dynasties, where pride of birth was particularly strong, and soon adopted by houses of lesser rank, was regarded henceforth as the monopoly of the families classed as noble. Finally, although tax exemptions were still far from being strictly defined, the military obligation—formerly the characteristic duty of the vassal, now the noble's duty *par excellence*—had henceforth the effect of relieving the nobleman of the usual pecuniary burdens; these being in his case replaced by warlike services.

However strong the rights acquired by birth, they were not so strong that they might not be lost by the exercise of certain occupations deemed to be incompatible with high rank. It is true that the conception of derogation (*dérogeance*) was as yet far from being fully developed.[1] The rule which forbade nobles to engage in trade seems at that time to have been imposed on them above all by certain urban statutes, which were intended to protect the virtual monopoly of the merchant communities rather than to serve the pride of a hostile caste. But by universal consent agricultural labour was regarded as contrary to the honour of the military class. Even with his own compliance—so the Parlement of Paris decided—a knight who had acquired a tenement in villeinage could not perform rural labour services. 'To plough, to dig, to carry a load of wood or manure'—these were actions which, according to a Provençal ordinance, automatically involved deprivation of knightly privileges. It was also in Provence that a noblewoman was characterized as one who goes 'neither to the oven, nor to the wash-house, nor to the mill'.[2] The nobility had ceased to be defined by the exercise of a function—that of the armed retainer. It was no longer a class of initiates. It remained, however, a class distinguished by its mode of life.

4 THE EXCEPTIONAL CASE OF ENGLAND

In England, where the institutions of vassalage and knighthood were all imported, the evolution of the *de facto* nobility at first followed almost the same lines as on the continent—only to take a very different direction in the thirteenth century.

As the very powerful masters of an island kingdom whose primary purpose, in their eyes, was to provide them with the means to pursue truly imperial ambitions, the Norman and later the Angevin kings set themselves to stretch to the limit the scope of military obligation. To this end they made use of two principles belonging to different ages: the general levy of all free men; and the specialized service required of vassals. As early as

---

[1] [*Dérogeance* was an act on the part of a nobleman which constituted an impairment of his rank and led to its forfeiture.]

[2] *Olim*, I, p. 427, no. XVII (Chandeleur, 1255); F. Benoit, *Recueil des actes*, passages cited above, p. 326, n.1; M. Z. Isnard, *Livre des privilèges de Manosque*, 1894, no. XLVII, p. 154.

1180 and 1181 we find Henry II, first in his continental dominions, then in England, compelling his subjects to provide themselves with arms, each man according to his rank. The English 'assize' specifies, among others, those required of the holder of a knight's fee. It does not mention dubbing to knighthood. Nevertheless, this ceremony, as we know, was regarded as a certain guarantee that the warrior would be properly equipped. Therefore in 1224 and 1234 Henry III judged it wise to compel every possessor of such a fief to undergo this initiation without delay, at least—the qualification was introduced by the second ordinance—if homage was done directly to the king.

So far, there was nothing in these measures which greatly differed from the Capetian legislation of the same period. Yet the English government, with its strong administrative traditions, could hardly have been unaware of the increasing ineffectiveness of the old system of feudal service. Many fiefs had been parcelled out; others underwent continual and always imperfect reassessments; finally, when all was said and done, their number was necessarily limited. Was it not more reasonable firmly to base the vassal's duty to serve, and consequently to equip himself, on a much more tangible reality—on landed wealth, whatever its nature? This, moreover, was the principle which already, in 1180, Henry II had striven to apply to his continental states, where the feudal organization was not nearly so regular as in England or the duchy of Normandy. The same thing was done in England, from 1254 onwards, by using varying economic criteria, the details of which need not concern us here. But, whereas Henry II had confined himself to the question of equipment, henceforth, in conformity with practices which had already taken root, the formal assumption of knighthood was required of all free possessors of a certain quantity of free land. The rule was doubtless imposed the more readily because the royal treasury could look forward to a welcome crop of fines from the expected contraventions.

Even in England, however, the machinery of government was not at that time sufficiently well organized to ensure the strict observance of such measures. As early as the end of the century, apparently, and certainly in the following century, they had become practically inoperative. They had to be abandoned; and the knighting ceremony, less and less regularly practised, was finally, as on the continent, relegated to a place among the accessories of a social code that was becoming more and more outmoded. But the policy of the crown, with its inevitable corollary, the absence of any attempt to stop the buying and selling of fiefs, had a very important result. In England knighthood, transformed into a fiscal institution, could not serve as the focal point for the formation of a class founded on the hereditary principle.

Such a class in fact never came into being across the Channel. In the French or German sense of the word, medieval England had no nobility;

that is to say that among the free men there was no intrinsically superior class enjoying a privileged legal status of its own, transmitted by descent. In appearance English society was an astonishingly egalitarian structure. Essentially, nevertheless, it was based on the existence of an extremely rigid hierarchic division, though the line was drawn at a lower level than elsewhere. In fact at a time when everywhere else the caste of nobles was being established above the growing mass of a population described as 'free', in England, the conception of serfdom had been extended to the point where the majority of peasants were branded with this stigma. On English soil the ordinary free man was in law scarcely distinguishable from the nobleman. But the free men themselves were an oligarchy.

Yet England had an aristocracy as powerful as any in Europe—more powerful perhaps, because the land of the peasants was still more at its mercy. It was a class of manorial lords, of warriors or chieftains, of royal officials and of 'knights of the shire'—all of them men whose mode of life differed greatly and consciously from that of the common run of free men. At the top was the narrow circle of earls and 'barons'. During the thirteenth century this highest group had begun to be endowed with fairly definite privileges, but these were of an almost exclusively political and honorific nature; and above all, being attached to the *fief de dignité*, to the 'honour', they were transmissible only to the eldest son. In short, the class of noblemen in England remained, as a whole, more a 'social' than a 'legal' class. Although, naturally, power and revenues were as a rule inherited, and although, as on the continent, the prestige of birth was greatly prized, this group was too ill-defined not to remain largely open. In the thirteenth century, the possession of landed wealth had been sufficient to authorize the assumption of knighthood, in fact to make it obligatory. Something like a century and a half later it officially conferred the right (always restricted by a characteristic rule to free tenure) to elect, in the shires, the representatives of the 'Commons of the Land'. And although in theory these same representatives—they were known by the significant name of 'knights of the shire' and had originally, in fact, to be chosen from among the dubbed knights—were required to furnish proof of hereditary armorial bearings, it does not appear that, in practice, any family of solid wealth and social distinction ever encountered much difficulty in obtaining per-mission to use such emblems.[1] There were no 'letters of nobility' among the English at this period (the creation of baronets by the needy House of Stuart was only a belated imitation of French practices). There was no need for them. The actual situation was enough.

It was mainly by keeping close to the practical things which give real power over men and avoiding the paralysis that overtakes social classes which are too sharply defined and too dependent on birth that the English aristocracy acquired the dominant position it retained for centuries.

[1] Cf. E. and A. G. Porritt, *The Unreformed House of Commons*, 2nd ed., 1909, I, p. 122.

XXV

CLASS DISTINCTIONS WITHIN THE NOBILITY

1 GRADATIONS OF POWER AND RANK

DESPITE the common characteristics of their military calling and their mode of life, the group of nobles *de facto*, and later *de jure*, was never in any sense a society of equals. Profound differences of wealth and power, and consequently of prestige, established a hierarchy among them, which was first tacitly recognized, and later confirmed by custom or statute.

At a time when the obligations of vassalage still retained their full force, the principle of this classification was sought by preference in the gradations of acts of homage themselves. At the lower end of the scale we have first of all the vavasour, the 'vassal of vassals' (*vassus vassorum*), who was not himself the lord of any other warrior—not, at least, when the term vavasour, which was common to all the Romance languages, was understood in its strict sense. Not to exercise authority or to exercise it only over rustics was to be entitled to but small consideration. In practice this status usually went with an extremely modest fortune and the needy life of a petty country nobleman, given up to adventure. Consider the portrait of the heroine's father in the *Erec* of Chrétien de Troyes—'very poor was his house'—or, in the poem of *Gaydon*, that of the great-hearted vavasour with his rude armour. Outside the realm of fiction we learn of the impoverished household from which Robert Guiscard escaped in search of war and plunder; the begging habits of Bertrand de Born; or again those knights depicted in various charters of a Provençal cartulary whose sole fief was a *mansus*, that is to say the equivalent of a peasant tenement. Sometimes the term 'bachelor', literally 'young man', was used in almost the same sense, for such was naturally the condition of many young men not yet enfeoffed or still insufficiently endowed, though it might be prolonged[1] till much later in life.

As soon as the noble became the chief of other nobles he increased in dignity. After having enumerated the various indemnities due to the knight

---

[1] For Provence, F. Kiener, *Verfassungsgeschichte der Provence seit der Ostgothenherrschaft bis zur Errichtung der Konsulate* (510–1200), Leipzig, 1900, p. 107. On the 'bachelors', cf. E. F. Jacob, *Studies in the Period of Baronial Reform*, 1925 (*Oxford Studies in Social and Legal History*, VIII), p. 127 *et seq*.

who had been struck, imprisoned, or in any way maltreated, the *Usages* of Barcelona continue: 'but if he has himself two other knights established on the lands of his fief and maintains another in his household, the compensation shall be doubled'.[1] Such a person might assemble under his banner a considerable body of armed retainers; in which case he was called a banneret. If no further step separated him from the king or territorial prince to whom he did homage directly, he was also called tenant-in-chief, *captal* or baron.

Borrowed from the Germanic languages, the term 'baron' first of all passed from its original meaning of 'man' to that of 'vassal': in swearing fealty to a lord, one acknowledged oneself his 'man'. Then the habit arose of applying it more particularly to the principal vassals of the great chiefs. In this sense it expressed what was only a relative superiority of status compared with other sworn retainers of the same group. The bishop of Chester or the lord of Bellême had his barons, just as the kings had. But even the most important feudatories of the crown—the mightiest among the mighty—were in common parlance simply 'barons'.

Almost synonymous with 'baron'—in fact, employed by certain texts as its exact equivalent—the term 'peer', though possessing from the outset a more precise legal significance, belonged properly speaking to the vocabulary of judicial institutions. One of the most cherished privileges of the vassal was that of being tried in his lord's court by the latter's other vassals. The common tie of vassalage made for equality, and 'peer' thus decided the fate of 'peer'. But among the persons who held their fiefs directly of the same master there were wide differences of power and prestige. Must the rich banneret be compelled to accept the judgments of the humblest nobleman, merely by virtue of an alleged similarity in their relationship to their lord? Once again the consequences of a legal situation conflicted with the sense of more concrete realities. At an early date, therefore, it became customary in many places to reserve for the leading vassals the right to sit in judgment in cases which concerned those who were genuinely their equals in rank, as well as to offer their counsel on serious issues. The circle of 'peers' *par excellence* was thus restricted, often by recourse to a traditional or mystical number—seven, like the assessors (*scabini*) in the public tribunals of the Carolingian epoch; twelve, like the Apostles. Such bodies were to be found in lordships of moderate size like that of the monks of Mont-Saint-Michel, as well as in the great principalities such as Flanders; and the epics pictured the peers of France gathered round Charlemagne in apostolic number.

There were also other names, merely expressive of power and wealth, which readily occurred to the chroniclers or the poets when they evoked the figures of the great aristocrats. 'Magnates', *poestatz, demeines* seemed to them to dominate the mass of knights from a high eminence. For

---

[1] *Us. Barc.*, c. 6.

contrasts of rank were, in truth, extremely sharp within the nobility. When a knight has wronged another knight, the Catalan *Usages* explain, if the guilty party is 'superior' to the victim, it will not be possible to exact expiatory homage from him personally.[1] In the *Poem of the Cid*, the sons-in-law of the hero, descended from a line of counts, regard their marriage with the daughters of an ordinary vassal as a *mésalliance*. 'We should not have taken them even as concubines, without being begged to do so. They were not our equals—to sleep in our arms.' From the other side, the memoirs of the 'poor knight' from Picardy, Robert de Clary, relating to the Fourth Crusade, have preserved for us the sharp echo of the grievances long cherished by the rank and file (*commun de l'ost*) against 'the great men', 'the rich men', 'the barons'.

It was reserved for the thirteenth century, an age of definition and hierarchy, to try to create a rigidly organized system from these social distinctions, which hitherto had been not so much defined as acutely felt. In carrying on this task the jurists displayed a zeal for mathematical precision ill-adapted to realities which continued to be much more subtle. Moreover, the course of evolution was very different from one country to another. We shall confine ourselves here, as usual, to the most characteristic examples.

In England, where the aristocracy had been able to fashion an instrument of government from the old feudal obligation of court service, the word 'baron' continued to be used to describe the principal feudatories of the king, summoned to his 'Great Council' by virtue of a *de facto* monopoly which was gradually transformed into a strictly hereditary right. These persons also liked to flatter themselves with the name of 'peers of the realm' and eventually succeeded in getting it adopted officially.[2]

In France, by contrast, the two terms diverged widely. There people still spoke of 'vavasours' and 'barons' but as a rule the distinction implied nothing more than a simple difference of wealth and prestige: the decay of the tie of vassalage rendered meaningless the criteria derived from the gradations of acts of homage. But in order to draw a clearer line of division between the two ranks the feudal lawyers devised a criterion based on the gradations of judicial authority: the exercise of 'high justice' was a distinguishing feature of the barony, while the fief of the vavasour was restricted to 'low' or 'middle' justice. In this sense—it was never unreservedly adopted in everyday speech—there were a great many French barons. On the other hand, there were very few peers of France. For since epic legend favoured the number twelve, the six most important vassals of the Capetian monarch succeeded—along with the six most powerful bishops or archbishops whose churches were directly dependent on the crown—in acquiring for themselves the exclusive right to the title of peer. They

---

[1] *Us. Barc.*, c. 6.
[2] Cf. T. F. Tout, *Chapters in Administrative History*, III, p. 136 *et seq.*

were much less successful, however, in their efforts to derive practical privileges from it; they even had to submit to the curtailment of their right to be tried by their own members by accepting the presence of royal officials in court. There were too few of them, their interests as great territorial princes were too remote from those of the greater nobility as a whole, and lay too far outside the kingdom itself, for them to be able to assert their primacy in the sphere of political realities; such pre-eminence as they enjoyed was destined to remain purely honorary. Moreover, as three of the six original lay peerages became extinct in the course of the century, as a result of the reversion to the crown of the fiefs on which they had been based, the kings began, from 1297 onwards, to create new ones on their own account.[1] The age of the spontaneous formation of the nobility was followed by one in which, from top to bottom of the social scale, the crown would henceforth have the power to determine and modify the status of its subjects.

A similar trend, so far as France is concerned, may be observed in the history of the old official titles (*titres de dignités*). At all times the counts —along with the dukes and marquises, each of them the head of several counties—had figured in the first rank of magnates, as did also their descendants, known in the south of France as *comtors*. But these terms, derived from Frankish nomenclature, originally expressed a well-defined type of authority. They were applied exclusively to the heirs of the great 'honours' of the Carolingian epoch, formerly public offices, now fiefs. If some usurpations had taken place at an early date, they had affected in the first place the nature of the power itself: and the name had gone with the power. Gradually, however, as we shall see, the body of rights appertaining to the counts was broken up and ceased to have any specific meaning. The holders of the different counties might continue to possess a great many rights which they had in fact inherited from ancestors who had been officials; but since the list of these rights varied greatly from one county to another and the counts seldom had the absolute monopoly of them, their exercise was no longer related to the notion of a count's authority as something universal in character. The title of count, in short, merely signified, in each case, a great deal of power and prestige. There was therefore now no valid reason for limiting its use to the successors of the provincial governors of long ago. From 1338, at the latest, the kings began to create counts.[2] In this way there came into existence a formal classification of the nobility, archaic in its terminology, but new in spirit, and becoming more and more complicated as time went on.

Yet among the French nobility these degrees of honour and sometimes

[1] In favour of the duke of Brittany: Dom Morice, *Histoire de Bretagne*, I, col. 1122. On the claims of the peers, cf. Petit-Dutaillis, *L'Essor des États d'Occident*, pp. 266–7.
[2] Borrelli de Serres, *Recherches sur divers services publics*, III, 1909, p. 276.

of privilege did not produce any profound breach in the unity of class consciousness. If, by contrast with England, where there existed no law of the nobles as distinct from that common to all free men, France in the thirteenth century gives the effect of a hierarchical society, at least in that country these specific rights were, in their essentials, common to all persons entitled to knighthood. Developments in Germany took a very different direction.

At the outset we encounter a rule peculiar to German feudalism. It appears that at an early date the view prevailed that, on pain of forfeiture of rank, a person of a given social level could not hold a fief of one who was considered his inferior. In other words, whereas in other countries gradations of acts of homage determined a man's rank, here the scale had to be modelled on pre-existing class distinctions. Although it was not always strictly respected in practice, this rigid ordering of the 'shields of knighthood' (*Heerschilde*) expressed very strongly the spirit of a society which, having accepted the ties of vassalage only with some reluctance, refused to let them interfere with a firmly rooted hierarchic sentiment. It remained to establish the degrees of nobility. At the summit of the lay aristocracy it was agreed to place those who were known as 'the first men', *Fürsten*. The Latin texts translated the word by *principes*, and in French it became customary to say *princes*. Here again it is characteristic that the criterion should not have depended originally on feudal relationships properly so called. For the earliest usage was to include under this name all who held the office of count, even when, having received investiture from a duke or a bishop, they did not figure among the immediate vassals of the king. In the Empire, where the Carolingian imprint remained so strong, the count was always regarded as exercising his office in the name of the crown, no matter what lord had enfeoffed him with it. All princes, so defined, sat in the great courts where the kings were elected.

Nevertheless, towards the middle of the twelfth century, the growing power of the great territorial lords, together with the increasingly marked permeation of German institutions with a genuinely feudal spirit, brought about a very pronounced shift of the dividing-lines between the social ranks. By a doubly significant restriction, it became customary henceforth to reserve the title of prince for the direct feudatories of the king; and, within that group itself, to those whose authority extended over several counties. Furthermore these magnates, together with their ecclesiastical colleagues, were the only ones empowered to elect the sovereign. This at least was so until by a second segregation which took place very shortly afterwards there was constituted above them a still more restricted group of hereditary Electors. Eventually the new class of lay princes, including the Electors, formed the third rank of 'shields', after the king and the princes of the Church (i.e. the bishops and the greater abbots directly dependent on the crown). But not even in Germany was inequality carried far enough to prevent the continuance, for a long time, of a sort of internal unity within the nobility, reinforced in particular by freedom of inter-marriage. An exception was the lowest grade of knights which as a legal group, if not as a social class, was highly characteristic of the stratification peculiar at that time to German society. This was the class of *Ministeriales*, or servile knights.

2 SERJEANTS AND SERF-KNIGHTS

A powerful man does not live without servants, nor does he exercise authority without assistance. Even on the smallest manor a representative of the master was needed to direct the cultivation of the estate, to call for the labour services and see that they were properly carried out, to levy taxes, and to keep good order among the tenants. Frequently this *maire*, *bayle*, *Bauermeister* or 'reeve' (as he was variously called according to the country) had assistance in his turn. It might be thought that such elementary duties would quite simply be exercised in rotation by the tenants, or even that the latter would be required to appoint temporary officials from among their own ranks. This was in fact a very common practice in England, but on the continent, as a rule, these functions—though also performed, as was natural, by the peasants—none the less constituted genuine offices, permanent and paid, and filled by men appointed by the lord alone. Then again, in his house itself, the petty nobleman, like the baron, was surrounded by a little world of retainers—varying greatly in number according to his wealth or rank. These comprised domestic servants, artisans attached to the workshops of the 'court', and officials who helped in the control of the men or in running the household. Language failed to make any clear distinction between these forms of service, so long as they were not included in the honourable category of knightly obligations. Artisans, domestic servants, messengers, estate officials, bailiffs in the lord's immediate circle—these were all comprised under a single head. The Latin of the charters (an international language) usually called them *ministeriales*; in French, they were known as *sergents*; in German, as *Dienstmänner*.[1]

As usual, there were two alternative methods of remunerating these various services: maintenance in the master's household ('prebend') or the grant of a tenement which, being burdened with professional duties, was called a fief. The rural serjeants, since they were peasants separated by their very functions from their much more nomadic lord, were by definition tenants; their 'fiefs', originally at least, were scarcely distinguishable from the surrounding villein tenements except for certain exemptions from taxes

---

[1] Since the references for this paragraph are easy to find among the various works listed in Section No. X, 8 of the bibliography, I have kept my notes to a bare minimum. To these works, however, should be added K. H. Roth von Schreckenstein, *Die Ritter-würde und der Ritterstand. Historisch-politische Studien über deutsch-mittelalterliche Standesverhältnisse auf dem Lande und in der Stadt*, Freiburg im Breisgau, 1886.

and labour services, a natural counterpart to the special obligations to which the man himself was subject. A certain percentage deducted from the taxes which it was their duty to collect completed their remuneration. The system of 'prebend' was undoubtedly much the best suited to the conditions of life of both the domestic craftsmen and the household officials. Nevertheless, the evolution which had led to the enfeoffment of so many vassals was paralleled at the lower level of service. A great number of *ministeriales* of this type were also enfeoffed at an early date; but they nevertheless continued to look to the customary distribution of food and clothing for a considerable part of their remuneration.

Many of the serjeants of every class were of servile status. The tradition went back a long way; in every period there had been slaves to whom positions of trust in the household of their masters had been confided, and we know that in the Frankish period some of these had found their way into the ranks of the early vassals. With the development of the relationships of personal and hereditary subjection, thenceforth described as serfdom, it was very naturally to dependants of this sort that the lord by preference assigned the offices which he did not reserve exclusively for his vassals. By their lowly status and the strictness of their hereditary bond, from which there was no escape, they seemed to offer a more certain guarantee of prompt and strict obedience than did the free man. Although the servile *ministeriales* never constituted the whole of the ministerial class—remember that there was nothing of mathematical precision about this society— their growing importance in the first feudal age cannot be doubted.

Of one person who was at first employed as a furrier by the monks of Saint-Père of Chartres and afterwards got himself put in charge of their store-room, the contemporary record says: he had wished 'to rise higher'. In its naivety, the remark is extremely significant. Although they were united by the idea of a common service, expressed by a common name, and were stamped, for the most part, with the same servile 'stigma', the serjeants formed a heterogeneous group and one that was becoming ever more hierarchic in structure. The duties were too diverse not to produce great inequalities in mode of life and prestige. It is true that the level to which a man might rise largely depended on the particular usages of his group, and on his opportunities or his skill. In a general way, nevertheless, three features—wealth, a share of authority, and the bearing of arms—raised the majority of the manorial stewards, on the one hand, and the principal court officials, on the other, well above the small fry of the petty rural serjeants, the servants properly so called and the domestic craftsmen.

Could the *maire*, the lord's steward, be described as a peasant? Undoubtedly he could—at the outset, at least, and sometimes to the end; but he was from the first a rich peasant who became progessively richer through his functions. For the lawful profits were already appreciable and still more so, doubtless, were the illicit ones. In this period, when the only

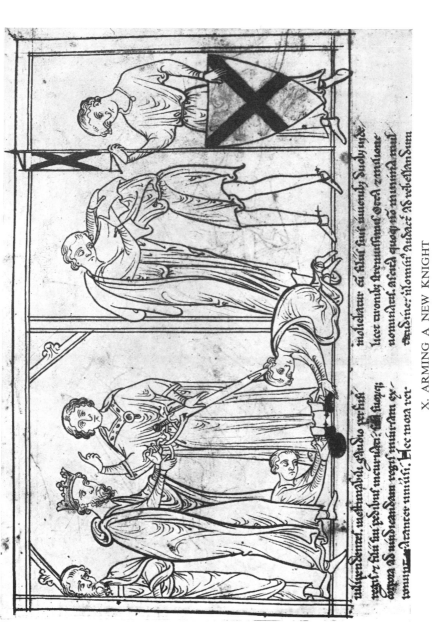

X. ARMING A NEW KNIGHT

The young Offa receives his arms from King Wermund; a pen-and-ink sketch in Matthew Paris, *Historia de Offa Rege*, perhaps by the author himself (about 1250), British Museum, Cotton MS., Nero D1, f. 3.

Tertio inter scapulas. Quarto in
scapulis. Quinto in compagibz
brachiorum. Dicens.

Ungo te in regem de oleo sci
ficato. in nomine patris
et filij et spe sancti. dicant omes.
Amen==J. Et cantetur hec antiph.

XI. THE ANOINTING OF A KING

Ordo of the Coronation Ceremony of the Kings of France. MS. dating from
the beginning of the 14th century; the miniatures perhaps copied from models of
slightly earlier date. Bibl. Nat., MS. Lat. 1246, f. 17.

effective authority was the one close at hand, it was only to be expected that the usurpations of rights which in practice made so many great royal officials sovereigns on their own account, would be repeated at the lower end of the scale in the humble setting of the village. Charlemagne himself had shown a well-founded mistrust of the stewards of his *villae* and had recommended that they should not be selected from among men who were too powerful. But although a few unscrupulous men might succeed here and there in completely usurping their lords' authority, such flagrant self-aggrandizement was always exceptional. On the other hand, how much produce was improperly retained, with a resulting loss to the lord's store-house or his pocket? 'An estate abandoned to serjeants, an estate lost,' was a maxim of the wise Suger. How many taxes and labour services were extorted from the villeins for his own benefit by this petty rural tyrant; how many chickens taken from their poultry-yards; how many casks of wine claimed from their cellars, or cuts of bacon from their storehouses; how much weaving imposed on their wives! All these were often, in origin, simple gifts; but gifts which could scarcely be refused, and which custom as a rule very soon changed into obligations. What is more, this man of peasant birth was, in his own sphere, a master. In theory, no doubt, his orders were given in the name of one more powerful than himself; they were orders none the less. What is more, he was a judge. He presided, alone, over the peasant courts; and occasionally he sat on more serious cases by the side of the abbot or the baron. Among his other duties was that of marking out the boundaries of the fields in cases of dispute. What function was more calculated to inspire respect in peasant minds? Finally, in the hour of peril, it was he who rode at the head of the contingent of villeins. By the side of Duke Garin, stricken unto death, the poet could place no better servant than a faithful steward.

There was, of course, immense variation in the steps that marked the social rise of this official. Nevertheless, we can hardly doubt the evidence of the many charters and monastic chronicles whose complaints, in exactly the same strain, echo from Swabia to Limousin; not to mention the testimony of the *fabliaux* themselves. From these sources a portrait emerges whose vivid colours may not have been true everywhere, but were so in many cases. It is the portrait, if you will, of the successful *maire*. He is not only very well off; his wealth, as such, has nothing in common with that of a peasant. He possesses tithes and mills. He has established tenants on his own lands, and in some cases even vassals. His dwelling is a fortified house. He dresses 'like a nobleman'. He keeps war-horses in his stables and hounds in his kennels. He is armed with sword, shield and lance.

The principal serjeants who, at the courts of the counts, formed as it were the general staff of the ministeriality were also rich men by virtue of their fiefs and the gifts they constantly received; they were raised still higher in dignity by their proximity to the master, by the important missions which the latter inevitably confided to them, by their military rôle when they were required to serve as a mounted escort and even as commanders of small contingents. Of this class, for example, were those 'non-noble knights' at the court of the lord of Talmont, whom a charter of the eleventh century mentions along with the 'noble knights'. They sat in law-courts and in councils; they served as witnesses to the most solemn legal acts. All this was true, occasionally, even of persons whose humble duties might have been expected to confine them to the class of menial servants. We find, for example, the 'kitchen-serjeants' of the monks of Arras taking part in judgments, and the locksmith of the monks of Saint-Trond (who was at the same time their glazier and their surgeon) trying to transform his tenement into a 'free military fief'. But it applied more frequently and in much greater degree to those whom we may call the head-servants: the seneschal, who in theory was responsible for the catering, the marshal, who had charge of the stables, the butler, and the chamberlain.

Originally most of these domestic offices had been filled by vassals, usually unenfeoffed ones. To the end the dividing line between the functions which were reserved for vassals and those which were not remained very vague. But as vassalage grew in honour and lost more and more of its primitive character, while the institution of the fief became more general, with a resulting dispersal of the old household group of knights, lords of every rank became accustomed to assign the duties of their courts to dependants of humbler birth—men who were closer to them, whom they regarded as easier to control. A charter of the Emperor Lothar for the abbey of St. Michael of Lüneburg, in 1135, prescribes that henceforward the abbot shall cease to distribute 'benefits' to free men and shall no longer grant them to any save *ministeriales* of the church. In this society, which had at first expected so much from the fealty of the vassal, the progress of the institution of court ministeriality was a symptom of disillusionment. Between the two types of service and the two classes of servants, a genuine rivalry thus developed, the echo of which has been preserved in epic and courtly literature. We find the poet Wace, for instance, congratulating one of his heroes on never having given the 'occupations of his household' to any but 'noblemen'. But in another poem we have the following portrait, also devised for the delectation of a castle audience (since its subject will finally be unmasked as a traitor) but certainly based on a familiar reality. 'A baron was seen there whom Girart thought the most faithful of his men. He was his serf and his seneschal for many a castle.'[1]

Everything contributed to make the highest class of serjeants a sharply defined social group, at least as to its lower boundary. In the first place, there was the factor of heritability; for, in spite of efforts to oppose it, notably on the part of the Church, the majority of the fiefs of serjeanty had rapidly become—frequently in law and generally in practice—transmissible

[1] *Girart de Roussillon*, trans. P. Meyer, § 620 (ed. Foerster, v. 9139).

from generation to generation. The son succeeded simultaneously to the estate and the office. Secondly, there was the practice of intermarriage, the evidence for which is to be found, from the twelfth century, in the agreements concluded between lords for the exchange of serfs. The son or daughter of a *maire* who could not find in his own village a partner of equal rank was obliged to look for one in the neighbouring manor. There could hardly be a more eloquent expression of class-consciousness than this refusal to marry outside one's own circle.

Nevertheless, this group, apparently so firmly constituted, suffered from a curious internal contradiction. In many features, it was similar to the 'nobility' of the vassals—authority, social habits, type of wealth, the military calling. As soldiers its members were naturally required to go through certain legal formalities. Homage 'of mouth and hands' was not required for all ministerial fiefs, but for many of the most important this characteristic rite of military vassals was regarded as indispensable. Then there was initiation into knighthood: more than one dubbed knight was to be found among the *maires* and court officials. But these knights, these powerful individuals whose mode of life was that of the nobility, were in most cases serfs at the same time, and as such subject to *mainmorte* and the prohibition against *formariage* (except where exemption was purchased, always at considerable cost); unless enfranchised, they were excluded from holy orders; they were deprived of the right to bear witness in court against free men; above all, they bore the humiliating stigma of a subordination which was not of their own choosing. In short, their *de jure* status was in stark contrast with their *de facto* status; and the remedies for these inconsistencies that were finally evolved differed widely from country to country.

In England serjeanty was of least importance, even as a mere social factor. The village serjeants, as we have seen, were not as a rule specialists. The court officials were not ordinarily recruited from the bondmen, originally too poor and too few; later on, as serjeants were specifically exempted from rural labour services, there could be no question of ranking them among the villeins. Thus for the most part they escaped both the old form of servitude and the new. As free men they were subject only to the common law of free men; as knights—if they were admitted to knighthood—they enjoyed the prestige peculiar to knights. Legal doctrine was content to elaborate the rules proper to the fiefs of serjeanty, as distinct from the exclusively military fiefs, and above all strove to establish among the former an ever clearer line of demarcation between the 'grand' and most honourable serjeanties which *ipso facto* entailed homage, and the 'petty' serjeanties, which were virtually assimilated to 'free' peasant tenements.

In France a cleavage occurred. The less powerful or less fortunate of the *maires* remained simply rich peasants; sometimes they became farmers of the demesne and the seignorial rights, and sometimes also they became gradually detached from any administrative rôle. For when economic conditions once more made possible the payment of money wages many of the lords bought back the offices from their holders, in order to entrust the management of their estates to genuine salaried officials. Of the officials of baronial courts a certain number, who had been for a long time concerned in the administration of urban lordships, finally took their place among the town patriciate. Many others, however, together with the most favoured of the rural serjeants, found their way into the nobility at the time when it was being formed into a legal class. The preliminary phases of this fusion appeared at an early date, notably in the form of ever more frequent marriages between the families of *ministeriales* and those of the knightly vassals. The chroniclers as well as the anecdotists of the thirteenth century found a frequent theme in the misadventures of the knight of servile birth who sought to live down this taint, only to fall back after all into the hard grip of his master.

Serfdom in fact was the only effective barrier to an assimilation favoured by so many common characteristics. In one sense, the obstacle might seem to have been more impassable than ever from the thirteenth century onwards. For, from that period, by a significant break with almost immemorial usage, jurisprudence decided to regard knighthood as incompatible with serfdom—so much stronger had the sense of hierarchy now become. But this was also the period of the great movement of enfranchisement. Better provided with money than the common run of serfs, the serjeants everywhere were among the first to purchase their freedom. There was therefore nothing now—since the law proved adaptable—to debar those of them who were nearest to a knightly mode of life, and who perhaps already counted knights among their ancestors, from admission to the order of persons whose birth entitled them to knighthood. Nor, since they entered it completely free from any stigma, was there anything to distinguish them from the rest of the nobility. They were destined to be the progenitors of a considerable section of the petty nobility of the countryside, and they did not always remain confined to it. The dukes of Saulx-Tavannes, who ranked towards the end of the Ancien Régime among the greatest members of the military aristocracy, were descended from a provost (*prévôt*) of the lord of Saulx, enfranchised by the latter in 1284.[1]

In Germany, the group of court *Dienstmänner*, together with some rural serjeants, early assumed an exceptional importance. Vassalage had never figured as largely in German society as in northern France and Lorraine. The decay of the tie had been rapid and no one had been much concerned to find a remedy, as is clearly proved by the absence of any effort such as was represented elsewhere by the practice of liege homage. More than in any other country, therefore, it seemed desirable in Germany to entrust

[1] *Sur les routes de l'émigration. Mémoires de la duchesse de Saulx-Tavannes*, ed. de Valous, 1934, Introduction, p. 10.

the duties of seignorial households to unfree dependants. As early as the beginning of the eleventh century these 'serfs living as knights' (as they are called in a Swabian text) were so numerous at the courts of the principal magnates, and the spirit of solidarity which animated their turbulent little communities was so active, that a whole series of group 'customs' was created in which their privileges were defined. Soon these customs were set down in writing and fused into the common law of a class. The lot of the *ministeriales* seemed so enviable that in the following century more than one free man of honourable rank entered into servitude in order to join their number. They played a rôle of the first importance in military expeditions. They made up the bulk of the judiciary, for by a decision of the diet of the Empire they were allowed to form the courts of the princes, provided that at least two 'noblemen' sat with them. They held such a high place in the counsels of the great that the sole condition laid down by an imperial decision of 1216 for the alienation, by the emperor, of the homage of a principality was—in addition to the consent of the prince himself—the approval of the *ministeriales*. In the ecclesiastical lordships they occasionally took part in the election of the bishop or the abbot, and when the latter was away they tyrannized over the monks.

In the first rank were the *Dienstmänner* of the sovereign; for the high offices of the court, which the Capetians entrusted to the members of the vassal dynasties, were committed by their German neighbours to simple serjeants, born into servitude. Philip I of France, it is true, had taken a serf as chamberlain.[1] But the office was a relatively modest one and the case, it seems, remained exceptional. As seneschal the French king occasionally employed a great baron; as marshals he regularly employed petty nobles from the region between Loire and Somme. In Germany—where the changes of dynasty, and as we shall see, certain peculiarities in the structure of the State, prevented the kings from ever creating an Île-de-France, reservoir of a faithful and stable nobility—neither seneschals nor marshals of the Empire were normally chosen from any but men of servile condition. Undoubtedly there was opposition to this policy among the aristocracy; and this opposition (which is constantly reflected in the literature of the courts) seems to have been at the root of certain rebellions. But in spite of everything the *ministeriales* continued to form the normal *entourage* of the Salian and Hohenstaufen monarchs. To them were entrusted the education of the young princes, the custody of the most important castles, and sometimes, in Italy, the great administrative offices; to them also belonged the purest tradition of imperial policy. In the history of Barbarossa and his first successors, few men stand out so prominently as the uncouth figure of the seneschal Markward of Anweiler, who died regent of Sicily; he had

---

[1] The servile status of this person—as W. M. Newman has rightly perceived (*Le Domaine royal sous les premiers Capétiens*, 1937, p. 24, n. 7)—may be deduced from the fact that after his death the king received his *mainmorte*.

only been enfranchised in 1197, on the day when his master invested him with the duchy of Ravenna and the marquisate of Ancona.

It goes without saying that nowhere did these *parvenus*, by virtue of their power and mode of life, approach nearer to the world of vassals than in Germany; yet they were not absorbed into it almost imperceptibly as in France. There were too many of them for that; they had been too long segregated from other classes by their special customs; too much importance was still attached in Germany to the old concept of freedom in public law; lastly, the German legal mind was too fond of hierarchic distinctions. Knighthood was not forbidden to serfs; but the serf-knights (sometimes themselves divided, by a further refinement, into an upper and a lower group) formed in the general class of nobles a rank apart—the lowest. And no problem was more troublesome to the legal theorists or to the courts than that of deciding the exact status in relation to ordinary free men which was to be accorded to these persons, so powerful and yet branded with the stigma of serfdom. For after all, even burghers and simple peasants, though lacking so many of the things that gave prestige to the *ministeriales*, were none the less their superiors by purity of birth. This was a serious difficulty, particularly when it was a question of the composition of courts of justice. 'That no men of servile status be in future set up to judge you': this promise is still to be read in the charter which Rudolf of Habsburg granted to the peasants of the original cantons of Switzerland.[1]

Nevertheless the inevitable development came about eventually, as in France; but, with the usual lack of synchronism between the two evolutions, a century or a century and a half later. The less fortunate of the families of *Dienstmänner* remained among the rich peasantry or infiltrated into the bourgeoisie of the towns. Those who had been admitted to the knightly dignity, though they might still be excluded from the highest nobility (for the German nobiliary law to the end remained imbued with the spirit of caste), were henceforth at least no longer separated by any peculiar distinguishing mark from the knighthood of free birth. So here again—and this is no doubt the most important lesson provided by the history of the ministeriality—legal tradition had finally yielded to facts.

[1] *Quellenwerk zur Entstehung der schweizerischen Eidgenossenschaft*, no. 1650.

XXVI

CLERGY AND BURGESSES

1 THE ECCLESIASTICAL SOCIETY WITHIN THE FEUDAL WORLD

IN the feudal period the dividing-line between the clergy and lay society was not so clear and firm as that which the Catholic reform movement endeavoured to draw about the time of the Council of Trent. A whole population of 'tonsured persons', whose status remained ill-defined, formed an indeterminate borderland on the frontiers of the two great groups. Nevertheless the clergy constituted in a high degree a legal class; for, as a body, it was characterized by its own peculiar law and jealously-guarded rights of jurisdiction. On the other hand, it was in no sense a social class; within its ranks coexisted human types differing widely in mode of life, power and prestige.

First of all we have the multitude of monks, all 'sons of St. Benedict', but subject in fact to increasingly varied versions of the primitive Benedictine Rule—a divided and pulsating world, ceaselessly tossed to and fro between pure asceticism and the more mundane cares inseparable from the administration of great wealth, or even from the humble business of gaining a livelihood. Moreover, we must not picture this body as separated from the laity by impassable barriers. Even those Rules which embodied the most uncompromising principles of reclusion had in the last resort to yield to practical necessity. Monks had the cure of souls in parishes. Monasteries opened their schools to pupils who would never assume the cowl; especially after the Gregorian reform they became a nursery of bishops and popes.

Socially in the lowest category of the secular clergy, the priests of country parishes, poorly educated and badly paid, led a life which differed little if at all from that of their flocks. Before Gregory VII they had almost all been married. Even after the great ascetic campaign instigated—in the words of one monastic text—by 'that teacher of impossible things',[1] the 'priestess', the priest's wife in fact and sometimes in law, long continued to figure among the familiar personages of village folklore. So much was this the case that here the word class could almost have been taken in its strictest sense: in the England of Thomas Becket, dynasties of priests do not

[1] K. Rost, *Die Historia pontificum Romanorum aus Zwettl*, Greifswald, 1932, p. 177, n. 4.

appear to have been much more uncommon than descendants of 'popes' are today in the Orthodox countries, nor as a general rule less respectable.[1] Then, higher up the scale there was the wealthier and more refined circle of the town priests, the canons attached to a cathedral, the clerks or dignitaries of episcopal courts.

Finally, at the summit, forming to some extent the link between the two hierarchies, the regular and the secular, stood the prelates: abbots, bishops, and archbishops. In wealth, power, and aptitude for command these great lords of the Church were the equals of the greatest military barons.

Now the sole problem with which we need to concern ourselves here is a social one. This body of servants of God, whose mission, inherited from what was already an old tradition, remained in theory remote from all temporal concerns, was nevertheless obliged to find a place for itself in the characteristic structure of feudal society. In what degree was it influenced by surrounding institutions, while influencing them in its turn? In other words, since historians are accustomed to speak of the 'feudalization' of the Church, what concrete meaning are we to attach to this phrase?

For the clergy, preoccupied with liturgical duties or the demands of the ascetic life, with the cure of souls or with study, it was impossible to seek a livelihood through directly productive forms of labour. The monastic reformers attempted at various times to induce the monks to live on the produce of fields cultivated by their own hands. But they invariably ran up against the same fundamental difficulty: time devoted to these material tasks was time taken from meditation or divine service. As for hired labour, we know very well that it was out of the question. It was therefore necessary that the monk and the priest should live—as Ramon Lull said of the knight[2]—by the 'weariness' of other men. The country parson himself, though no doubt he did not disdain on occasion to handle the plough or the spade, derived the best part of his meagre income from the share of fees or tithe which the lord of the village had agreed to allot to him.

Formed by the accumulated alms of the faithful, augmented by purchases, often at a price which took into account the benefit of the prayers promised for the soul of the vendor, the patrimony of the great churches, or rather the patrimony of the 'saints' (for this, so far from being a mere legal fiction, was then the prevailing notion), was essentially of a seignorial nature. Immense fortunes were amassed by monastic communities or prelates, sometimes amounting to those almost princely agglomerations of estates and varied rights whose rôle in the establishment of territorial lordships we shall consider later. Now, lordship meant not only rents, but also authority. The heads of the clergy had therefore under their orders a great many lay dependants of every rank, from military vassals, indispensable

---

[1] See, especially, Z. N. Brooke in *Cambridge Historical Journal*, II, p. 222.
[2] See above, p. 319.

for the protection of such great properties, to villeins and 'commended men' of inferior degree.

The latter group, in particular, gravitated to the church estates in large numbers. Was it really because to live 'under the cross', rather than the sword, seemed an enviable lot? The controversy went back a long way: as early as the twelfth century, we find the critical Abelard opposing the views of the abbot of Cluny, eager to extol the mildness of the monastic régime.[1] In so far as it is permissible to leave the individual factor out of account, what it amounts to, after all, is the question whether a strict master (such as the clergy generally were) is better than an unreliable one. The problem is really insoluble; but two things are certain. The perennial character of ecclesiastical establishments and the respect which surrounded them caused them to be much sought after as protectors by the poor. Moreover, he who gave himself to a saint gained both protection against earthly perils and the no less precious benefits of an act of piety. It was a double advantage which the charters, drawn up in the monasteries, frequently expressed by asserting that the man who became the serf of a church was in reality entering into true freedom. By this was meant—though the distinction between the two ideas was not always very clearly drawn—that in this world he would share in the immunities of a privileged corporation, and in the next be guaranteed 'the eternal freedom which is in Christ'.[2] There are cases on record of grateful pilgrims earnestly seeking permission from their original lord to subject themselves and their posterity to the representatives of the powerful intercessor who had healed them.[3] Thus, in the formation of the network of personal subjections so characteristic of the age, the houses of prayer were among the most powerful centres of attraction.

Nevertheless, by thus transforming itself into a great earthly power, the Church of the feudal era exposed itself to two risks of which contemporaries were fully aware. In the first place, it was in danger of being too readily forgetful of its proper function. 'What a fine thing it would be to be archbishop of Rheims, if only one did not have to sing mass!' Public rumour attributed this remark to Archbishop Manasses, deposed in 1080 by the papal legates. Whether true or slanderous, the anecdote is symbolic of the period when the recruitment of the French episcopate was more scandalous than at any other time in its history. After the Gregorian reform, such cynicism would have made the story incredible. But the type of warrior prelate—those 'good knights of the clergy', as one German bishop called them—was to be found in all periods. Moreover, the spectacle of so much wealth amassed by churchmen, the resentment awakened in the hearts of 'impoverished' heirs at the thought of so many fine estates but

---

[1] Migne, *P.L.*, CLXXXIX, col. 146; P. Abaelardi, *Opera*, ed. V. Cousin, I, p. 572.

[2] A. Wauters, *Les Libertés communales. Preuves*, Brussels, 1869, p. 83 (1221, April). Cf. Marc Bloch, in *Anuario de historia del derecho español*, 1933, p. 79 *et seq.*

[3] L. Raynal, *Histoire du Berry*, I, 1845, p. 477, no. XI (23rd April 1071—22nd April 1093. Saint-Silvain de Levroux).

lately surrendered by their ancestors to monks skilled in making capital out of the fear of hell, together with the contempt of the warrior for so sheltered a mode of life, produced that brand of anticlericalism which found such forthright expression in many passages of the epics.[1] Though quite compatible with the renewal of generous alms-giving in moments of remorse, or in the anguish of death, these sentiments none the less underlay certain political attitudes as well as some genuinely religious movements.

In a world which was inclined to conceive of all ties between one man and another in terms of the most binding of them, it was almost inevitable that in the very heart of ecclesiastical society the practices of vassalage should impregnate relationships of subordination of a much older and essentially very different kind. The bishop demanded homage from the dignitaries of his chapter or the abbots of his diocese; the canons who held the largest prebends required it from their less well-provided colleagues; and the parish priests had to do homage to the head of the religious community on which their parishes were dependent.[2] The introduction into the spiritual citadel of customs so plainly borrowed from the secular world could not fail to arouse the protests of the rigorists. But the evil became much graver when the hands in which those of the priest, sanctified by the consecrated oil of ordination and the contact of the Eucharist, were placed for the rite of submission were the hands of a layman. The problem here is inseparable from another and much vaster one—one of the most anxious, certainly, which ever confronted the Church: the problem of appointments to the various posts in the ecclesiastical hierarchy.

It was not the feudal era which originated the practice of handing over to the temporal powers the responsibility for choosing the shepherds of souls. In the case of the village cures, of which the lords disposed more or less freely, the practice went back to the very origins of the parochial system. What of the bishops or abbots? The sole procedure conformable to the canonical rule was unquestionably election: by the clergy and people of the city, in the case of the former; by the monks, in the case of the latter. But as far back as the last days of the Roman Empire, the emperors had not hesitated to impose their will on the electors in the cities and even occasionally to appoint bishops directly. The sovereigns of the barbarian kingdoms followed suit, and the bishops were appointed by the rulers much more generally than hitherto. Abbots of monasteries which were not also directly

---

[1] Guibert de Nogent, *Histoire de sa vie*, I, 11 (ed. Bourgin, p. 31); Thietmar of Merseburg, *Chronicon*, II, 27 (ed. Holtzmann, pp. 72-3). For a characteristic reference in the epics, see *Garin le Lorrain*, ed. P. Paris, I, p. 2.

[2] The popes of the great Gregorian period have sometimes been credited with the design of making themselves the feudal lords of certain kings. It appears, in fact, that they confined themselves to claiming and sometimes obtaining an oath of fealty and a tribute—forms of subjection, undoubtedly, but with nothing peculiarly feudal about them. Homage was at that time demanded only of territorial princes (such as Norman leaders in southern Italy and the count of Substantion in Languedoc). John Lackland performed it, it is true; but at a much later date (1213).

dependent on the king were frequently appointed by the founder of the house or his heirs. The truth was that no serious government could afford to leave outside its control the assignment of offices which—apart from a heavy religious responsibility, from which no ruler solicitous for the welfare of his people had the right to dissociate himself—involved so great a measure of purely secular authority. Confirmed by Carolingian practice, the idea that it was for the kings to 'designate' the bishops ended by becoming a recognized principle. In the tenth century and the beginning of the eleventh, popes and prelates unanimously concurred in it.[1]

Nevertheless, in this sphere as in others, the institutions and practices inherited from the past were to come under the influence of a new social atmosphere.

In the feudal era every transfer of property—an estate, a right, or an office—was effected by the handing over of a material object which represented the subject of the grant. The cleric appointed by a layman to take charge of a parish, a diocese, or a monastery therefore received from this collator an 'investiture' in the usual forms. For the bishop the favourite symbol, from the time of the first Carolingians, was very naturally a crosier:[2] to this was later added a pastoral ring. It goes without saying that this delivery of insignia by a temporal chief by no means dispensed with the liturgical consecration; in this sense, it was powerless to create a bishop. But we should be gravely mistaken were we to imagine that its rôle was limited to marking the transfer to the prelate of the property attached to his new dignity. Both the right to the office and the right to the stipend that went with it—though no one felt the need to distinguish between two indissoluble elements—were thereby simultaneously conveyed. Moreover this ceremony, if it underlined somewhat crudely the preponderant part claimed by the secular authorities in ecclesiastical appointments, in itself added almost nothing to a state of things that had long been recognized. It was otherwise with another gesture charged with much deeper human significance.

From the cleric to whom he had just confided an ecclesiastical office, the local potentate or the sovereign expected in return an unwavering loyalty. Now, since the formation of Carolingian vassalage, no engagement of this nature—at least among the upper classes—was considered really binding unless it was contracted according to the forms developed by the Frankish practice of commendation. The kings and the princes were therefore accustomed to require from the bishops or abbots nominated by them an act of homage; and the lords of villages sometimes required the same of their parish priests. But homage, in the strict sense, was a rite of subjection;

---

[1] Jaffé-Wattenbach, *Regesta pontificum*, I, no. 3564; Rathier of Verona, in Migne' *P.L.*, CXXXVI, col. 249; Thietmar, *Chronicon*, I, 26 (pp. 34–5).

[2] For one of the earliest examples, often overlooked, see G. Busson and Ledru, *Actus pontificum Cenomannensium*, p. 299 (832).

and a much respected rite, moreover. By its means the subordination of the representatives of the spiritual power to the lay power was not only strikingly displayed; it was also reinforced, inasmuch as the combination of the two formal acts—homage and investiture—fostered a dangerous assimilation of the office of the prelate to the fief of the vassal.

The right to appoint the bishops and greater abbots, essentially a regalian attribute, was necessarily involved in the subdivision of sovereign rights in general, characteristic of feudal societies. But this fragmentation did not take place everywhere in equal degree, so that the effects on the recruitment of ecclesiastical officials varied widely. In regions where, as in France—especially in the South and Centre—many bishoprics fell under the control of the great barons and even of those of middle rank, the worst abuses found their favourite soil: from the hereditary succession of the father by the son to the open sale of the episcopal office. Note the contrast with Germany, where the kings were able to retain their grip on almost all the episcopal sees. Certainly their choice of bishops was not inspired by exclusively spiritual motives. Before all else, they needed prelates capable of governing, and even on occasion of fighting. Bruno of Toul, who under the name of Leo IX was to become a very saintly pope, owed his episcopal see primarily to qualities of which he had given proof as a military commander. To poor churches the sovereign by preference appointed rich bishops, nor was he himself above accepting the gifts which custom tended to make obligatory for newly invested persons, whether the object of the investiture was a military fief or a religious office. There is no doubt, however, that taken as a whole the imperial episcopate, under the Saxons and the first Salians, was far superior in education and moral tone to that of neighbouring countries. Once it became necessary for the Church to submit to a lay ruler it was evidently better for it to depend on one of higher rank, which tended to produce a broader outlook.

And now the Gregorian impulse began to be felt. There is no need here to recount the vicissitudes of this impassioned attempt to wrest the spiritual forces from the grip of the world and reduce the secular powers to the discreetly subordinate function of auxiliaries enrolled in the great work of salvation. The final balance-sheet, if we leave out of account many slight variations in the different countries, can be summarized in a few words.

It was not towards the parochial system that the principal effort of the reformers was directed. In the legal control of the parishes few changes were in fact made. A more respectable name, 'patronage', was finally substituted for the crude expression 'property', and there was a stricter control by the episcopal authority over the selection of priests; but these modest innovations did not count for much as against the right of nomination, which in practice was retained by the lords. The only new feature of any significance belonged to the domain of fact rather than of law: by gift or by sale, a great number of village churches had passed from the hands of laymen into those of ecclesiastical establishments, especially monasteries. The seignorial supremacy continued, even though it was now exercised by masters who ranked among the soldiers of the Church. It was one more proof that the manor, though essentially older than the rest of the social structure of feudalism, was one of its most indestructible parts.

So far as the great offices of the Church were concerned the most scandalous forms of subjection to the temporal power had been eliminated. There were no more monasteries openly 'appropriated' by local dynasts; no more military barons constituting themselves abbots or 'arch-abbots' of religious houses; no more investitures by the distinctive insignia of the spiritual power. The sceptre replaced the crosier and the ring, and the canonists laid it down in principle that the sole object of the ceremony was to grant the enjoyment of the material rights attached to the exercise of a religious function independently conferred. Election was universally recognized as the rule and laymen, even in the capacity of simple electors, were finally excluded from all regular participation in the choice of the bishop. The latter, as a consequence of a revolution which occupied the whole of the twelfth century, was henceforth designated by a college restricted to the canons of the cathedral church—a new feature, absolutely contrary to the primitive law and one which, more than any other, reveals the growing schism between the priesthood and the lay multitude.

Nevertheless, the elective principle functioned with difficulty, because of a reluctance merely to count votes. The decision was considered to belong, not to the majority pure and simple, but, according to the traditional formula, to the fraction which was at once 'the most numerous and the most sound'. It is doubtful if any minority resisted the temptation of denying to its adversaries, victorious according to the rule of number, the less ponderable of these two qualities. Hence the frequency of disputed elections, which favoured the intervention of authorities of higher rank— popes, assuredly, but also kings. Add to this that no one could cherish any illusions about the bias of very restricted electoral colleges, often closely subject to the influence of the least reputable local interests. The most intelligent canonists scarcely denied that a control exercised over a wider field would be in their view beneficial; and here the supreme head of the Church and the heads of state were in agreement. Under cover of a general reorganization of political forces the small fry among the barons in the greater part of the West were in fact gradually eliminated to the advantage of the king or a few particularly powerful princes; but the sovereigns who thus remained sole masters of the field were all the more capable of handling effectively the various means at their disposal for exerting pressure on the ecclesiastical bodies. One method of intimidation, the presence of the sovereign at the election, had been recognized as legal in 1122 by the Concordat concluded between the Pope and the Emperor. The monarchs most sure of their strength did not hesitate to resort occasionally to direct appointment. The history of the second feudal age, as of the centuries which followed, reverberated with the sound of the innumerable quarrels provoked, from one end of the Catholic world to the other, by appointments to bishoprics or abbacies. All in all, the Gregorian reform had shown itself powerless to wrest from the great temporal powers this means of control—in truth almost indispensable to their very existence—which consisted in the right to choose the principal dignitaries of the Church or, at the very least, to supervise the choice.

The bishop or abbot of the new age was endowed with vast manorial estates which imposed on him the normal obligations of every great baron to the king or prince, and which even involved services of more than ordinary importance; for ecclesiastical estates were, as we shall see, considered to be attached to the royal domain by a particularly close tie. Thus the ecclesiastical dignitary remained bound to his sovereign by duties of fidelity whose legitimate force could not be denied, and the reformers confined themselves to stipulating that these be expressed in a manner consistent with the high office of the churchman. That the prelate should pronounce the oath of fealty, well and good; but for him there must be no homage. Such was the theory—very logical and clear-cut—which, from the end of the eleventh century, councils, popes and theologians vied with each other in developing. For a long time it was disregarded in practice; but little by little it gained ground, and towards the middle of the thirteenth century, it had triumphed almost everywhere—with one important exception. France, the chosen home of vassalage, had remained on this point obstinately devoted to the traditional practices, and apart from a few special privileges, it remained attached to them till the sixteenth century. That St. Louis, calling one of his bishops to order, should not have hesitated to say to him 'you are my man, of your hands' is eloquent testimony to the persistence of the most characteristic concepts of feudalism, even when extended to an essentially spiritual society.[1]

2 THE BURGESSES

Beneath the noble and the churchman the literature of knightly inspiration affected to see only a uniform population of 'rustics' or 'villeins'. But really this vast multitude was deeply divided by various social distinctions. Even among the 'rustics', in the exact and restricted sense of the term, such distinctions prevailed. Not only did the different degrees of subjection create within their ranks fluctuating legal divisions, gradually reduced to the antithesis between 'servitude' and 'freedom'; side by side with those differences of status and unconnected with them, substantial economic inequalities also divided the small rural communities. To mention only the

[1] Joinville, c. CXXXVI.

simplest and most readily formulated contrast, what plough-owning peasant, proud of his draught animals, would have accepted as his equals the poor cultivators of his village who had to rely on their muscles to exploit their meagre plots?

Above all, apart from both the peasant population and the groups engaged in the honourable tasks connected with the exercise of authority, there had always existed isolated nuclei of merchants and craftsmen. From these beginnings, fostered by the economic revolution in the second feudal age, there arose the powerful and well-differentiated social group of the urban classes, swollen with innumerable additional elements. The study of a class so distinctively professional in character could not be undertaken without an intensive examination of its economics. A rapid sketch will be sufficient here to indicate its position against the backcloth of feudalism.

None of the languages spoken in feudal Europe possessed terms which allowed a clear distinction to be made between the town and the village. *Ville*, town, *Stadt* applied indifferently to both types of community. *Burg* designated any fortified area. *Cité* was reserved for the diocesan centres or, by extension, to some other centres of exceptional importance. On the other hand, as early as the eleventh century the name *bourgeois*, burgess, French by origin, but quickly adopted by international usage, was employed in unequivocal opposition to the words knight, cleric, villein. If the agglomeration as such remained anonymous, the most active of its denizens, those whose occupations as merchants and craftsmen were most typically urban, came to be recognized as a distinctive group in society, with a distinctive name. It was perceived that the dominant characteristic of the town was that it was inhabited by a special type of human being.

Of course it would be easy to exaggerate the contrast. The burgess of the early phases of town life shared with the knight a warlike disposition and the practice of bearing arms. For a long time he might be seen, like a peasant, attending to the cultivation of fields whose furrows were sometimes prolonged even inside the fortified enclosure, or one might find him outside the walls, driving his herds to graze on the jealously guarded common pastures. If he became rich he acquired rural manors in his turn. But for the burgess the activities which thus seemed to approximate him to the other classes were in fact only secondary and, most often, the survivals, as it were, of former modes of existence which he had gradually discarded.

Essentially the burgess lived by commerce. He derived his subsistence from the difference between the price at which he bought and the price at which he sold; or between the capital lent and the amount of repayment. And since the legality of such intermediate profit—unless it were merely a question of the wages of a workman or a carrier—was denied by the theologians and its nature ill-understood by knightly society, his code of conduct was in flagrant conflict with prevailing moral notions. For his part, as a speculator in real estate he found the feudal restrictions on his landed property intolerable. Because his business had to be handled rapidly and, as it grew, continued to set new legal problems, the delays, the complications, the archaism of the traditional judicial procedures exasperated him. The multiplicity of authorities governing the town itself offended him as obstacles to the proper control of business transactions and as an insult to the solidarity of his class. The diverse immunities enjoyed by his ecclesiastical or knightly neighbours seemed to him so many hindrances to the free pursuit of profit. On the roads which he ceaselessly traversed, he regarded with equal abhorrence rapacious toll-collectors and the predatory nobles who swooped down from their castles on the merchant caravans. In short he was harassed or annoyed by almost everything in the institutions created by a society in which he as yet had only a very small place. With franchises won by violence or purchased with hard cash, organized and equipped for economic expansion as well as for the necessary reprisals, the town which it was his ambition to build would be as it were a foreign body in feudal society.

In the last resort the collective independence which was the ideal of so many eager communities rarely went beyond varying degrees of limited administrative autonomy; but in order to escape the unintelligent restrictions of local tyrannies another course was available to the burgesses which, although it might seem little more than a desperate remedy, was often proved by experience to be the most effective. This was to place themselves under the protection of the great royal or princely governments, guardians of law and order over vast areas. Their very concern for their finances gave these authorities—as they came to appreciate more and more—an interest in the prosperity of rich taxpayers. In this way again, and perhaps more decisively, the increasing power of the burgesses tended to undermine one of the most characteristic features of feudalism—the subdivision of authority.

One act of outstanding significance generally marked the entry on the scene of the new urban community, whether in a mood of revolt or for peaceful organization. This was the communal oath of the burgesses. Hitherto they had been only isolated individuals: henceforth they had a collective being. It was the sworn association thus created which in France was given the literal name of *commune*. No word ever evoked more passionate emotions. The rallying cry of the bourgeoisies in the hour of revolt, the call for help of the burgess in peril, it awakened in what were previously the only ruling classes prolonged echoes of hatred. Why was there so much hostility towards 'this new and detestable name', as Guibert de Nogent called it? Many feelings no doubt contributed to it: the apprehensions of the powerful, directly threatened in their authority, their revenues, their prestige; the fears, not wholly groundless, aroused in the heads of the Church by the ambitions of groups with little respect for ecclesiastical 'liberties', which stood in their way; the contempt or ill-will

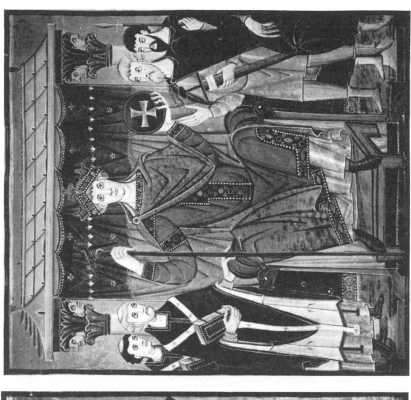

XII. The Land of the Slavs, Germania, Gaul (i.e. the Imperial Territories on the left bank of the Rhine) and Rome do obeisance to the Emperor Otto III. From Otto III's Gospelbook, School of Reichenau, end of the 10th century. Munich, Staatsbibliothek, Latin 4453.

XIII. THE LORD OF THE HILLS BECOMES THE LORD OF THE PLAIN

The Castle of Canossa in the Emilian Apennines.

of the knight for the trader; the virtuous indignation provoked in the heart of the cleric by the audacity of these 'usurers', of these 'engrossers' whose gains seemed to spring from tainted sources.[1] There was, however, another, and a deeper cause.

In feudal society the oath of aid and 'friendship' had figured from the beginning as one of the main elements of the system. But it was an engagement between inferior and superior, which made the one the subject of the other. The distinctive feature of the communal oath, on the other hand, was that it united *equals*. Certainly engagements of this type were not absolutely unknown. Of this nature, as we shall see, were the oaths taken 'one to another' by the fellow-members of those popular 'gilds' which Charlemagne prohibited; and later by the members of the peace associations of whom, in more ways than one, the urban communes were the heirs. Such again were the oaths which, before the first efforts of the towns to achieve autonomy, bound together the merchants in little societies, also sometimes called 'gilds'. These, although formed simply to serve the needs of commercial enterprise, constituted one of the earliest manifestations of burgess solidarity. But never, before the communal movement, had the practice of these mutual fealties been so widespread or displayed such strength. The 'conspiracies' which had arisen on every hand were truly like so many 'bundles of thorns intertwined', as one writer of sermons expressed it.[2] It was there, in the commune, that the really revolutionary ferment was to be seen, with its violent hostility to a stratified society. Certainly these primitive urban groups were in no sense democratic. The 'greater bourgeois', who were their real founders and whom the lesser bourgeois were not always eager to follow, were often in their treatment of the poor hard masters and merciless creditors. But by substituting for the promise of obedience, paid for by protection, the promise of mutual aid, they contributed to the social life of Europe a new element, profoundly alien to the feudal spirit properly so called.

[1] Cf. the synod of Paris, 1212: Mansi, *Concilia*, XXII, col. 851, c. 8 (*feneratoribus et exactoribus*).

[2] A. Giry, *Documents sur les relations de la royauté avec les villes*, 1885, no. XX, p. 58.

PART VII
Political Organization

XXVII

JUDICIAL INSTITUTIONS

1 GENERAL CHARACTERISTICS OF THE JUDICIAL SYSTEM

HOW were men tried? There is no better touchstone for a social system than this question. Let us therefore see how matters stood in this respect in the Europe of about the year 1000; on a first scrutiny, a few dominant features stand out in strong relief from the mass of legal detail. First, we may note the tremendous fragmentation of judicial powers; next, their tangled interconnections; and lastly, their ineffectiveness. The most serious cases could be heard in many different courts exercising parallel jurisdiction. Undoubtedly there were certain rules which, in theory, determined the limits of competence of the various courts; but in spite of them uncertainty persisted. The feudal records that have come down to us abound in charters relating to disputes between rival jurisdictions. Despairing of knowing before which authority to bring their suits, litigants often agreed to set up arbitrators of their own or else, instead of seeking a court judgment, they preferred to come to a private agreement—even at the risk that subsequently it might not be respected. Uncertain of its competence and doubtful of its strength, the court sometimes did not disdain to ask the parties to accept its judgment, either in advance or after it had been pronounced. Even if one had obtained a favourable decision there was often no other way to get it executed than to come to terms with a recalcitrant opponent. Nothing reminds us more forcibly than these conflicts that disorder can be a most important historic fact: a fact which nevertheless needs to be explained. In the present case it was clearly due in large part to the coexistence of contradictory principles which, being derived from diverse traditions and compelled to adapt themselves in a somewhat rough and ready fashion to the needs of a highly unstable society, were incessantly in conflict with each other. But it also had its source in the actual conditions imposed on the exercise of justice by the human environment.

In this society, in which protective relationships had multiplied, every chief—and there were certainly enough of them—desired to be a judge. One reason was that the right to sit in judgment on his subordinates, to the exclusion of other courts, alone enabled a lord both to protect them and to maintain effective control over them. Another was that this right was also essentially lucrative. Not only did it carry with it the proceeds of judicial fines and costs, it also favoured, more than any other right, that transformation of usages into legal obligations which the lords found so profitable. It was no accident that the meaning of the word *justitia* was sometimes extended so as to describe a lord's powers as a whole. It is true that this was merely the recognition of a necessity common to almost all group activity: even in our own day, is not every employer in his business, every military commander, a judge after his fashion? But his powers in this capacity are limited to a well-defined sphere of activity. He must confine himself to judging the workman or the soldier as such. The chief of feudal times had greater scope, because the ties of subjection tended at that time to fetter the whole man.

Moreover, in feudal times the administration of justice was not a very complicated task, though it naturally called for a modicum of legal knowledge. Where written codes existed this amounted to knowing their rules more or less by heart or having them read to one; though often numerous and detailed, these rules were too rigid to require in most cases any personal effort of thought. If, on the other hand, written law had been superseded by oral custom, it sufficed to have some acquaintance with this diffuse tradition. Finally, it was important to know the prescribed gestures and the necessary phrases, which imposed a rigid formality on procedure. In short, it was all a matter of memory and practice. The means of proof were rudimentary and easily applied. The court seldom heard evidence, and when it did, confined itself to recording the statements of witnesses rather than examining them. To take cognizance of the contents of a legal document (which for a long time was rarely necessary), to receive the oath of one of the parties or of the oath-helpers, to declare the result of an ordeal or a trial by battle (the latter was increasingly favoured at the expense of other forms of 'judgment of God')—such duties required but little technical training. The matters with which the actions themselves were concerned were few and simple. The anaemic condition of commerce greatly reduced the number of cases relating to contracts. When in certain quarters, a more active economy of exchange once more developed, the inefficiency of the common law and the ordinary courts in dealing with such disputes early led the merchant groups to settle these among themselves, at first by unofficial arbitration, later by means of their own courts. Seisin (that is to say, possession sanctioned by long usage), powers over things and men—such were the constant subjects of almost all litigation. In addition, of course, there were crimes and civil wrongs to be dealt with; but here the action of the courts was, in practice, greatly restricted by private vengeance. In short, there was no intellectual obstacle to prevent anyone who had the necessary power from setting up himself or his representative as a judge.

Side by side with the ordinary courts, however, there existed a system of special courts—those of the Church. (We refer to the courts of the Church in the exercise of its proper function; for the judicial powers which bishops and monasteries exercised over their dependants, on the same basis as so many lay lords, naturally did not come under the heading of ecclesiastical jurisdiction in the true sense of the word.) These courts had a twofold sphere of action. They sought to embrace under their jurisdiction all tonsured persons, clerics and monks alike. In addition, they had more or less completely appropriated certain cases which, even when they concerned laymen exclusively, were considered to be of a religious nature— from heresy to the swearing of oaths and marriage. The growth of this jurisdiction during the feudal era not only reveals the weakness of the great temporal powers (the Carolingian monarchy had allowed much less independence to its clergy); it also bears witness to the tendency of the ecclesiastical world increasingly to widen the gulf between the small body of God's servants and the profane multitude. Here again the question of competence provoked lively quarrels about the limits of jurisdictions, which became especially fierce from the time when genuine state governments once again began to oppose the encroachments of the spiritual power.

Among the institutions peculiar to feudalism, both the judicial system of the Church and its law were thus a sort of empire within an empire, and for this reason it is logical that, having briefly recalled their rôle and their importance, we should exclude them from our review.

2 THE DISINTEGRATION OF JUDICIAL AUTHORITY

Like the law of persons, the judicial system in barbarian Europe had been dominated by the traditional antithesis between free men and slaves. The former were in theory tried by courts composed of other free men and the trials were conducted by a representative of the king. Over the slaves the master exercised a power of decision (in disputes among themselves) and a power of correction, which were too exclusively dependent on his personal discretion to be fitly described as justice. There were, it is true, exceptional cases of slaves being brought before the public courts, either because their owner voluntarily chose this method of relieving himself of responsibility, or even in certain cases because the law in the interests of good order compelled him to do so. But even then it was by superiors and not by equals that their fate was decided. Nothing was clearer than this contrast. Yet, at an early date, it had to give way before the irresistible pressure of circumstances.

In practice, as we know, the gulf between the two legal categories tended gradually to lessen. Many slaves had become tenants, as had many free men. Numbers of free men lived under the authority of a lord and held their fields from him; thus it is not surprising that the master frequently

361

came to extend his right of correction uniformly over this mixed body of humble folk, and also appointed himself judge in the lawsuits which arose within the group. As early as the end of the Roman period, these private jurisdictions of the 'powerful', often with their own prisons, were springing up on the margin of the law. When the biographer of Caesarius of Arles, who died in 542, praises his hero for never having allotted more than twenty-nine strokes with a stick to any of his dependants (at least not at one time), he makes it clear that the saint showed this mildness not only towards his slaves but also towards 'the free men of his obedience'. It was left to the barbarian monarchies to give legal recognition to this *de facto* situation.

This from the outset was one of the principal objects of the Frankish 'immunity', and soon became its real *raison d'être*. Of great antiquity in Gaul, this institution was disseminated by the efforts of the Carolingians throughout their vast empire. The term designated the combination of two privileges: exemption from certain fiscal burdens; and the immunity of a territory from visitation by the royal officials, for any reason whatsoever. It thus almost necessarily involved the delegation to the lord of certain judicial powers over the population.

It is true that the grant of immunities by specific charter appears to have been strictly limited to ecclesiastical authorities, and the rare examples to the contrary which one might be tempted to cite are not only of late date, but are clearly accounted for by wholly exceptional circumstances. Moreover, even if the silence of the cartularies, always suspect, does not carry conviction, that of the formularies employed by the Frankish chancellery should do so; and there we should look in vain for a form of document of this type in favour of laymen. In practice, nevertheless, a large number of the latter had attained the same advantages by other means. Traditionally, the royal estates were also classed as 'immunities'; in other words, being run directly for the benefit of the prince and administered by a special body of agents, they were outside the control of the ordinary royal officials. The count and his subordinates were forbidden to levy any taxes on them and even to enter them. Now, when the king, in return for services rendered or to be rendered, granted away one of these estates, he ordinarily allowed it to retain the privilege of exemption previously enjoyed. In theory the 'benefit', as a temporary grant, continued to form part of the domain of the crown, so that the powerful men, whose wealth was in very large part derived from these liberalities, enjoyed on many of their manors exactly the same legal privileges as the ecclesiastical immunists. Moreover, there can be no doubt that they often succeeded, less legitimately, in extending them to their patrimonial possessions, which they had so long been accustomed to rule as masters.

These grants continued to be made throughout the first feudal age, and till a much later date the chancelleries still handed down their formulas, which by that time had become rather meaningless. The sovereigns had been led to resort to them for various reasons all equally cogent. In the case of the churches, to load them with favours was a pious duty which came near to being identified with a duty of good government, since the prince thereby called down upon his peoples the dew of heavenly blessings. As for the magnates and the vassals, these gifts were considered the necessary price of their fickle loyalty. Moreover, there was something to be said for restricting the scope of the royal officials. Harsh in their treatment of their master's subjects, and often not particularly submissive to the master himself, their conduct gave only too much ground for mistrust. Henceforth, it was on the chiefs of the little groups into which the mass of its subjects was divided, as much as on the royal officials, that the crown laid the responsibility for ensuring order and obedience; by strengthening their authority it hoped to consolidate its own police system. Finally, the encroachments of private jurisdictions had been growing for a long time, and since they arose from the mere exercise of force, it was force alone which determined their limits. By legalizing them they could be brought within proper bounds. This concern, very evident in the Carolingian immunity, was bound up with the general reform of the judicial system undertaken by Charlemagne, which was destined to exercise a strong influence on all subsequent developments.

In the Merovingian state the fundamental judicial division had been a comparatively small territory: allowing, needless to say, for innumerable local variations, it was more or less the equivalent in size of the smallest of the *arrondissements*, the districts into which the French departments were divided by Napoleon. It was generally known by Romance or Germanic names signifying 'a hundred'—a designation of rather mysterious origin, which went back to the old institutions of the Germanic peoples and perhaps to a numerical system different from ours (the earliest meaning of the word which in modern German is written as *hundert* seems to have been 'one hundred and twenty'). In Romance-speaking regions, the terms *voirie* or *viguerie* (Latin, *vicaria*) were also used. The count, in the course of his circuit through the various hundreds placed under his authority, summoned all the free men to his court. There judgment was rendered by a small group of 'jurors' taken from the assembly; the rôle of the royal official was confined to presiding over the proceedings and getting the sentences carried out.

In practice, however, this system seemed to suffer from a double drawback: for the local inhabitants it involved too frequent summonses, and on the count it imposed a responsibility too heavy for him to fulfil satisfactorily. Charlemagne therefore substituted for it a system in which there were two courts at different levels, each enjoying full powers within its own sphere. The count continued to visit the hundred regularly to hold his court, and this, as in the past, the whole population was obliged to attend.

But these plenary sessions of the count's court now took place only three times a year—an arrangement which made possible a limitation of competence. For henceforward the only cases brought before these general assemblies were those turning on the most important matters—the 'major causes'. As for the 'minor causes', they were reserved for less infrequent and more restricted sittings, which only the jurors were obliged to attend and which were presided over by a simple subordinate of the count—his representative in the district, the 'hundred-man', known in France as the *centenier* or *voyer*.

Now, despite the appalling vagueness of our documents, there can be scarcely any doubt that in the reign of Charlemagne and his immediate successors the extent of the jurisdiction conceded to the immunists over the free men of their territories coincided generally with the 'minor causes'. In other words, the lord enjoying this privilege acted within his own territory in the capacity of *centenier*. What happened if a 'major' cause were in question? The immunity stood in the way of any attempt by the count himself to seize the accused, the defendant, or the oath-helpers in exempt territory. But the lord was obliged on his own responsibility to deliver the persons summoned to the count's court. Thus, cutting his losses, the sovereign hoped at least to preserve the most serious decisions for the public law courts.

The distinction between major and minor causes was to have prolonged repercussions. It is this distinction, in fact, which we find persisting throughout the feudal era and much later still under the new names of 'high' and 'low' justice. This fundamental antithesis, common to all the countries which had been subject to Carolingian domination and to those alone, continued to distinguish between two degrees of competence which, within the same territory, were not necessarily united in the same hands. But neither the limits of the judicial powers thus superimposed, nor their distribution, remained at all as they had been when first established.

In criminal justice, the Carolingians had, after some uncertainty, established a criterion for 'major causes' based on the nature of the punishment: the count's court alone could pronounce sentence of death or reduction to slavery. This principle, a very clear one, passed down through the ages. As a result of changes in the conception of freedom, penal enslavement proper rapidly disappeared (where we find the murderer of a serf being enslaved to the lord of his victim the case comes under quite a different heading—it is classed as compensation). Crimes 'of blood', however—that is, crimes punishable by death—always remained within the normal jurisdiction of those who exercised 'high justice'. But these 'pleas of the sword', as they were called in Norman law, ceased to be the privilege of a few great counts. One of the most striking features of the first feudal age everywhere, but particularly in France—and one most decisive for the future—was the multitude of petty chiefs thus provided with powers of life and death. What then had happened? It is clear that neither the fragmentation of certain powers of the count by inheritance or gift, nor even usurpations pure and simple, can suffice to explain the phenomemon. What is more, there are various indications which clearly point to an actual change in juridical values. All the great ecclesiastical authorities exercised judgment of blood, either on their own account or through their representatives; this right had in fact become a natural consequence of the privilege of immunity, in defiance of the ancient rules. It was sometimes called *centaine* or *voirie*—a sort of official recognition that it was henceforth regarded as being within the competence of the lower courts. In other words, the barrier raised not so long before by the Carolingians had on this point given way. And this development can without doubt be explained.

It would indeed be a mistake to imagine that these death sentences, formerly reserved for the count's courts—or, at a higher level still, for the king's court or the assizes held by the *missi*—had ever been very numerous in the Frankish period. Only crimes considered particularly heinous from the point of view of the public peace were at that time visited with such punishments. Much more often, the rôle of the judges was confined to proposing or imposing a settlement, and then ordering the payment, in accordance with the legal tariff, of an indemnity, of which the judicial authority took a share. But in the period when governments were at their weakest, there were continual vendettas and acts of violence, and it was not long before a reaction set in against the old system of criminal justice, whose dangerous inefficiency seemed to be demonstrated by events. This reaction was closely bound up with the movement which gave rise to the peace associations. It found its most characteristic expression in the entirely new attitude adopted by the most influential ecclesiastical circles. Not so long before, through their horror of bloodshed and feuds, they had favoured the practice of pecuniary settlements. But now they began to insist that these too lenient measures should be replaced by afflictive penalties, which in their view were alone capable of frightening evil-doers. It was in this period—about the tenth century—that the European penal code began to assume that aspect of extreme harshness which it was destined to retain until the humanitarian movement of comparatively recent times. This grim development, which was to result in increased indifference to human suffering, had nevertheless been originally inspired by the desire to alleviate it.

Now in all criminal cases, however serious, in which the executioner had no part the inferior jurisdictions, courts of hundreds or immunity, had always been competent. When money compensation gradually gave way to punishment, the judges remained the same; the only change was in the nature of the sentences pronounced, and the death penalty ceased to be the monopoly of the counts. The transition, moreover, was facilitated by two features of the earlier system. The hundred courts had always possessed the right to punish with death criminals caught *in flagrante delicto*. So much concern for public order had seemed to require. This same concern now induced these courts to pass beyond the limit previously fixed. As for the immunists, they had always had the power of life and death over their slaves. Where henceforth, among dependants, was the dividing line between freedom and slavery?

Apart from crimes, the count's courts had had exclusive jurisdiction over two classes of cases: those which turned on the status, free or unfree, of one of the parties, or which concerned the possession of slaves; and those which related to the possession of allodial lands. This double heritage was not to pass intact to the much greater number of courts exercising high justice in the succeeding age. Lawsuits relating to allods—which were becoming increasingly rare—often remained the monopoly of the real heirs of the count's rights; this was the case until the twelfth century at Laon, where the count was the bishop.[1] As for questions relating to servile status or slaves, the virtual disappearance of household slavery, as well as the emergence of a new conception of freedom, led to their being merged in the mass of disputes on property in general and personal dependence—a type of dispute which had never been included among 'major causes'. Despoiled, as it were, at the lower end as well as the upper, it might be thought that 'high justice' was now confined to the rôle of a purely criminal jurisdiction; but the 'civil' side—in the modern sense of the word—returned to it through the medium of procedure. In the feudal era a very great number of disputes of every kind were decided by single combat. Now, by a natural association of ideas, it was admitted—not invariably, but very frequently —that this sanguinary solution could only be effected before courts having jurisdiction in the case of crimes punishable by death.

In feudal times everyone who exercised the rights of 'high justice' also possessed those of 'low justice' over the territories under his direct control. But the converse was not true, except in certain regions and only there at a later stage—as in Beauvaisis in the thirteenth century, if Beaumanoir is to be believed. Thus it was for a long time not exceptional for men subject to the jurisdiction of their local lord in minor cases to take their more serious actions to a neighbouring court. Extensive as had been the subdivision of judicial powers, it had not done away with the system whereby two degrees of competence, a higher and a lower, reposed in different hands; though it had moved it one step down all along the line. Just as the successors of the *voyers* or *centeniers* and the immunists (not to mention a great many powerful men, with no official position) had taken from the count—save in matters relating to allods—the monopoly of major causes and thus come to exercise 'high justice', so in their turn they lost the monopoly of minor causes, to the advantage of the great body of manorial lords. Whoever

[1] For the peace institution of Laon (26th August, 1128), see Warnkoenig and Stein, *Französische Staats- und Rechtsgeschichte*, I, *Urkundenbuch*, p. 31, c. 2.

found himself the master of a small group of humble dependants, whoever derived rents and services from a small group of rural tenements, henceforth possessed at least the right of 'low justice'. In this right many elements of different date and different kinds were mingled.

It included in the first place the trial of all disputes between the lord himself and his tenants—particularly as regards the obligations of the latter. It is useless to try to explain this right as a legacy of official judicial systems. Its real source was in an ancient yet increasingly prevalent conception of the powers proper to the chief, or rather to the person, whoever he might be, who was in a position to exact from another man an obligation which savoured of inferiority. In France in the twelfth century we find the holder of a modest tenement in villeinage, which he in turn had rented to a cultivator, getting his own lord to grant him, in the event of the rent not being paid, 'the exercise of jurisdiction in this matter only and in none other'.[1] From jurisdiction properly so called to distraint carried out personally by the creditor—so frequently practised at that time and often legally recognized—the transitions were not always very perceptible and most people no doubt failed to make any very clear distinction between the two ideas. This jurisdiction over tenants' obligations—called *justice foncière* by French jurists of a later age—did not, however, constitute the whole of 'low justice'. He who exercised the latter was, for the men who lived on his land, the normal judge of practically all the civil actions which they could institute among themselves (unless there was recourse to trial by battle), as well as of all except the most serious of their offences. His function was thus a mixture of the legacy of 'minor causes' and that of the rights of decision and correction which had for so long been exercised in fact by the masters.

Both high justice and low justice were essentially territorial: he who resided within their boundaries was subject to them; he who lived outside was not. But, in a society in which the ties between man and man were so strong, this territorial principle had constantly to compete with a personal principle. Whoever in the Frankish period extended his *maimbour* over someone weaker than himself assumed both the right and the duty of accompanying his protégé to court, of defending him there and of standing surety for him. From this to claiming the power of pronouncing sentence upon him was an easy step; and it was in fact taken at all levels of the hierarchy.

Among the personal dependants, the humblest and most subordinate were those who, on account of the hereditary character of the bond, it had become customary to describe as unfree. It was in general considered that they could only be tried, at any rate for crimes punishable by death, by the lord to whom they were personally bound—this even when they did not live on his land, or when the lord did not exercise high justice over his

---

[1] *Cartulaire du prieuré de Notre-Dame de Longpont*, ed. Marion, no. 25.

other tenants. It was often sought to apply similar principles to other types of humble dependant who, though not in hereditary bondage to the master, were none the less considered to be very close to his person: servants of both sexes, for example, or again the merchants who, in the cities, acted as buying and selling agents for ecclesiastical lords. These claims, of which it was difficult to obtain practical recognition, were a constant source of uncertainty and conflict.

In so far as the new form of servitude had retained the imprint of the old, the exclusive jurisdiction of the lord over his serfs might be regarded as the natural consequence of the old right of correction—such, moreover, is the idea which seems still to be expressed in one German text of the twelfth century.[1] The military vassals, on the other hand, as free men, were in the Carolingian epoch subject only to the jurisdiction of the public courts. This at least was their position in law. Can it be doubted that in fact the lord himself tried to settle the differences which threatened to sow discord among his vassals, or that persons injured by the henchmen of a powerful man ordinarily considered that they were more sure of obtaining redress by going to him? From the tenth century onwards, these practices gave rise to a genuine right of jurisdiction. The change, moreover, had been favoured and sometimes rendered almost imperceptible by the way in which the general evolution of powers had affected the public tribunals. In the form of 'honours', and later as patrimonial fiefs, these courts had for the most part fallen into the hands of the magnates, who filled them with their retainers; and in certain principalities we can follow clearly the process by which the count's court, thus composed, was gradually transformed into a really feudal court, in which it was the vassals themselves who decided the cases of other vassals.

3 TRIAL BY PEERS OR TRIAL BY THE LORD

The free man tried by an assembly of free men, the slave punished by his master alone—this division could scarcely survive the drastic changes in social classifications nor, in particular, the entry into servitude of so many men formerly free who in their new bonds still retained many of the features of their original status. The right to be tried by their 'peers' was never disputed in the case of persons of even the most modest rank—despite the introduction of hierarchic distinctions which seriously impaired the old principle of judicial equality, born simply of a common freedom. What is more, in many places customary law extended to dependants and even to serfs the right of trial, if not always by exact equals, at least by bodies composed of subjects of the same master. In the regions between Seine and Loire, high justice continued ordinarily to be dispensed in general assemblies (*plaids généraux*), which the entire popula-

[1] Ortlieb of Zwiefalten, *Chronicon*, I, c. 9, in *M.G.H.*, SS. X, p. 78.

tion of the territory was required to attend. As for the jurors, they were still frequently appointed for life by the holder of the judicial rights, in conformity with the purest Carolingian tradition, and were still known as *échevins* (*scabini*); in other cases, as a result of the feudalization of offices, the hereditary obligation to sit in the court was finally attached to certain tenements. Elsewhere, the lord or his representative appears to have been content to surround himself, in a somewhat haphazard way, with the chief personages, the 'good men and true' of the locality. Over and above these divergences, a central fact remains. To speak of royal, baronial, or seignorial justice may be convenient. But it is only legitimate provided that we do not forget that the king or the great baron almost never decided a case personally and that the same was true even of many manorial lords or stewards. Convoked by the chief, who frequently presided over it, it was his court which 'declared' or 'found' the law; that is, it recalled the rules and incorporated them in its judgment. 'The court passes judgment; not the lord', one English text declares, in so many words.[1] And no doubt it would be as unwise to exaggerate as to deny altogether the protection thus afforded to the litigants. 'Quick, quick, hasten ye to get me a judgment'—thus spoke the impatient Henry Plantagenet, demanding of his vassals the condemnation of Thomas Becket.[2] The command neatly reflects the limitations—varying immensely from case to case—imposed by the power of the chief on the impartiality of the judges; at the same time it shows that even the most imperious of tyrants found it impossible to dispense with a collective judgment.

But the idea that the unfree and, by a natural assimilation, the humblest dependants should have no other judge than their master was too deeply rooted in men's minds to be easily obliterated. In the countries that were formerly Romanized, moreover, it found support in what had remained of the imprint or the memories of Roman organization; there the magistrates had been the superiors, not the equals, of those subject to their jurisdiction. Once more the existence of contrary principles, between which it was necessary to choose, produced a diversity of customs. According to the region or even the village, the peasants were tried sometimes by the whole body of the court, sometimes by the lord or his steward alone. The latter system does not appear to have been the most usual at first, though during the second feudal age the course of development turned clearly in its favour. 'Court baron', composed of free tenants who decided the fate of other free tenants; 'customary court', in which the villein, henceforth regarded as unfree, submitted to the judgment of the lord's steward—such was the distinction, pregnant with consequences, which in the thirteenth century English jurists strove to introduce into the hitherto much simpler judicial structure of the English manor. Similarly in

---

[1] *Monumenta Gildhallae Londoniensis* (Rolls Series), 1, p. 66.
[2] Roger of Hoveden, *Chronica* (Rolls Series), Vol. I, p. 228.

France, in defiance of what was still a widespread practice, legal doctrine as interpreted by Beaumanoir chose to regard trial by peers as the monopoly of noblemen. The hierarchization, which was one of the marks of the period, forced even the judicial system to subserve its ends.

4 ON THE EDGE OF DISINTEGRATION: SURVIVALS AND NEW FACTORS

Subdivided and manorialized though judicial authority was, it would be a grave mistake to imagine that in the feudal world nothing survived of the old courts of popular or public law, though their power of resistance to change, nowhere negligible, varied greatly from country to country. The time has therefore come to emphasize national contrasts more clearly than has been done so far.

Despite its distinctive features, the course of development in England presented some obvious analogies with that in the Frankish state. Here again we find, at the base of the organization, the hundred with its court of free men. Above the hundreds, and comprising a varying number of them, were the counties (called in the native speech 'shires'). In the south they corresponded to actual ethnic divisions, ancient kingdoms such as Kent or Sussex which had gradually been absorbed in larger monarchies, or else groups spontaneously formed within a people in the course of settlement, like Suffolk and Norfolk ('southern folk' and 'northern folk') which represented the two halves of the original East Anglia. In the centre and north, on the other hand, the counties were at the outset only administrative and military districts created more recently and more arbitrarily at the time of the struggle with the Danes, each with a citadel as its centre, which explains why in this part of the country they mostly bear the name of the county town. Henceforth, the shire also had its court of free men; but the division of competence between county and hundred was here much less clearly marked than in the Carolingian Empire. Despite some efforts to reserve for the county court the trial of certain crimes particularly inimical to the public peace, it appears to have intervened mainly in cases where the lower court had proved powerless to act. This explains why the distinction between high and low justice always remained foreign to the English system.

As on the continent, these public tribunals had to compete with the courts of the chiefs. At an early date we find mention of sessions held by the lord in his house, his 'hall'. Later the kings legalized this *de facto* situation, and from the tenth century onwards we find them granting rights of jurisdiction known as 'sake and soke' (*sake*, which corresponds to the German noun *Sache*, signified 'case' or 'action'; *soke*, which is to be compared with the German verb *suchen*, meant seeking a judge, that is, having recourse to his judgment). The powers thus granted, which applied sometimes to a particular territory, sometimes to a group of persons, coincided more or less with what we know to have been the very wide competence of the Anglo-Saxon hundred. This gave them, from the beginning, a larger sphere of application than that which, in theory, went with the Carolingian immunity, though it was approximately equal to the rights which the immunists had contrived to appropriate in the tenth century. The influence of these rights upon social ties was such that the free tenant derived from his submission to the master's court his ordinary title of sokeman, literally 'suitor'. Sometimes certain churches or certain magnates received as a gift in perpetuity the right to hold a hundred court; and a few monasteries—though very few—were even accorded the right to try all crimes, including those normally reserved for the king.

Nevertheless, these grants, important as they were, never completely superseded the old communal courts of public law. Even where the hundred court was in the hands of a baron it continued to meet, as in the days when it had been presided over by a representative of the king. As for the county court, it continued to function without interruption according to the ancient forms. It is true that the great men, too exalted in rank to submit to the judgments of these tribunals, and the peasants—even the free ones—who had been snapped up by the manorial courts, ceased generally to appear at these assemblies (though for the humble folk of the villages it was still obligatory, in theory, to be represented by the priest, the reeve, and four men). But all who occupied an intermediate position in power and freedom were still required to attend. Stifled between the lords' courts and—after the Norman Conquest—the encroachments of royal justice, the old courts were progressively reduced to relative insignificance. Nevertheless it was there—within the framework of the county, mainly, but also in the more restricted sphere of the hundred—that the most vital elements in the nation preserved the habit of meeting to determine the customary law of the territorial group, reply in its name to all manner of inquiries and even, if the need arose, bear the responsibility for its collective offences. And so it continued till the time when, summoned to meet as one body, the representatives of the shire courts formed the earliest nucleus of what was later to be the House of Commons. Assuredly the English parliamentary system was not cradled in 'the forests of Germania'. It bore the deep imprint of the feudal environment from which it sprang. But the peculiar quality which distinguished it so sharply from the continental systems of 'Estates', and, more generally, that collaboration of the well-to-do classes in power, so characteristic of the English political structure as long ago as the Middle Ages—the origin of these is surely to be found in the firm establishment on English soil of the system of assemblies composed of the free men of the territory, in accordance with the ancient practice of the barbarian epoch.

Over and above the infinite variety of local or regional customs, two great facts dominated the evolution of the German judicial system. First, since the 'law of fiefs' remained distinct from the 'law of the land', the feudal courts developed side by side with the ancient tribunals, without absorbing them. Secondly, the maintenance of a more stratified social hierarchy, and more especially, the long survival of the idea that to enjoy freedom was to be subject directly to the authority of the State, preserved for the ancient courts of county and hundred (whose respective jurisdictions were somewhat imperfectly delimited) a very extensive sphere of action. This was especially the case in the Swabian Alps and in Saxony, regions of many allods and of incomplete feudalization. It was nevertheless customary, as a general rule, to require the jurors or *scabini* (German, *Schöffen*) to be possessed of a certain amount of landed wealth. Sometimes, in accordance with what was then an almost universal tendency, their offices were even regarded as hereditary; so that the very respect for the old principle that a free man should be tried by a court of free men often resulted in the long run in the composition of the courts being more oligarchic than elsewhere.

France (along with northern Italy, of course) was the land of feudalized justice in its purest form. It is true that the Carolingian system left deep and lasting traces, especially in the northern parts of the country, but their influence was chiefly felt in the hierarchization of the seignorial courts—in terms of high and low justice—and their internal organization. The hundred or district courts disappeared very rapidly and very completely. It is characteristic that the jurisdiction of the lord who exercised high justice ordinarily acquired the name of 'castellany'—as if the only source of judicial rights that common opinion now recognized was the possession of a fortified dwelling, at once the origin and the symbol of actual power. This is not to say, however, that nothing survived of the old jurisdictions of the counts. In the great territorial principalities the prince was sometimes able to reserve for himself the monopoly of cases where the death penalty was involved—as in Flanders, Normandy, Béarn. Frequently, as we have seen, the count had jurisdiction over allodial estates; he decided lawsuits in which the churches, imperfectly incorporated in the feudal hierarchy, figured as parties; and, in theory, he possessed jurisdiction over markets and public highways, except where these rights had been granted away or usurped. Here already, at least in embryo, was a powerful antidote to the dispersal of judicial powers.

Furthermore, two great forces throughout Europe were working to limit or counteract the disintegration of judicial powers; both for a long time had only a modest success, but both were rich in promise.

First, there were the monarchies. That the king was by his very nature the supreme judge of his people—on this point all were agreed. It remained to deduce the practical consequences of this principle; and here it became a question of action and effective power. In the eleventh century the functions of the Capetian royal court were largely confined to trying cases involving the ruler's immediate dependants and his churches, or (on exceptional occasions and much less effectively) acting as a feudal court with jurisdiction, in theory, over the great feudatories of the crown. On the other hand the tribunal of the German king, conceived on the Carolingian model, still attracted a large number of important cases. But even when relatively active, these courts attached to the person of the sovereign obviously remained inaccessible to the mass of his subjects. It was not enough that, as in Germany, wherever the king passed in the course of his official visitations his jurisdiction should supersede all others. The power of the monarchy could become a decisive element in the judicial system only by extending its grip over the entire realm by means of a complete network of itinerant justices or permanent representatives. This was achieved at the time of the general reconcentration of authority during the second feudal age, first by the Norman and Angevin kings of England, later and much more slowly by the Capetians. In both countries, but in France especially, the monarchy was to find a valuable buttress in the system of vassalage itself. For feudalism, which had had the effect of dividing judicial authority among so many hands, nevertheless provided a remedy for this process in the practice of appeals.

At this period, no lawsuit, once decided, could be begun again between the same adversaries in a different court, since it was held that for a genuine error, committed in good faith, there was no redress. Suppose, however, that one of the litigants believed that the court had deliberately rendered false judgment, or else that he charged it with having bluntly refused to try the action at all. There was nothing to prevent him from proceeding against the members of this court in a higher one. If, in this action, absolutely distinct from the previous one, he won his case, the bad judges were generally punished and their judgment was in any case annulled. This form of appeal—we should today call it 'suing the judge'— existed as early as the era of the barbarian kingdoms. But at that time it could only be brought before the sole tribunal which stood above the assemblies of free men—namely the royal court. Thus the procedure was an unusual and a difficult one. The system of vassalage opened up new possibilities; every vassal's feudal lord was henceforth his normal judge; and the denial of justice was a crime, like other crimes. Quite naturally, the common rule was applied to it and appeals ascended, step by step, through the gradations of homage. The procedure continued to require delicate handling; above all it was dangerous, for the customary mode of proof was trial by battle. However, the feudal court, recourse to which was henceforth necessary, proved much more accessible than that of a king too far removed from his subjects; if a case eventually reached the sovereign's court it did so by successive stages. In the legal affairs of the upper classes appeals became less and less exceptional. Because it involved a hierarchy of ties of dependence and established a series of direct contacts between chiefs ranged one above the other, the system of vassalage and the fief permitted the reintroduction into the judicial organization of an element of unity which monarchies of the earlier type, out of touch with the mass of their nominal subjects, had shown themselves powerless to safeguard.

XXVIII

THE TRADITIONAL POWERS:
KINGDOMS AND EMPIRE

1 GEOGRAPHICAL DISTRIBUTION OF THE MONARCHIES

ABOVE the profusion of manors, family or village communities, and vassal groups, there were in feudal Europe various powers whose wider range was for a long time counter-balanced by much less effective action; it was nevertheless their destiny to maintain in this divided society certain principles of order and unity. At the summit, kingdoms and Empire derived their strength and their ambitions from a long past. Lower down, younger powers were ranged one above another, by an almost imperceptible gradation, from the territorial principality to the simple barony or castellany. We must first consider the position of the powers with a long history behind them.

After the fall of the Roman Empire, the West had been divided up into kingdoms ruled by Germanic dynasties. It was from these 'barbarian' monarchies that almost all those of feudal Europe were more or less directly descended. The line of descent was particularly clear in Anglo-Saxon England, which towards the first half of the ninth century was still divided into five or six kingdoms; genuine heirs—although their number was much smaller—of the states founded not so long before by the invaders. We have seen how the Scandinavian invasions left in the end only Wessex, enlarged at the expense of its neighbours. In the tenth century its sovereign took to calling himself either king of all Britain, or more frequently and with more lasting effect, king of the Angles or English. On the frontiers of this *regnum Anglorum* there nevertheless subsisted, at the time of the Norman Conquest, a Celtic fringe. The Britons of Wales were divided among several little principalities. Towards the north a family of Scottish —that is to say, Irish—chiefs, conquering in turn the other Celtic tribes of the Highlands and the Germanic or Germanized populations of Lothian, had bit by bit established a large realm, which took from the conquerors the name of Scotland.

In the Iberian peninsula a number of Gothic nobles, who had taken refuge in Asturias after the Moslem invasion, had set up a king. Several times partitioned among the heirs of the founder, but considerably enlarged by the Reconquest, the state thus formed had its capital transferred, about the beginning of the tenth century, to Leon, on the plateau to the south of the mountains. In the course of the same century a military command which had been established to the east in Castile, and which had at first been dependent on the kingdoms of Asturias and Leon, gradually made itself autonomous and its chief, in 1035, took the title of king. Then a century or so later a similar secession in the west gave birth to Portugal. Meanwhile, the Basques of the Central Pyrenees, who were known as the Navarrese, were living apart in their valleys. They also finally formed themselves into a kingdom which emerged clearly about the year 900 and from which, in 1037, another tiny monarchy detached itself, taking the name of 'Aragon' from the torrent which watered its territory. Finally, to the north of the lower course of the Ebro was a 'march' created by the Franks, which under the name of the county of Barcelona was considered, until the time of St. Louis, to be legally a fief of the king of France. These were the political formations—with fluctuating frontiers and subject to all the vicissitudes of partitions, conquests and political marriages—from which 'the Spains' were born.

To the north of the Pyrenees the barbarian kingdom of the Franks had been vastly enlarged by the Carolingians. The deposition of Charles the Fat in November 887, shortly followed by his death on 13th January of the following year, marked the failure of the final effort to restore the unity of the Empire. It was not through a mere whim that the new king of the East Franks, Arnulf, declined to take over the rule of the western kingdom, offered to him by the archbishop of Rheims. Plainly, the heritage of Charlemagne seemed too great a burden. Broadly speaking, the division followed the lines laid down by the first partition, that of Verdun, in 843. The kingdom of Lewis the German, formed at that date by the union of three dioceses on the left bank of the Rhine—Mainz, Worms and Speyer —with the vast Germanic territories on the east bank subdued not long before by the two Frankish dynasties, was in 888 re-established for the benefit of his only surviving descendant, Arnulf of Carinthia. This formed 'East Francia' which, by an anachronism that is harmless provided we are conscious of it, we may here and now call 'Germany'.

In the former kingdom of Charles the Bald, 'West Francia', or simply France as we call it today, two great lords were proclaimed king almost at the same time—Guy of Spoleto, an Italian duke of Frankish ancestry, and Odo, a Neustrian count, probably of Saxon origin. The latter, who commanded a much larger following and had distinguished himself in the war against the Northmen, was successful in securing recognition. Here again the frontier was approximately that of Verdun. Based on a juxtaposition of county boundaries, it crossed and recrossed the Scheldt several times and reached the Meuse a little downstream from its junction with the Semois; after which it ran almost parallel with the river, a few miles distant from the left bank. It then reached the Saône, below Port-sur-

Saône, and followed its course for a fairly long distance, hardly leaving it save for a sharp bend towards the east, opposite Châlon. Finally, to the south of the Mâconnais, it abandoned the line Saône-Rhône, in such a way as to leave to the neighbouring power all the riparian counties on the western bank and only rejoined the stream at the delta, to skirt the Petit Rhône as far as the sea. There remained the intermediate strip which, to the north of the Alps, was wedged between the states of Lewis the German and Charles the Bald, and then extended down the Italian peninsula as far as Rome. This territory had in 843 formed the ill-balanced kingdom of Lothar; but no descendant of that prince in the male line now survived, and the whole of his heritage was eventually annexed to East Francia, though the annexation took place piecemeal.

The kingdom of Italy, the successor of the former Lombard state, covered the north and centre of the peninsula with the exception of the Byzantine Venice, and for nearly a century it had a very stormy history. Several dynasties disputed the crown: dukes of Spoleto in the south and, above all, the masters of those Alpine passes towards the north whence it was so easy and so tempting to swoop down upon the plain—marquises of Friuli or Ivrea, kings of Burgundy, who held the passes of the Pennine Alps, kings or counts of Provence, and dukes of Bavaria. Several of these claimants, in addition, got themselves crowned emperor by the pope; for after the first partition of the Empire in the reign of Louis the Pious, the possession of Italy, on account of the rights of protection and domination which it conveyed over Rome and the Roman Church, seemed at once the necessary condition of this august office and the best title to it. Nevertheless, unlike the kings of West Francia, who were kept by their very remoteness from cherishing Italian or imperial ambitions, the sovereigns of East Francia were also among the near neighbours of the beautiful neglected realm. Already, in 894 and 896, Arnulf, strong in his Carolingian ancestry, had descended into Italy, secured his recognition as king and received the imperial crown. In 951 one of his successors, Otto I, a Saxon whose grandfather had perhaps accompanied Arnulf across the Alps, once more took the same road. He was acclaimed king of the Lombards in the old capital of Pavia; then—having been obliged in the meantime to turn his attention to other tasks—he returned ten years later, subjugated the country more thoroughly and finally pressed on to Rome, where the pope crowned him 'Imperator Augustus' (2nd February 962). Henceforth, except for short periods of crisis, Italy as such had no other lawful monarch than the German king right down to modern times.

In 888 a very great personage of Bavarian origin, the Welf Rudolf, was at the head of the great military command which the Carolingians, in the course of the preceding years, had established between the Jura and the Alps and which was ordinarily called the duchy of Transjurania—a position of first importance, since it commanded some of the principal internal routes of the Empire. Rudolf also hoped to find a crown by fishing in troubled waters and, to this end, chose the 'no man's land' between West Francia and East Francia formed by the regions which were later to be called, so appropriately, *Entre Deux*. The fact that he was crowned at Toul is a sufficient indication of the direction of his hopes. Nevertheless, at such a distance from his own duchy, he lacked followers. Beaten by Arnulf, he was obliged, while retaining the royal title, to content himself with joining to Transjurania the greater part of the ecclesiastical province of Besançon.

To the north of this territory a whole portion of the heritage of Lothar therefore remained vacant. This was the region which, for the lack of an appropriate geographical term, was frequently called 'Lotharingia' from a second Lothar, the son of the first, who had ruled it for some time. It was a large territory bounded on the west by the frontiers of West Francia, as they have already been defined, and on the east by the course of the Rhine, except for about 125 miles, where the boundary left the river to allow East Francia its three left-bank dioceses; a country of great abbeys and rich bishoprics, of fine rivers, alive with merchant craft; a venerable land, moreover, for it had been the cradle of the Carolingian house and the very heart of the great empire. Its vivid memories of the legitimate lines were probably the obstacle which prevented any native sovereigns from establishing themselves in this region. Since, however, ambitious men were present here as elsewhere, their game was to play off one neighbouring monarchy against the other. Nominally subject at first to Arnulf, who in 888 was the only one of Charlemagne's descendants to wear the crown, and subsequently very refractory towards the king whom Arnulf soon created for it in the person of one of his bastards, Lotharingia, after the extinction of the German branch of the Carolingians in 911, was for a long time disputed by the neighbouring princes. Although different blood flowed in their veins, the kings of East Francia regarded themselves as the heirs of Arnulf. As for the sovereigns of West Francia—so long, at least, as they belonged to the Carolingian line, which was the case from 898 to 923, and from 936 till 987—it is hardly surprising that they should have claimed the inheritance of their ancestors on the Meuse and the Rhine. Nevertheless, East Francia was plainly the stronger; so that when in 987 the Capetians, in their turn, took the place of the ancient race in the opposing kingdom, they quite naturally abandoned the prosecution of a design that was alien to their own family traditions and for which, moreover, they would no longer have found ready support in the territory itself. For long centuries—indeed permanently as regards the north-eastern part, Aachen and Cologne, Trier and Coblenz—Lotharingia was incorporated in the German political constellation.[1]

On the borders of Transjurania, an extensive area—Lyonnais and

[1] See Plate XII.

Viennois together with Provence and the Alpine dioceses—recognized no king for nearly two years. In these regions, however, there survived the memory and the retainers of an ambitious person called Boso who, before 887, in disregard of the legitimate claims of the Carolingians, had succeeded in carving out a kingdom for himself—the kingdom of Provence. His son Louis (who, moreover, was descended through his mother from the Emperor Lothar) was able at length to get himself crowned at Valence towards the end of 890. But the kingship thus founded proved ephemeral. Neither Louis, who in 905 had his eyes put out at Verona by Berengar of Friuli, nor his kinsman Hugh of Arles, who after this tragedy ruled for a long time in the name of the unfortunate victim, seems ever to have seen in their lands between the Rhône and the mountains anything but a convenient starting point for the fascinating project of Italian conquest. Hence after the death of Louis in 928, Hugh, proclaimed king in Lombardy, left the Welfs virtually free to extend their dominion to the sea. From about the middle of the tenth century therefore the kingdom of Burgundy—as the state founded by Rudolph was generally called—stretched from Basle to the Mediterranean. Nevertheless from this time on its weak kings figured as little more than vassals of the German kings or emperors. Finally—though not without much reluctance and vacillation—the last of the line, who died in 1032, recognized the sovereign of Germany as his successor. Moreover, unlike Lotharingia, but like Italy, 'Burgundy'—usually known from the thirteenth century onwards as the kingdom of Arles—was not exactly absorbed in the former East Francia. The union was conceived of rather as that of three distinct kingdoms indissolubly united in the same hands.

Thus the feudal era witnessed the emergence of the first lineaments of a political map of Europe, certain features of which are still perceptible; it also saw debated those problems of frontier zones which were destined till our own day to be responsible for the spilling of both ink and blood. But perhaps, all things considered, the most characteristic feature of this geography of kingdoms was that though their territorial limits were so fluctuating, their number varied remarkably little. Although in the former Carolingian Empire a crowd of virtually independent powers arose, only to fall into decay one after another, not even the most powerful of these local tyrants—after Rudolf and Louis the Blind—dared to assume the royal title or to deny that he was legally the subject or the vassal of a king. There could be no more eloquent testimony to the continued strength of the monarchic tradition, much older than feudalism and destined long to survive it.

2 TRADITIONS AND NATURE OF THE ROYAL POWER

The kings of ancient Germania liked to claim descent from the gods. Themselves like 'Aesir or demi-gods', in the words of Jordanes, it was from the mystic virtue with which their persons were imbued that their peoples looked for victory in battle, and in time of peace fertility for their fields. The Roman emperors had also worn the halo of divinity, and from this double heritage, but especially from the Germanic element, the kingships of the feudal age derived their sacred character. Christianity had sanctioned it, while borrowing from the Bible an old Hebraic or Syriac accession rite. In the states which had succeeded the Carolingian Empire, in England and in Asturias, the kings on their accession received from the hands of prelates the traditional insignia of their office, including the crown which was thereafter worn formally at the courts held on the occasion of the great feasts—the 'crowned courts' which are called to mind by a charter of Louis VI of France.[1] Moreover, it was a bishop, a new Samuel, who anointed these new Davids on various parts of the body with a consecrated oil—a rite whose universal significance in the Catholic liturgy is that it invests with a sacred character the person or object so anointed.[2] This rite was to prove a double-edged weapon. 'He that blesseth is superior to him that is blessed,' St. Paul had said, and thus it might be argued that the consecration of the king by the priests clearly signified the supremacy of the spiritual power. Such at least, almost from the beginning, was the view of some ecclesiastical writers. Awareness of the dangers inherent in this interpretation doubtless explains the fact that among the first sovereigns of East Francia several neglected, or refused, to have themselves anointed. Their successors, however, were not slow to make amends, for they were naturally loath to abandon to their rivals of the West the sole privilege of this wondrous chrism. The ecclesiastical ceremony of the delivery of the insignia—ring, sword, standard, crown itself—was imitated, somewhat tardily, in various principalities: Aquitaine, Normandy, the duchies of Burgundy and Brittany. It is characteristic, on the other hand, that no great feudatory, however powerful he might be, ever dared to demand the most sacred part of the ceremony, the anointing. Apart from priests, the 'Lord's anointed' were to be found only among kings.

This supernatural quality, of which the anointing was the confirmation rather than the origin, was deeply felt in an age accustomed to associate the influences of the Beyond with everyday life; yet a genuinely sacerdotal kingship would have been incompatible with the religion which prevailed throughout western Europe. The powers of the Catholic priest are perfectly defined; he and he alone can transform the bread and wine into the body and blood of Christ. Not having been ordained, the kings were incapable of celebrating the Blessed Sacrament, and were not therefore in the strict sense priests. But still less were they pure laymen. It is difficult to express clearly conceptions by their very nature opposed to logic. One may nevertheless give an approximate idea of them by saying that, although not

---

[1] Warnkoenig and Stein, *Französische Staats- und Rechtsgeschichte*, vol. I, *Urkundenbuch*, p. 34, c. 22.
[2] See Plate XI.

invested with the priesthood, the kings, in the phrase of an eleventh-century writer, 'participated' in its ministry. The consequence of this—and an extremely serious one—was that in their efforts to govern the Church they believed, and others believed, that they acted as members of it, though this view never found general acceptance in ecclesiastical circles. In the eleventh century the Gregorian reformers attacked it with great vigour and perspicacity. They argued for that distinction between the spiritual and the temporal which Rousseau and Renan have taught us to recognize as one of the greatest innovations introduced by Christianity. Moreover their purpose in separating the two powers so completely was to humble the rulers of men's bodies before the rulers of their souls—'the moon', which is only bright through reflection, before 'the sun', the source of all light. But in this they had little success. Many centuries were to elapse before kingship was reduced in the eyes of the people to the rôle of an ordinary human power.

In the popular mind the sacred character of kingship was expressed not only by the abstract notion of a right to govern the Church but also by a whole cycle of legends and superstitions about kingship in general and the various individual monarchies. It is true that it only attained its full expansion in the period when the majority of monarchical powers had grown actually stronger—that is, about the twelfth and thirteenth centuries—but its origins went back to the first feudal age. From the end of the ninth century the archbishops of Rheims claimed to have the custody of a miraculous oil, brought down to Clovis of old by a dove from the vault of heaven—a wonderful privilege which at once enabled these prelates to claim the monopoly of the coronation and their kings to declare and to believe that they had been consecrated by God himself. The kings of France, certainly from Philip I and probably from Robert the Pious, and the kings of England, from Henry I, were believed to possess the power to cure certain sicknesses by the touch of their hands. When in 1081 the excommunicated Emperor Henry IV passed through Tuscany, the peasants crowded the route and strove to touch his garments, convinced that by so doing they were making sure of good harvests.[1]

It would be easy to cast doubt on the effectiveness of this popular conception of kingship by contrasting the marvellous aura which surrounded the persons of kings with the scant respect which was often paid to the royal authority. But this would be to misinterpret the evidence. The examples of kings whose vassals disobeyed them, fought against or flouted them, and even held them prisoner, are indeed numberless. But of kings who died a violent death at the hands of their subjects in the period we are considering there are, unless I am mistaken, exactly three cases: in England, Edward the Martyr, the victim of a palace revolution fomented on behalf of his own brother; in France, Robert I, a usurper slain in

[1] Rangerius, *Vita Anselmi*, in *M.G.H.*, SS. XXX, 2, p. 1256, v. 4777 *et seq.*

combat by a partisan of the legitimate king; and in Italy, the scene of so many dynastic struggles, Berengar I. By comparison with the hecatombs of Islamic history, or with what the West itself could show in the number of great vassals murdered, and considering the general moral outlook of this age of violence, this number seems small indeed.

These religious or magical ideas of kingship were only the expression, on the plane of the supernatural, of the political mission recognized as belonging peculiarly to kings—the king as 'head of the people', *thiudans*, to use the old Germanic term. In the proliferation of lordships characteristic of the feudal world, the kingdoms, as Guizot rightly said, constituted a unique type of authority—not only superior, theoretically, to all others, but also of a genuinely different order. It was a significant feature that, while the other powers were for the most part mere agglomerations of various rights so intertwined that any attempt to delineate on the map the extent of these 'fiefs', great or small, is bound to be inaccurate, the kingdoms, on the contrary, were separated by what might legitimately be called frontiers. Not indeed that these boundaries could be, or needed to be, drawn with rigorous exactitude, for the soil was still too loosely occupied. To separate France from the Empire in the marches of the Meuse, what more was needed than the uninhabited thickets of the Argonne? But at least, no town or village, however much its ownership might occasionally be disputed, ever appeared to be legally dependent on more than one of the contiguous kingdoms, whereas one might very well find in the same place one potentate exercising high justice, another possessing serfs, a third having quit-rents with the jurisdiction which went with them, and a fourth with the right to tithe. In other words, for a piece of land, as for a man, to have several lords was almost a normal thing; to have several kings was impossible.

Outside Europe, in distant Japan, it so happened that a system of personal and territorial subordination, very similar to Western feudalism, was gradually formed over against a monarchy which, as in the West, was much older than itself. But there the two institutions coexisted without interpenetration. In the land of the Rising Sun the emperor—like the kings of Europe a sacred personage, but much nearer to divinity—remained legally the sovereign of the whole people. Below him the hierarchy of vassals culminated in the shogun, their supreme head. The result was that for long centuries the shogun monopolized all real power. In Europe, on the contrary, the monarchies, though older than the system of vassalage and by their nature foreign to it, none the less took their place at its summit. Yet they were able to avoid being themselves enveloped in the network of dependence. What happened when an estate previously held from a private lord or a church became, by inheritance, part of the royal domain? The invariable rule was that the king, though he might succeed to certain obligations, was nevertheless dispensed from doing homage;

for he could not acknowledge himself the vassal of one of his subjects. On the other hand, nothing ever prevented him from choosing among his subjects (who, as such, were all his *protégés*) certain privileged persons over whom he extended a special protection in accordance with the rite of homage.

Now from the ninth century onwards, as we have seen, there figured among these royal *commendati*, alongside a crowd of petty 'satellites', all the great men of the realm, soon to be transformed into regional princes; so that the monarch was not only the ruler of the whole people, but also, by a series of ascending steps, the ultimate lord of an immense number of vassals and, through them, of a still greater multitude of humble dependants. In the countries where an exceptionally close feudal structure excluded allodial estates—as in England after the Norman Conquest—there was no poor wretch so far down the ladder of subjection that he could not perceive, on looking upwards, the king on the topmost rung. Elsewhere, before reaching this height, the continuity was sometimes broken. But even so this feudalization of the monarchies contributed everywhere to their preservation. Wherever he was unable to exercise authority as head of the state the king could at least use to his own advantage the weapons of the law of vassalage, sustained by the sentiment of the strongest human tie known to that age. In the *Chanson de Roland*, is it for his sovereign or for the lord to whom he has done homage that Roland fights? Doubtless he does not know himself; but he fights with such selfless devotion for his sovereign only because the latter is at the same time his lord. Later, when Philip Augustus disputed the pope's right to dispose of the property of a heretic count, he could still say quite naturally, 'this county is held of me as a fief'; not, 'it is part of my realm'. In this sense the policy of the Carolingians, who had dreamed of building their government on vassalage, did not perhaps, on a long view, prove so vain as its early failures would lead one to believe. We have already noted (and we shall return to the point later) that many factors conspired during the first feudal age to reduce to insignificance the really effective action of the royal power. But at least it had at its disposal two great latent forces, all ready to expand under more favourable conditions—the inviolate heritage of its ancient prestige, and the rejuvenation which it enjoyed through adapting itself to the new social system.

3 THE TRANSMISSION OF THE ROYAL POWER: DYNASTIC PROBLEMS

How was this monarchical office, with its weight of mixed traditions, handed on—by hereditary succession or by election? Today we are apt to regard the two methods as strictly incompatible; but we have the evidence of innumerable texts that they did not appear so to the same degree in the Middle Ages. 'We have obtained the unanimous election of the peoples and the princes and the hereditary succession to the undivided realm'—declared Henry II of Germany in 1003. And in France, according to that excellent canonist Ivo of Chartres: 'That man was rightly crowned king, to whom the kingdom fell by hereditary right and who was designated by the unanimous consent of the bishops and great men.'[1] The fact is that neither of the two principles was interpreted in an absolute sense. It is true that pure election, regarded less as the exercise of free choice than as obedience to a sort of private revelation which led to the discovery of the true chief, had its champions among the churchmen. Not only were they hostile to the quasi-pagan idea of a sacred virtue residing in a particular family; they were also inclined to see the legitimate source of all power in a method of appointment which the Church, for its own part, maintained was the only one consistent with its law: must not the abbot be chosen by his monks, the bishop by the clergy and people of the cathedral city? On this point, these theologians were of the same mind as the great feudatories, who desired nothing so much as to see the monarchy come under their control. But the prevailing opinion, dictated by a whole world of ideas which the Middle Ages had received principally from Germania, was altogether different. Men believed in the hereditary vocation not of an individual but of a dynasty; this alone they thought capable of producing able leaders.

The logical conclusion would doubtless have been the exercise of authority in common by all the sons of the dead king, or the division of the realm among them. These practices, as we know, had been familiar to the barbarian world, and they have sometimes been interpreted, quite wrongly, as proving the hereditary character of kingship, whereas they really only embodied the principle of the participation of all descendants in the same dynastic privilege. They were continued for a long time in the feudal period by the Anglo-Saxon and Spanish states. Nevertheless, they seemed injurious to the public welfare. They ran counter to that concept of an indivisible monarchy which Henry II very consciously emphasized and which corresponded with the survival, amidst all the disorders, of a feeling for the State which was still very much alive. Another solution therefore gained general acceptance; one which, moreover, had always worked on more or less parallel lines to the first. Within the predestinate family—and occasionally, if the male line was extinct, in families allied to it by marriage—the principal personages of the realm, the natural representatives of the whole body of subjects, named the new king. 'The usage of the Franks', wrote Archbishop Fulk of Rheims, very pertinently in 893 (the year in which he crowned Charles the Simple), 'was always on the death of their king to elect another within the royal house.'[2]

---

[1] *M.G.H., Diplom. regum et imp.*, III, no. 34; *Histor. de France*, XV, p. 144, no. CXIV.

[2] Flodoard, *Historia Remensis ecclesiae*, IV, 5, in *M.G.H.*, SS. XIII, p. 563.

This collective heritability, moreover, tended almost inevitably to result in individual heritability in the direct line. Did not the sons of the late king share in a high degree the virtues of his blood? The decisive factor here, however, was another usage, which the Church employed in its own affairs as a useful corrective to the hazards of election. An abbot would induce his monks to recognize, during his own lifetime, the person designated by him as his successor: this was the procedure followed by the first heads of the great monastery of Cluny. Similarly the king or the prince got his vassals to agree that one of his sons should be associated in his office during his lifetime, and even—if it were a question of a king—crowned there and then. This was a very general practice during the feudal era and one which was followed by the doges of Venice and the 'consuls' of Gaeta in common with all the Western monarchs. Again there might be several sons. How was one to choose from among them the fortunate beneficiary of this advance election? The law of monarchy did not at first recognize primogeniture, any more than did the feudal law. Frequently it conflicted with the rights of the child 'born in the purple'—born, that is to say, when his father was already king; or else more personal reasons might tip the scale. Nevertheless, the right of primogeniture was a convenient fiction; moreover, it was gradually imposed by the example of the fief itself, and in France, in spite of some opposition, it became the rule almost from the outset. Germany, more faithful to the spirit of the old Germanic customs, never admitted it without reservation. Even in the middle of the twelfth century Frederick Barbarossa appointed his second son as his successor.

This, moreover, was only the symptom of more profound divergences. For, starting from similar conceptions, involving the two principles of election and dynastic right, monarchic custom in the various states evolved in very different directions. It will suffice here to recall two typical cases: that of France, on the one hand, and that of Germany, on the other.

The history of West Francia was inaugurated in 888 by a startling break with dynastic tradition. In the person of King Odo the magnates had chosen a new man, in the fullest sense of the term; for the only remaining descendant of Charles the Bald at that date was a child of eight who on account of his youth had already been twice passed over for the throne. Scarcely, however, had this youngster—he also was called Charles and nicknamed by uncharitable historians 'the Simple'—reached the age of twelve (the age of majority as fixed by the Salian Franks) than he was crowned at Rheims, on 28th January 893. War between the two kings continued for a long time. But shortly before his death on 1st January 898, Odo, in accordance, it seems, with an agreement concluded a few months earlier, urged his supporters to rally, when he had gone, to the Carolingian. It was twenty-four years before Charles was again faced with a rival; but then, provoked by the favour he showed to a petty knight, and naturally inclined to rebelliousness, a number of the greatest personages in the land began to look for another king. Since Odo had left no son, his brother Robert had inherited his family honours and his following, and he was elected by the rebels on 29th June 922. Having already occupied the throne, this family was considered half-sacred. When the following year Robert was killed on the field of battle, his son-in-law Raoul, duke of Burgundy, was crowned in his turn; and when a little later Charles was ambushed by one of the principal rebels and afterwards imprisoned for the rest of his life, the victory of the usurper was assured. Nevertheless the death of Raoul, who also left no male descendants, was the signal for a Carolingian restoration. The son of Charles the Simple, Louis IV, was recalled from England where he had taken refuge (June 936), and his son, and subsequently his grandson, succeeded him without serious opposition; so that towards the end of the tenth century everything seemed to point to the final re-establishment of legitimacy.

It needed the chance factor of the death in the hunting-field of the young king Louis V to raise the question of the succession once more. On 1st June 987 the grandson of King Robert, Hugh Capet, was proclaimed king by the assembly of Noyon. However, there was still living a son of Louis IV named Charles, whom the Emperor had made duke of Lower Lorraine, and he was not slow to take up arms in prosecution of his claim. Many people doubtless saw in Hugh only a king *ad interim*, as Gerbert expressed it. A successful surprise attack decided otherwise, and betrayed by the bishop of Laon, Charles was captured in that city on Palm Sunday, 991, to die eventually in captivity like his grandfather before him. Thenceforth all France's kings till the day when she no longer acknowledged any at all were of the Capetian line.

From this long tragedy, brought to an end by chance, it seems clear that the sentiment in favour of legitimacy remained fairly strong over a considerable period. The Aquitanian charters of the reigns of Raoul and Hugh Capet display in their system of dating an unwillingness to recognize the usurpers; but then the regions south of the Loire had always led a life apart and the baronage there was naturally hostile to chiefs sprung from Burgundy or France proper. More important than this—or the conventional or partisan indignation of certain chroniclers—is the evidence on this point of the facts themselves. The experiences of Odo, of Robert, and of Raoul may well have discouraged others from running the risk of repeating them. Though Robert's son, Hugh the Great, had no scruples about keeping Louis IV a prisoner for more than a year, it is significant that he did not dare to assume the crown himself.

The accession of Hugh Capet in 987 was brought about by an utterly unforeseen death and was not, whatever may have been said about it, 'primarily the work of the Church'. Though the archbishop of Rheims, Adalbero, was unquestionably its chief contriver, he did not have the whole of the Church behind him. To all appearance the threads of intrigue led back to the imperial court of Germany, to which the archbishop and his counsellor, Gerbert, were bound by both personal interest and political convictions. For in the eyes of these learned priests Empire was synonymous with Christian unity. The Saxon monarchs, who at that time reigned over Germany and Italy, were afraid of the Carolingians of France as representing the dynasty of Charlemagne, whose august heritage they had acquired, though they were not descended from him. More particularly, they expected with good reason that a change of dynasty would give them the peaceful possession of Lorraine, which the Carolingians, who looked on it as their homeland, had never ceased to dispute with them. Their success was assisted by the balance of power within France itself. Not only was Charles of Lorraine obliged to seek his fortune outside his native land, where he had almost no personal followers; in a more general way, the Carolingian cause suffered from the inability of the last kings to retain the direct control of enough lands or churches to guarantee them the hereditary support of a great body of vassals, constantly kept faithful by the promise of new rewards. In this sense the triumph of the Capetians represented the victory of a young power—that of a territorial prince, the lord and distributor of many fiefs—over the traditional authority of kingship pure and simple.

The surprising thing, moreover, is not so much their initial success as the cessation, from as early as 991, of all dynastic strife. The Carolingian line did not become extinct with Charles of Lorraine. He left sons who, sooner or later, escaped from captivity. But they seem never to have attempted any move against the Capetians; nor, despite their turbulence, did the counts of Vermandois whose house, which was descended from a son of Charlemagne, came to an end only in the second half of the eleventh century. Perhaps by a sort of contraction of loyalty to the crown, there was a reluctance to extend hereditary rights to these collaterals who, if it had been the case of a fief, would at that time have been generally considered to be excluded from the succession. The argument seems to have been employed in 987 against Charles, though at that date and in the mouth of adversaries it is suspect. It may nevertheless account in some measure for the abstention of the Vermandois branch, as early as 888. And who knows what would have been the fate of the Capetians without the remarkable good fortune which they enjoyed from 987 to 1316, in that each king had a son to succeed him? Above all, the respect for Carolingian legitimacy, overshadowed among the great by their own ambitions and deprived of the support which a large body of personal followers could have given it, could scarcely have been maintained save in those clerical circles which, alone or almost alone at that time, had intellectual horizons wide enough to see beyond the petty intrigues of everyday life. That the most energetic and intelligent of the leaders of the Church, an Adalbero and a Gerbert, through their devotion to the imperial idea deemed it necessary to support the current representatives of that idea at the expense of the dynasty of Charlemagne—this was undoubtedly the decisive factor in a balance of forces no longer material but moral.

How are we to explain nevertheless that, even apart from the last representatives of the Carolingians, no rival ever raised his head against the Capetians? The principle of election did not disappear for a long time. Consider the testimony of Ivo of Chartres, mentioned above; it relates to Louis VI, who was crowned in 1108. A solemn court assembled and proclaimed a king; then on the day of the coronation the prelate, before proceeding to the anointing, once more asked the consent of those present. But such ostensibly free choice invariably fell on the son of the previous sovereign, generally in the latter's lifetime, thanks to the practice of association. It sometimes happened that this or that great feudatory was by no means eager to do homage, and rebellions were frequent; but no anti-king was set up.

It is significant that the new dynasty at once showed its desire—as Pepin and his successors had done in regard to the Merovingians—to link itself with the tradition of the line which it had supplanted. The kings spoke of the Carolingians as their predecessors, and at an early date they appeared to have prided themselves on being descended from them through a female line—a claim that was no doubt correct, since a little of the blood of Charlemagne probably flowed in the veins of Hugh Capet's wife. Then from the time of Louis VI at the latest, we find the entourage of the reigning family seeking to exploit for the latter's benefit the legend of the great Emperor which, thanks to the epics, flourished in France at that time; they may even have contributed to its diffusion. From this heritage, the Capetians derived above all the high prestige of sacred kingship. They were not long in adding to it a particularly impressive miracle of their own devising—the power of healing. Respect for an anointed king did not prevent revolts, but it prevented usurpation. Almost unknown to the Roman world, the sense of the mysterious virtue residing in a predestined royal race had reached the West, via Germania, from remote primitive ages. It continued to exercise such an influence that when, after the accession of the Capetians, it was reinforced by an uninterrupted succession of male births and fostered by the presence of numerous vassals around the royal house, it enabled a completely new form of legitimacy to be built on the ruins of the old.

In Germany, the history of succession to the crown was at the outset much less complicated. When in 911 the German branch of the Carolingian dynasty came to an end, the choice of the magnates fell on a great Frankish lord, Conrad I, who was related by marriage to the extinct line. Unable to command much obedience, though no other claimant ever rose against him, this prince himself designated Henry, duke of Saxony, to reign after his death. Despite the rival claims of the duke of Bavaria, Henry was elected and recognized without much trouble, and while the western kingdom was engaged in a long dynastic struggle the sovereigns of this Saxon family succeeded each other for more than a century (919–1024), from father to son and even, in one case, from cousin to cousin. Election, which continued to take place in accordance with the proper forms, seemed merely to confirm hereditary succession. If we now jump forward about a century and a half, we find that the contrast between the two countries persists, but in inverse sense. In Europe it came to be one of the common-places of political discussion to contrast France, where the monarchy was now entirely hereditary, with Germany, where it was—at least in principle —elective.

Three main causes had brought about the change in Germany. The accidents of procreation, so favourable to the Capetians, here proved detrimental to dynastic continuity. Successively there died, without male issue or descendants in the male line, the fifth of the Saxon kings, then the fourth of the 'Salian' (Frankish) dynasty, which had succeeded them. Furthermore, the German monarchy since Otto I seemed tied to the imperial office; and whereas the monarchies were based on the funda-mentally Germanic tradition of hereditary succession—if not by an individual, at least by a family—the Empire was based on the Roman tradition, which had never fully recognized the hereditary right of par-ticular families. That tradition was moreover supported by a body of historical or pseudo-historical literature which became increasingly influential from the end of the eleventh century onwards. 'It is the army which makes the Emperor' was an oft-repeated saying; and the great barons were naturally quite ready to assume the rôle of the legions or even, as they were also fond of saying, of the 'Senate'. Finally, the violent struggle which at the time of the Gregorian movement broke out between the sovereigns of Germany and the papacy, recently reformed by their efforts, led the popes to use the principle of election, so conformable to the sentiment of the Church, as a weapon against the enemy monarch whose deposition they wished to bring about. The first anti-king whom Germany had known since 888 was elected against the Salian Henry IV on 15th March 1077, in the presence of the papal legates. He was not by any means to be the last; and though it is doubtless untrue that this assembly pro-nounced expressly in favour of the permanent adoption of the elective principle, the rumour to this effect which at once swept through the monas-teries might at least be called prophetic. But the very bitterness of the quarrel which thus divided the German kings and the Curia can, in its turn, only be explained by the fact that those kings were also emperors. While the popes could reproach other sovereigns only with the oppression of partic-ular churches, they found in the successors of Augustus and Charlemagne rivals for the mastery of Rome, of the Holy See, and of Christendom.

4 THE EMPIRE

The collapse of the Carolingian state had had the effect of handing over to local factions the two universal offices of Western Christendom: the papacy to the clans of the Roman aristocracy; the Empire to the parties that were ceaselessly being formed and dissolved within the Italian nobility. For as we have already seen, the imperial title seemed associated with the possession of the kingdom of Italy. It was only after its appropriation (from 962 onwards) by the German sovereigns, whose claims could be backed by what was, for those times, considerable strength, that it once again acquired some meaning.

Not that the two titles, royal and imperial, were ever confused. The period from Louis the Pious to Otto I had witnessed the definitive affirmation of the dual character—at once Roman and pontifical—of the Western Empire. To call oneself emperor, it was therefore not enough to have been acknowledged and crowned in Germany. It was absolutely necessary to have received, at Rome itself, a specific consecration from the hands of the pope through a second anointing, and investiture with the imperial insignia. The new development was that henceforth the choice of the German magnates was regarded as the sole legitimate candidate for this august rite. In the words of a monk of Alsace, writing towards the end of the twelfth century, 'whichever prince Germany has chosen as her chief, before him gilded Rome bows the head and adopts him as her master'. Soon it was even considered that from the moment of his accession to the German throne the monarch *ipso facto* succeeded immediately to the government not only of East Francia and Lotharingia, but also of all the imperial territories—Italy, and later the kingdom of Burgundy. In other words, being, as Gregory VII put it, the 'future Emperor', he already exercised command within the Empire—a provisional status expressed from the end of the eleventh century by the title 'king of the Romans'. This title was borne by the German sovereign from the day of his election on the banks of the Rhine and exchanged for a more splendid one only when, having at last undertaken the classic 'Roman expedition', the traditional *Römerzug*, he was able, on the banks of the Tiber, to put on the crown of the Caesars; and if circumstances prevented him from making the long and difficult journey he was obliged to content himself for the rest of his life with being only the king of an empire. However, all the monarchs called to reign over Germany were made emperor, prior to Conrad III (1138–52).

What was the significance of this coveted title? There is no doubt that it was considered to express a superiority over the common run of kings— the 'kinglets' (*reguli*), as they were fond of saying at the imperial court, in the twelfth century. For this reason the title of emperor was occasionally assumed, outside the limits of the old Carolingian Empire, by various sovereigns who thereby intended to mark both their independence of any so-called universal monarchy and their own hegemony over neighbouring kingdoms or former kingdoms. This was done, in England, by certain kings of Mercia or Wessex, and (more frequently) in Spain, by the kings of Leon. But, there was no authentic emperor in the West, except the emperor 'of the Romans'—this was the formula which, from 982 on, the Ottonian chancery had resumed, in opposition to Byzantium. The memory of the Caesars nourished the myth of the Empire; and especially the memory of the Christian Caesars. Rome was not only 'the head of the world'; it was also the city of the apostles, 'renewed' by the precious blood of the martyrs. Mingled with the echoes of Roman universalism and strengthening them with the memory of things less remote was the image of Charlemagne also, in the words of an imperialist bishop, a 'conqueror of the World'.[1] Otto III inscribed on his seal the motto 'Renewal of the Roman Empire', already employed by Charlemagne himself; what is more, he had a search made at Aachen for the tomb of the great Carolingian, which had been neglected by generations more indifferent to history, and while providing for these glorious bones a sepulchre worthy of their renown kept for his own use as relics a jewel and some fragments of clothing from the corpse. These gestures expressed his fidelity to a dual and indissoluble tradition.

These were, of course, above all clerical ideas—at least in origin—and it is not at all certain that rather uneducated warriors like an Otto I or a Conrad II were ever completely receptive to them. But the clerics who surrounded and counselled the kings and had sometimes been their tutors were not without influence on their actions. Otto III, because he was young, educated, and of a mystical temperament, and because he had been born in the purple and brought up by a Byzantine princess, his mother, was completely intoxicated by the imperial dream. 'Roman, Saxon and Italian victor (*triumphator*), slave of the Apostles, by the gift of God august emperor of the World'—the notary who rolled off this list of titles at the beginning of one of his diplomas surely must have been certain in advance of his master's concurrence. Like a refrain, the expressions 'ruler of the World', 'lord of the lords of the World' are repeated, a little more than a century later, by the official historiographer of the first of the Salians.[2]

Yet this ideology was in reality a tissue of contradictions. Nothing was more attractive, at first sight, than to allow oneself (like Otto I) to be described as the successor of the great Constantine. But the forged 'Donation', which the Curia had attributed to the maker of the Peace of the Church and by which he was supposed to have granted Italy and even the whole of the West to the pope, proved such an embarrassment to the imperial power that at the court of Otto III its authenticity began to be

[1] Liutprand, *Antapodosis*, II, c. 26.
[2] Wipo *Opera*, ed. Bresslau, pp. 3 (5) and 106 (11).

called in question; partisan sentiments had awakened the critical sense. The German kings from Otto I onwards, in having themselves crowned by preference at Aachen, indicated that they regarded themselves as the legitimate heirs of Charlemagne; yet we know from the chroniclers that in Saxony, whence the reigning dynasty had sprung, the memory of the terrible war waged there by the conqueror had left an abiding bitterness. The view that the Roman Empire was still in existence found much support among the clergy, especially since the usual interpretation of the Apocalypse required them to see in it the last of the four Empires, preceding the End of the World. Other writers, however, questioned its survival; according to them, the partition of Verdun marked the beginning of an entirely new era. Finally, these Saxons, Franks, Bavarians or Swabians—emperors or great lords of the Empire—who wished to march in the steps of the Romans of old felt themselves to be in reality strangers and conquerors where the Romans of their own day were concerned. They neither liked nor respected them, and were detested by them in return. The case of Otto III, truly Roman at heart, was exceptional, and his reign ended in the tragedy of a shattered dream. He did not die at Rome, for he had been driven from the city by a revolt of the citizens; and the Germans, for their part, accused him of having neglected for the sake of Italy 'the land of his birth, delectable Germania'.

As for the claims to universal monarchy, they obviously lacked all material support from sovereigns whose effective control of their own territories was often imperilled by—not to mention more serious difficulties—a revolt of the Romans or the people of Tivoli, the fact that a castle at a point of transit was held by a rebel lord, or even the recalcitrance of their own troops. In fact till the time of Frederick Barbarossa (whose accession took place in 1152), these claims do not seem to have gone beyond the sphere of chancery formulas. They do not appear ever to have been advanced in the course of the numerous interventions of the first Saxon emperors in the West Frankish kingdom. If these vast ambitions manifested themselves at all at that time, it was in an indirect way. As the supreme master of Rome, and consequently *advocatus* (that is defender) of St. Peter, above all heir to all the traditional rights which the Roman emperors and the first Carolingians had exercised over the papacy, and finally guardian of the Christian faith wherever he exercised (or claimed to exercise) dominion, the Saxon or Salian emperor had in his own eyes no higher mission nor one more closely attached to his office than to protect, reform and direct the Roman Church. As a bishop of Vercelli expressed it, 'it is in the shadow of Caesar's power' that 'the pope washes away the sins of the ages'.[1] More precisely, this 'Caesar' regards himself as having the right to appoint the sovereign pontiff, or at least to require that he be appointed only with his consent. 'For love of St. Peter we have chosen as

[1] Hermann Bloch, in *Neues Archiv*, 1897, p. 115.

pope our teacher, the lord Sylvester, and with the approbation of God, we have ordained and established him as pope'—thus Otto III in one of his diplomas. In this way, since the pope was not only bishop of Rome but also and above all head of the Church Universal—*Universalis papa* is the phrase used on two occasions in the privilege accorded by Otto the Great to the Holy See—the Emperor reserved for himself over the whole of Christendom a sort of right of control which, if it could have been made effective, would have made him much more than a king. In this way, too, the germ of discord between the spiritual and the temporal was introduced into the Empire—a lethal germ, as it proved.

XXIX

FROM TERRITORIAL PRINCIPALITIES TO CASTELLANIES

1 THE TERRITORIAL PRINCIPALITIES

THERE had long been a tendency in the West for the greater states to split up into smaller political formations. The insubordination of the city aristocracies, sometimes organized in regional leagues, had constituted almost as great a threat to the unity of the Roman Empire in its last days as the ambitions of military commanders. In certain parts of feudal Europe some of these little oligarchic *Romaniae* still survived as witnesses of an age that had elsewhere come to an end. One of these was the 'community of the Venetians', an association of townships founded in the lagoons by refugees from the mainland, and whose collective name, borrowed from the province where they originated, only tardily became attached to the island of Rialto, our Venice, which was gradually promoted to the rank of capital. Other such survivals, in southern Italy, were Naples and Gaeta. In Sardinia, dynasties of native chiefs had divided the island into 'judicatures'. Elsewhere the establishment of the barbarian monarchies had prevented this fragmentation, though not without some concessions having to be made to the irresistible pressure of local forces. The Merovingian kings had been obliged at various times to grant to the aristocracy of a particular county the right to elect the count, and to the great men of Burgundy the privilege of appointing their own mayor of the palace. Thus the establishment of provincial governments, which occurred all over the continent at the time of the collapse of the Carolingian Empire, and which had its counterpart among the Anglo-Saxons a little later, might appear in one sense simply a reversion to earlier practice. But in this age the influence of the very strong public institutions of the period immediately preceding it gave the phenomenon an original cast.

Throughout the Frankish Empire we regularly find that the territorial principalities are based on agglomerations of counties. Thus, since the Carolingian count was a genuine official, it would hardly be anachronistic to picture the men into whose hands the new powers had fallen as a kind of super-prefects each of whom (supposing that such officials existed in modern France), in addition to exercising the military command, would be responsible for the administration of several *départements*. Charlemagne is said to have made it a principle never to entrust several districts at the same time to the same count; but we cannot be sure that even during his lifetime this wise precaution was always observed. It is certain that under his successors and particularly after the death of Louis the Pious the rule ceased altogether to be followed. Not only was it opposed by the greed of the magnates but circumstances made it difficult to apply. The invasions, together with the quarrels of rival kings, had carried war to the heart of the Frankish world, and it therefore became necessary nearly everywhere to set up great military commands similar to those which had always existed on its borders. Sometimes they owed their origin to one of those tours of inspection instituted by Charlemagne; the temporary inspector, the *missus*, would transform himself into a permanent governor—as did for example Robert the Strong, between Seine and Loire, or farther south, the ancestor of the counts of Toulouse.

The grant of a county was as a rule supplemented by the grant of the principal royal monasteries of the region. Having become their protector, perhaps even their 'lay abbot', the great chief derived substantial resources from them in property and men. Often he already had possessions of his own in the province; to these he added new fiefs or new allods; and he built up for himself locally—particularly by usurping the homage of the royal vassals—a large body of followers. Incapable of exercising direct control over the territories legally subject to his authority and consequently forced to instal or at least to accept in some of them either subordinate counts or simply viscounts (literally delegates of the count), he at any rate bound those subordinates to him by ties of homage. To describe those who controlled several counties, ancient usage provided no precise label. They were called and they called themselves, more or less indiscriminately, 'arch-counts', 'principal counts', 'marquises' (that is to say, commanders of a march, by analogy with the governments of frontier regions which had provided the model for those of the interior), and finally 'dukes', a borrowing from Merovingian and Roman terminology. But this last term was seldom used except where an old provincial or ethnic unity served as a basis for the new power. Force of habit slowly led to the adoption in this place or that of one or other of these titles; or else, as at Toulouse and in Flanders, the simple title of count was retained.

Needless to say, these clusters of powers only acquired a real stability from the time—very early, as we know, in West Francia, appreciably later in the Empire—when the heritability of 'honours' in general was introduced. Till then an untimely death, the changing designs of a king capable perhaps of effectively asserting his authority, or the hostility of powerful or crafty neighbours might at any moment ruin the edifice. In the north of France at least two attempts were made by two different dynasties to effect a union of counties, before the 'marquises of Flanders' brought their effort to a successful conclusion from their citadel of Bruges. In short, chance certainly played a great part in the success or failure of such efforts. Nevertheless it does not explain everything.

The founders of principalities were doubtless not very subtle geographers. But their work was only effective where geography did not run counter to their ambitions; where they were able to join together territories between which communications were sufficiently easy and of established frequency; and where, above all, they could make themselves masters of those points of transit whose importance the study of the monarchies has already shown us, both as vital military positions and as sources of handsome revenues from tolls. Threatened as it was by many unfavourable circumstances, the Burgundian princedom could hardly have survived and prospered if the dukes had not held the routes through the bleak upland solitudes of the Côte d'Or—from Autun to the valley of the Ouche—which joined France proper to the Rhône basin. 'He longed to possess the citadel of Dijon,' said the monk Richer of one claimant, 'thinking that, as soon as this place was in his hands, he could bring the greater part of Burgundy under his sway.' The lords of Canossa, in the Apennines, were not slow to extend their power from the mountain-tops over the neighbouring lowlands, towards the Arno as well as the Po.[1]

In many cases also the way was prepared by the ancient traditions of a common way of life among the people. This explains why old national names reappeared in the titles of many new chiefs; though in fact, where the group so designated was too widely scattered, nothing more of it survived in the long run than a label somewhat arbitrarily applied to a fragment of the whole.

Of the great traditional subdivisions of the Frankish state, which more than once had formed separate kingdoms, almost the whole of Austrasia had been absorbed by Lorraine. But the memory of the three others— Aquitaine, Burgundy, Neustria, the last of which it gradually became customary to call simply 'France'—had not yet, about the year 900, been effaced from the minds of men. Consequently various persons placed at the head of vast regional commands styled themselves dukes of the Aquitanians, of the Burgundians, or of the Franks. Because the union of those three principalities seemed to cover the whole realm, the king himself was sometimes called 'king of the Franks, of the Aquitanians and of the Burgundians', and Robert I's son Hugh the Great, aspiring to rule the whole, believed that there was no surer means of achieving this end than to unite the duchies of Burgundy and Aquitaine to that of France, in which he had succeeded his father. But this was a concentration too vast to endure.[2]

---

[1] See Plate XIII.

[2] It has sometimes been held that the title of duke of France, borne by the Robertians from the time of Robert I, expressed a sort of viceroyalty over the whole kingdom. It is possible that certain contemporaries may have held this view, though nowhere in

In point of fact the dukes of France, when later they became the Capetian kings, never exercised real authority except over the counties which they kept in their own hands and which—those of the Lower Loire having been usurped by their own viscounts—were reduced, about 987, to some six or eight districts in the neighbourhood of Paris and Orleans. As for the ancient land of the Burgundians, its name was finally divided in the feudal period between the kingdom of Rudolf's heirs, a great fief held of those kings (the 'county' of Burgundy, later known as Franche-Comté), and a French duchy. Moreover, the last-named territory, which extended from the Saône to the regions of Autun and Avallon, was far from including all the regions—those of Sens and Troyes, for example—which in West Francia itself continued to be spoken of as 'in Burgundy'. The kingdom of Aquitaine had been extended to the north as far as the Loire and for a long time the centre of gravity of the duchy which succeeded it remained near that river. It was from Bourges, in 910, that Duke William the Pious dated the foundation charter of Cluny. Nevertheless, after the title had been disputed by several rival houses, the one which retained it found its effective power limited at first to the plains of Poitou and the western parts of the Massif Central. Then about 1060 a fortunate inheritance enabled it to join to its original patrimony the principality founded between Bordeaux and the Pyrenees by a family of native rulers, who—since this region had not long before been occupied in part by invaders of Eskuaran speech— were called dukes of the Basques or Gascons. The feudal state born of this fusion was certainly large, but a great part of the original Aquitaine remained outside its frontiers.

Elsewhere the ethnic basis was more definite. By this is meant—leaving out of account all so-called racial factors—the presence, as substratum, of a group possessing a certain traditional unity of civilization. Amidst many setbacks the duchy of Brittany had inherited the 'kingdom' which Celtic chiefs of Armorica, profiting by the troubles of the Carolingian Empire, had created by uniting—like the Scottish kings, far away in the North— the areas of Celtic population with their border regions, where another language was spoken; these were the old Romance-speaking marches of Rennes and Nantes. Normandy owed its origin to the Scandinavian

---

the texts do I find any very clear expression of it (the term *dux Galliarum* employed by Richer, II, 2, is only a pedantic translation of *dux Franciae*; 11, 39, *omnium Galliarum ducem constituit* refers to the investiture of Hugh the Great with the duchy of Burgundy, in addition to the duchy of France). But there is no doubt that the original meaning was territorial. It is surely impossible, on the contrary hypothesis, to understand Hugh's attempt to unite the three duchies. Perhaps the office of count of the palace (i.e. the royal palace) had also been divided, as in Germany, on the same lines, each duchy having henceforth its own count of the palace; this would explain the title of count palatine which was claimed, in 'France' by the count of Flanders, in Burgundy by the count of Troyes (later described as 'of Champagne'), and in Aquitaine by the count of Toulouse. For the tripartite royal title, see *Rec. des Hist. de France*, IX, pp. 578 and 580 (933 and 935).

'pirates'. In England, the ancient divisions of the island resulting from the settlement of the various Germanic peoples served approximately as limits for the great administrative districts which, from the tenth century onwards, the kings were accustomed to set up for the benefit of a few great men. But nowhere was this character more pronounced than in the German duchies.

We find that these duchies originated in the same way as the principalities of West Francia or Italy: through the union of several counties in military commands; and here too names were at first indefinite, though in this case the nomenclature was much more quickly decided and with much greater uniformity. In a remarkably short interval of time—roughly between 905 and 915—there arose the duchies of Alemannia or Swabia, of Bavaria, of Saxony, and of Franconia (the riparian dioceses on the left bank of the Rhine and the lands of Frankish colonization on the Lower Main), without counting that of Lorraine, where the duke was nothing but the diminished successor of a king. These names are significant. In East Francia, which had not, like the old Romania, gone through the melting-pot of the invasions, the ancient divisions of the Germanic peoples persisted beneath the theoretical unity of a very recently founded state. Magnates taking part in the election of the king—or abstaining from it—were grouped in accordance with these ethnic affinities. Particularist sentiment, maintained by the use of codified customs peculiar to each people and, in practice, to its territory, was fostered by memories derived from a recent past. Alemannia, Bavaria, and Saxony had been successively annexed to the Carolingian state in the second half of the eighth century, and the title of duke itself, revived by the feudal princes, reproduced that which had long been borne, under an intermittent Frankish hegemony, by the hereditary sovereigns of the first two of the above-mentioned countries. Thuringia provides by contrast the perfect negative example: since the collapse of the native monarchy, as early as 534, it had had no independent national existence, and no stable ducal power succeeded in establishing itself there.

To such an extent was the duke regarded as the head of a people, rather than the mere administrator of a provincial area, that the aristocracy of the duchy frequently claimed the right to elect him, and in Bavaria it sometimes got the kings to recognize its right to share in the appointment at least to the extent of approving it. Nevertheless, the tradition of the Carolingian state was still too much a living thing in Germany for the kings to cease treating the persons vested with these great governmental powers as being, above all, their representatives, and for a long time, as we have seen, they refused to recognize their right to hereditary succession.

Now this character of a public office, which the ducal power had thus preserved, combined with the persistence of ethnic particularism to make the German duchy of the tenth century something very different from a French principality: something, so to speak, much less feudal and consequently very typical of a country which had not, to the same degree as France, reached the stage where the vassal relationship constituted among the powerful almost the only effective organization of command and obedience. In France (despite the efforts of the first dukes of the Franks, of the Aquitanians and the Burgundians) dukes, marquises and arch-counts very soon came to exercise real power only over the counties which belonged to them personally or were held of them in fee. The German duke, on the other hand, while evidently drawing a great part of his power from his own 'honours', nevertheless remained the supreme head of a much larger territory. It might very well be that among the counts whose districts were situated within the frontiers of the ducal territory there were some who owed homage directly to the king. They were none the less in some measure subordinated to the duke, rather in the way that—if I may venture to employ such a comparison—in France today a sub-prefect, in spite of being appointed by the central government, remains the subordinate of the prefect. The duke summoned to his formal courts all the great men of the duchy, commanded its army, and being responsible for the maintenance of peace within its boundaries, extended over it a right of jurisdiction, somewhat ill-defined in scope, but not incapable of being enforced.

Nevertheless, these great 'ethnic' duchies—the *Stammesherzogtümer* of the German historians—were threatened from above by the king, whose power was greatly limited by them, and from below by all the forces of disintegration, increasingly active in a society which was moving away from its origins, as well as from the memory of the primitive peoples, in the direction of a progressive feudalization. Sometimes they were simply suppressed by the kings as in the case of Franconia in 939; more often they were broken up and, deprived of all authority over the principal churches and over the counties which had been attached to these, they progressively lost their original characteristics. After the ducal title of Lower Lorraine or 'Lothier' had passed in 1106 to the House of Louvain, the holder of this dignity tried, forty-five years later, to establish his rights throughout the former extent of the duchy. The reply of the imperial court was that according to usage duly ascertained 'he had ducal authority only in the counties which he held himself or which were held of him'. This a contemporary chronicler translated by saying that the dukes of that line 'had never exercised jurisdiction outside the limits of their own estates'.[1] It would be impossible to express better the new direction of development. Of the duchies of the earlier type there subsisted a few titles and sometimes more than a title. But the few principalities so described could now scarcely be distinguished from the crowd of 'territorial' powers which, taking

[1] Gislebert of Mons, ed. Pertz, pp. 223–4 and 58.

advantage of the growing weakness of the monarchy, firmly established themselves in Germany at the end of the twelfth century, and above all in the thirteenth, to give rise finally to the federated states which survived into the present century. As political organisms they were much nearer to the French type, since they too were merely conglomerations of the rights of counts and various other powers. By one of those time-lags in evolution with which we are already familiar, Germany, after an interval of something like two centuries, entered on the same course from which her western neighbour seemed already to be emerging.

2 COUNTIES AND CASTELLANIES

In the states born of the Carolingian Empire the counties, which had sooner or later become hereditary, had not all been absorbed by the great principalities. Some long continued to lead an independent existence—as did for example Maine until 1110, although perpetually menaced by its Angevin and Norman neighbours. But as a result of partitions and the establishment of many immunities, not to mention plain usurpation, the counts' rights disintegrated; so that the difference between the legitimate heirs of the Frankish officials and the ordinary 'powerful men', lucky enough or clever enough to have gathered into their hands a great number of lordships and judicial rights, came more and more to be merely a question of whether or not they used the title of count; which title itself was sometimes usurped by certain lay representatives of churches (as, for example, the *advocati* of Saint-Riquier, who became counts of Ponthieu), and even, in Germany, by a few rich allodialists. Thus did the idea of the public office yield to the undisguised realities of power.

In the establishment and strengthening of these lordships of varying title and extent, a common feature is to be observed—the part played by the castles as focal points. 'He was powerful,' said Ordericus Vitalis of the sire de Montfort, 'like a man who possessed strong castles, guarded by strong garrisons.' These castles were not the mere fortified houses such as the common run of knights, as we have seen, were content to live in. The fortresses of the magnates were virtually small entrenched camps. There was indeed a tower which served both as the lord's living quarters and the defenders' last redoubt; but around it were one or more *enceintes*, enclosing a fairly large area where stood buildings reserved as quarters for troops, servants and craftsmen, or as storehouses for provisions and the produce contributed by the peasants. The count's *castrum* at Warcq-sur-Meuse seems, as early as the tenth century, to have been a fortress of this type, as also two centuries later those of Bruges and Ardres, though these latter were much better constructed.

The first of these citadels had been built at the time of the invasions of the Northmen and the Hungarians by the kings or the heads of the great military commands, and the idea that the right to build fortifications belonged essentially to the State never completely disappeared. For generations the castles built without the permission of the king or prince were described as unlawful or, according to the Anglo-Norman expression, 'adulterine'. But the ban had no sanction save the physical power of the authority concerned to see that it was observed, and in most countries it only became effective as a result of the consolidation of monarchic and territorial powers, from the twelfth century onwards. More serious still, the kings and princes, powerless to prevent the erection of new fortresses, were hardly more successful in keeping the control of those which they had built themselves and subsequently handed over as fiefs to the care of vassals; the dukes and greater counts even found themselves defied by their own castellans, who were also officials or vassals ambitious to transform themselves into dynasts.

Now these castles were not only a safe refuge for the master and some-times for his subjects; they also constituted, for the whole of the sur-rounding district, an administrative capital and the centre of a net-work of dependencies. There the peasants carried out the compulsory labour of fortress-building and deposited their contributions in kind; there the vassals of the neighbourhood performed their garrison duties, and their fiefs were often said to be held of the fortress itself—as, for example, in Berry, from the 'great tower' of Issoudun. The castle was the seat of justice, and the source of all visible authority. So much was this so that in Germany, from the end of the eleventh century, many counts who had become incapable of controlling the whole of an irremediably sub-divided territory, became accustomed to substitute in their title the name of their principal patrimonial fortress for that of the district or *Gau*. This practice sometimes extended to persons of still higher rank: for instance Frederick I, duke of Swabia, called himself duke of Staufen.[1] In France at about the same time it became customary to give the name of *châtellenie* to the territory over which high justice was exercised. An outstanding example was the castle of Bourbon-l'Archambault in Aquitaine. Al-though its possessors were not of the rank of counts, it gave rise in the end to an actual territorial principality, whose name survives in one of the French provinces, the Bourbonnais, as well as in the patronymic of an illustrious family. The towers and the walls which were the visible source of the power also gave it its name.

3 THE ECCLESIASTICAL LORDSHIPS

Following the Merovingian and Roman tradition, the Carolingians had always regarded as normal and desirable the participation of the bishop

[1] *Monumenta Boica*, XXIX, 1, No. CCCCXCI: *Würtemberger Urkundenbuch*, II, No. CCCLXXXIII.

in the temporal administration of his diocese, but only as a colleague or, occasionally, as a sort of supervisor of the representative of the crown, i.e. of the count. The monarchies of the first feudal age went farther; they sometimes made the bishop the count as well.

This development took place in two phases. More than the rest of the diocese, the city where the cathedral church stood was considered to be under the special protection and authority of its pastor. Whereas the count had innumerable occasions to roam about the country districts, the bishop by preference resided in his *cité*. In the hour of danger, while his followers helped to man the ramparts—which were often built or repaired at his expense—and while his granaries were opened to provide food for the besieged, he himself often assumed the command. By recognizing the bishop's right to exercise the powers of a count over this urban fortress and its immediate approaches (together with other rights such as that of mintage, or even the possession of the fortified enclosure), the kings sanctioned a *de facto* situation considered favourable to defence. Such was the case at Langres as early as 887; at Bergamo, certainly, in 904; at Toul in 927: at Speyer in 946—to mention only the earliest known example in each country. To the count was reserved the government of the surrounding territory. This division was sometimes permanent. For centuries, the city of Tournai had its bishop or its cathedral chapter as count, while the count of Flanders was the count of the surrounding territory. Elsewhere the whole territory was eventually granted to the bishop. Thus, after an interval of sixty years, the grant of the county of Langres followed that of the countship *in* Langres. Once the practice of these gifts of whole counties had been introduced, it became customary to speed up the process: without apparently ever having been counts of the city of Rheims, the archbishops became in 940 counts of Rheims and the surrounding territory.

The motives which drove the kings to make these grants are obvious. They were hoping to have the best of both worlds. In heaven, the saints would certainly rejoice to see their servants not only provided with lucrative revenues but also relieved of inconvenient neighbours. On earth, to give the county to the bishop was to place the command in the most reliable hands. The prelate was not likely to transform his office into a hereditary patrimony; his appointment was subject to the approval of the king (when indeed it was not made by the latter directly); and both his culture and his interests tended to make him side with the monarchic party. Amidst the disorder of the feudal states, he proved to be, all things considered, the least insubordinate of the officials. It is significant that the first counties entrusted to the episcopate by the German kings should have been certain Alpine districts—far from cathedral cities—whose loss, by closing the mountain passes, would have gravely jeopardized imperial policy. Nevertheless, originating from needs which were the same everywhere, the institution evolved in very different directions in different countries.

PRINCIPALITIES TO CASTELLANIES

In the French kingdom many bishoprics as early as the tenth century had fallen under the domination of territorial princes, and even of ordinary counts. The result was that the number of bishops who themselves obtained the powers of counts was fairly small; they were concentrated above all in France proper and Burgundy. Two of them at least, at Rheims and at Langres, appeared at one time to be on the point of forming genuine principalities, by assembling round the central district which they governed themselves a cluster of vassal counties. In the records of the wars of the tenth century no military force is mentioned more often or with more respect than the 'knights of the church of Rheims'. But, subjected to pressure from the neighbouring lay principalities, and victims of the faithlessness of their feudatories, these vast ecclesiastical lordships seem to have rapidly decayed. From the eleventh century onwards, none of these bishop-counts had any resource against the power of their enemies but to attach themselves more and more closely to the crown.

Faithful to the Frankish tradition, the German sovereigns seem to have long hesitated to touch the old county organization. Nevertheless, towards the end of the tenth century we find frequent grants of entire counties, and even groups of counties, in favour of bishops; so that, since these gifts were supplemented by grants of immunity and a whole variety of concessions, substantial territorial lordships belonging to the Church were created in a few years. Clearly the kings had accepted, although reluctantly, the idea that in their struggle against the monopolization of local powers by unruly magnates and especially by the dukes, they had no better weapon than the temporal power of the prelates. It is notable that these ecclesiastical territories were especially numerous and strong where the duchies had been either removed from the map—as in Franconia —or, as in the former Rhenish Lorraine or East Saxony, deprived of all effective control over a part of their old territory. But as things turned out, the policy of the sovereigns proved in the long run to have been illadvised. The long quarrel of the popes and the emperors and the at least partial triumph of ecclesiastical reform caused the German bishops from the twelfth century onwards to look on themselves less and less as officials of the monarchy and, at most, as its vassals. In Germany the ecclesiastical princedom ended by simply taking its place among the elements of disunion in the national state.

In Lombard Italy and—though to a less degree—in Tuscany, imperial policy followed at first the same lines as in Germany. Nevertheless, the concentration of several counties in the hands of the same church was much less common in these regions, and the course of evolution produced very different results. Behind the bishop-count, a new power very quickly arose—that of the urban commune. It was, in many respects, a rival power, but one which was able in the end to use for the furtherance of its own ambitions the weapons prepared by the former lords of the city. It was often as heirs of the bishop or under cover of his name that from the twelfth century the great oligarchic republics of the Lombard cities asserted their independence and extended their lordship over the plain.

In no country was there any very strict legal distinction between a church possessed of counties and one which, while it had received no grants of this kind, none the less had sufficient immunities, sufficient vassals, villeins, persons subject to its jurisdiction to figure as a real territorial power. On every hand the soil of the West was traversed by the frontiers of these great ecclesiastical 'liberties'. Often lines of crosses marked their limits, like so many 'pillars of Hercules' (as Suger put it), impassable for the profane.[1] Impassable, at any rate, in theory. Practice, however, was somewhat different. The patrimony of the saints and the poor provided the lay aristocracy with a favourite form of sustenance for its appetite for wealth and power—by means of enfeoffments, extorted by threats or obtained through the complaisance of over-accommodating friends; sometimes by the most plainly brutal sort of spoliation; lastly— at least within the limits of the former Carolingian state—by the expedient of the *avouerie* or system of lay 'advocacy'.[2]

At the time when the working of immunities was first regularized by Carolingian legislation, it was deemed necessary to provide each im- munist church with a lay representative, responsible both for holding the authorized pleas in the lordship itself and for bringing before the count's court those who were required to appear there but who could no longer be directly sought out by the king's own officers on an estate from which the latter were henceforth excluded. The creation of this office answered a double purpose, conformable in its very duality to the fundamental trends of a policy which was very conscious of its ends. It was intended, on the one hand, to prevent the clergy, and in particular the monks, from being diverted by worldly obligations from the duties of their order, and on the other, by giving official recognition to seignorial jurisdictions, to secure their incorporation in a regular, properly supervised, and clearly defined judicial system. Not only, therefore, must every church enjoying immunity possess its 'advocate' (*avoué*) or 'advocates'; but the very choice of these officials was closely supervised by the government. The Carolingian advocate, in short, though he was in the service of the bishop or the monastery, none the less fulfilled in relation to them the rôle of a sort of representative of the crown.

The collapse of the administrative edifice erected by Charlemagne did not entail the disappearance of this institution; but profound changes took place in it. From the beginning, no doubt, the advocate had been re-

[1] Suger, *Vie de Louis VI*, ed. Waquet, p. 228.
[2] There is no detailed study of the post-Carolingian *avouerie* in France. This is one of the most serious *lacunae* in research on the Middle Ages and one of the easiest to fill. In Germany the institution has been examined especially in its relation to the judicial system, though perhaps from a too theoretical point of view.

munerated by the grant of a 'benefit', carved out from the patrimony of the Church. When the notion of public office came to be overshadowed by ties of personal dependence, he ceased as a rule to be regarded as being attached to the king, to whom he did not do homage, and came to be looked on merely as the vassal of the bishop or the monks. His appointment was henceforth entirely in their hands until—and this came about very quickly, in spite of some legal reservations—his fief, like the rest, became in practice hereditary together with his office.

Meanwhile, the rôle of the advocate had grown to a remarkable degree. In the first place, his judicial function had expanded. Since the immunities had monopolized cases involving the death penalty, the advocate henceforth, instead of bringing criminals before the county court, himself exercised the formidable powers of high justice. Above all, he was no longer only a judge. In the troubles of the time the churches were in need of captains to lead their men to battle under the banner of the saint. Since the State had ceased to afford effective protection they needed defenders nearer at hand to protect property which was constantly in danger. They believed that they had found both of these in the lay representatives assigned to them by the legislation of the great Emperor; and these professional warriors themselves were apparently not slow to offer and even to impose their services for tasks which held out a rich prospect of honour and profit. The result was a shifting of the centre of gravity of the office. More and more, when the texts attempt to define the nature of the advocate's office (*avouerie*) or to justify the remuneration claimed by the advocate, they emphasize the factor of protection. There was a corresponding change in the recruitment of these officials. The Carolingian advocate had been an official of fairly modest rank; but in the eleventh century the most powerful individuals, even the members of dynasties of counts, did not disdain to seek a title which only a little while before they would have thought very much beneath them.

Nevertheless, the disintegration which affected so many rights at that time did not spare this one either. In the case of establishments whose possessions were spread over a wide area, Carolingian legislation seems to have provided for one advocate in each county. But soon their number multiplied. In Germany and Lotharingia, where the institution departed least from its original character, these local advocates, frequently called 'sub-advocates' (*sous-avoués*), remained in theory the representatives and as a rule the vassals either of the general advocate of the church, or of one or other of the two or three general advocates between whom it had divided its property. In France, as one might expect, the fragmentation was carried farther: so much so that in the end there was scarcely an estate or group of estates of any size which did not have its particular 'defender' recruited among the neighbouring potentates of middle rank. There again, however, the person—he was usually of higher rank—appointed to protect the bishopric or monastery far surpassed in the extent of his revenues and power the host of petty local protectors. Moreover, this magnate might be not only the advocate of the religious community, but also its 'proprietor' (meaning, principally, that it was he who appointed the abbot), and even occasionally he might himself, although a layman, have assumed the abbot's title—a confusion of ideas very characteristic of an age more impressed by tangible realities than by legal subtleties.

The advocate not only possessed fiefs—frequently very large ones—attached to his office; the office itself allowed him to extend his authority even over the estates of the church and to collect lucrative rents from them. Particularly in Germany, while becoming a protector he remained a judge. Arguing from the old principle which forbade the clergy to shed blood, many a German *Vogt* succeeded in monopolizing almost completely the exercise of high justice within the monastic lordships, and the relative strength of the monarchy and its loyalty to the Carolingian tradition helped to facilitate this appropriation of judicial rights. For, although in Germany also the kings had had to abandon the appointment of the advocates, at least they continued to accord them in theory the investiture of the *ban*, that is to say the right of coercion. Without this delegation of power, which thus passed directly from the sovereign to their vassal, the monks would scarcely have been able to exercise high justice. In practice they barely succeeded in keeping the right to punish the dependants who were attached to them by the closest bonds, their domestics or their serfs. In France, where all ties had been severed between the royal authority and the advocates, the subdivision of jurisdictions worked along more varied lines; and this disorder no doubt served the interests of the Church better than German order.

On the other hand, how many 'exactions'—the term used in the charters —were everywhere levied on the villeins of the churches by their 'defenders', real or pretended! It is true that even in France, where the office of advocate had fallen into the hands of innumerable rural tyrants eager for gain, this protection was not perhaps always as ineffectual as clerical historians would have us believe. A charter of Louis VI, though to all appearance drawn up in an abbey, admits that 'it is extremely necessary and of the greatest utility'.[1] But it was undoubtedly bought at a high price. Service in all its forms, from compulsory labour in the fields to purveyance, from military service to castle-building; dues in oats, in wine, in chickens, in coin, levied on the fields and still more frequently (for it was above all the village that had to be defended) on the cottages—the list of everything that the ingenuity of the advocates was able to extract from peasants of whom they were not the direct lords would be almost interminable. Indeed, as Suger wrote, they devoured them whole.[2]

[1] *Mém. Soc. archéol. Eure-et-Loir*, X, p. 36, and *Gallia christ.*, VIII, *instr.*, col. 323.
[2] *De rebus*, ed. Lecoy de la Marche, p. 168.

The tenth century and the first half of the eleventh was the golden age of the advocate system for the continent (England, where the Carolingian example had not been followed, never knew the institution). Then the Church, revitalized by the Gregorian reform, passed to the offensive. By agreements, by judicial decisions, by redemptions, thanks also to the free grants prompted by repentance or piety, it succeeded in gradually restricting the advocates to the exercise of rights which were strictly defined and progressively reduced. It is true that it had to abandon to them large slices of its ancient patrimony. It is true that the advocates continued to exercise their judicial authority over a number of Church estates and to levy on these certain dues whose origin had come to be less and less understood. Nor did the peasants always derive much benefit from the patient work of their clerical masters; for a rent redeemed by a church did not thereby cease to be collected; it was merely that thenceforth it was paid to the episcopal lord or the monastic lords, instead of going to enrich some neighbouring lay landlord. But once the inevitable sacrifices had been accepted the seignorial power of the Church escaped from one of the most insidious dangers with which it had been threatened.

Those who suffered most from the reform were the petty dynasts and those of middle rank, for they were compelled to abandon the exploitation of resources which were formerly almost indefinitely available to them and without which more than one knightly family of the past would never have succeeded in emerging from its original obscurity. Towards the end of the second feudal age, the local advocates had been rendered practically harmless, but the general advocateships survived. These had always been mainly in the hands of the kings and the greater barons; and the kings had already begun to claim a universal 'guardianship' over the churches within their own realms. Moreover, bishops, cathedral chapters, and monasteries had dared to reject the onerous services of all these petty defenders only because they were henceforth able to depend for their security on the support (which had once more become effective) of the great monarchic or princely governments. Now this protection also, under whatever name it went, had always had to be paid for by very onerous services and money contributions which constantly grew heavier. 'It is fitting that the churches should be rich,' is the naive remark attributed to Henry II of Germany in a forged document; 'for the more that is entrusted to one, the more is demanded.'[1] In theory inalienable, and preserved by their very nature from the perpetual danger of divided succession, the ecclesiastical lordships had constituted from the beginning a remarkable element of stability in an unstable world. From this point of view they were to prove an even more valuable instrument in the hands of the great powers, at the time of the general reconcentration of authority.

[1] *M.G.H., Diplom. regum et imperatorum*, III, no. 509.

XXX

DISORDER AND THE EFFORTS TO
COMBAT IT

1 THE LIMITS OF STATE ACTION

WE are accustomed to speak of feudal states, and to the learned in
medieval times the idea of the State was certainly not unfamiliar; the texts
sometimes employ the old word *respublica*. In addition to obligations
to the immediate master, political morality recognized those owed to thus
higher authority. A knight, says Bonizo of Sutri, must 'be prepared to die
in defence of his lord and to fight to the death for the commonwealth'.[1]
But the idea thus evoked was very different from what it would be today;
in particular, it was much less comprehensive.

A long list could be made of the activities which we consider inseparable
from the idea of the State, but which the feudal states completely ignored.
Education belonged to the Church, and the same was true of poor relief,
which was identified with charity. Public works were left to the initiative
of the users or of petty local authorities—a most palpable breach with
Roman tradition and even with that of Charlemagne. Only in the twelfth
century did the rulers begin once more to take an interest in such matters,
and then less in the kingdoms than in certain precociously developed
principalities such as the Anjou of Henry Plantagenet, who built the Loire
levees, and Flanders, which owed some of its canals to its count, Philip of
Alsace. It was not till the following century that kings and princes intervened, as the Carolingians had done, to fix prices and hesitantly outline an
economic policy. Indeed from the second feudal age onwards the real
champions of welfare legislation had been almost exclusively authorities
of much more limited range, by nature completely alien to feudalism
properly so called—namely the towns, which almost from the time when
they became autonomous communities concerned themselves with schools,
hospitals, and economic regulations.

For the king or the great baron there were virtually only three fundamental duties. He had to ensure the spiritual salvation of his people by
pious foundations and by the protection of the true faith; to defend them
from foreign foes (a tutelary function to which, when possible, was added

---

[1] Bonizo, *Liber de vita christiana*, ed. Perels, 1930 (*Texte zur Geschichte des römischen und kanonischen Rechts*, I), VII, 28, p. 248.

conquest, prompted as much by considerations of honour as the desire for power); and lastly to maintain justice and internal peace. Therefore, since his mission required him above all to smite the invader or the evil-doer, he was engaged in making war, meting out punishment, and repressing disorder rather than in the administration of his realm. And this was a sufficiently heavy task.

For one of the common features of all the governments was, not exactly their weakness, but the fact that they were never more than intermittently effective; and this blemish was never more strikingly manifest than where ambitions were greatest and the professed sphere of action widest. When in 1127 a duke of Brittany confessed that he was incapable of protecting one of his monasteries against his own knights, he was merely proclaiming the weakness of a second-rate territorial principality. But even among the sovereigns whose power is most vaunted by the chroniclers, it would be impossible to find one who did not have to spend long years in suppressing rebellions. The least grain of sand was enough to jam the machinery. A petty rebel count entrenches himself in his lair and lo! the Emperor Henry II is held up for three months.[1] We have already noted the principal reasons for this lack of stamina: the slowness and the general difficulties of communication; the absence of monetary reserves; the need for direct contact with men, indispensable to the exercise of genuine authority. In 1157, says Otto of Freising, in the naive belief that he is thereby exalting his hero, Frederick Barbarossa 'returned north of the Alps; by his presence peace was restored to the Franks (i.e. the Germans); by his absence it was denied to the Italians'. To these reasons, naturally, we must add the stubborn competition of personal ties with wider obligations. In the middle of the thirteenth century a French customary still recognizes that there are cases in which the liege vassal of a baron can lawfully make war on the king, by embracing the cause of his lord.[2]

The best minds clearly appreciated the permanence of the State. Conrad II of Germany is credited by his chaplain with having said: 'When the king dies, the kingdom remains, like a ship whose captain has perished.' But the people of Pavia, to whom this admonition was addressed, were undoubtedly much nearer the common opinion when they said that the destruction of the royal palace could not be imputed to them as a crime, because it had taken place during the interregnum. 'We served our emperor while he lived; when he died, we no longer had a sovereign.' Prudent persons always persuaded the new monarch to confirm the privileges granted to them by his predecessor, and in the middle of the twelfth century certain English monks maintained in the king's court that an edict not in conformity with an old custom should be valid only during the

---

[1] *Cartulaire de Redon*, ed. de Courson, p. 298, no. CCCXLVII; cf. p. 449; S. Hirsch, *Jahrbücher des d. Reiches unter Heinrich II*, III, p. 174.
[2] *Ét. de Saint-Louis*, I, 53.

FEUDAL SOCIETY

lifetime of its author.[1] In other words, no clear distinction was made between the concrete image of the chief and the abstract idea of power. The kings themselves had difficulty in rising above a strictly limited family sentiment. Consider the terms in which Philip Augustus, on setting out for the Crusade arranges for the disposal of his treasure—the indispensable basis of all monarchic power—in the event of his death on the way to the Holy Land. If his son survives him one half only shall be distributed as alms; but if the child dies before the father the whole shall be so distributed.

But let us not picture a régime of personal absolutism either in law or in fact. According to the code of good government universally accepted at that time, no chief, whatever his rank, could make any serious decision without first taking counsel. This did not mean, of course, taking counsel with the people, which no one considered it necessary to consult either directly or through its elected representatives: were not the rich and the powerful its natural representatives, according to the divine plan? The king or the prince had therefore merely to seek the advice of his principal subjects and personal vassals—in a word, his court, in the feudal sense of the term. The proudest monarchs never failed to recall this necessary consultation in their charters. The Emperor Otto I admitted that a law whose promulgation had been arranged for a particular assembly could not be published there 'on account of the absence of some great men'.[2] How strictly the rule was applied depended on the balance of forces. But it would never have been prudent to violate it too openly; for the sole orders which subjects of a certain social standing believed themselves really bound to respect were those which had been given, if not with their consent, at least in their presence. In this inability to conceive of the political tie otherwise than in terms of personal contact we recognize once again one of the deep-seated causes of feudal disintegration.

2 VIOLENCE AND THE LONGING FOR PEACE

A picture of feudal society, especially in its first age, would inevitably give but an inaccurate idea of the reality if it were concerned exclusively with legal institutions and allowed one to forget that men in those times lived in constant and painful insecurity. It was not, as it is today, the agony of the terrible, but intermittent and collective, dangers inherent in a world of nations in arms. Nor was it—or at least not mainly—the fear of the economic forces which crush the poor or unfortunate. The ever-present threat was one which lay heavy on each individual. It affected one's possessions and, indeed, one's very life. War, murder, the abuse of power—these have cast their shadow over almost every page of our analysis. The reasons why

[1] Bigelow, *Placita Anglo-Normannica*, p. 145.
[2] *M.G.H.*, *Constitutiones regum et imp.*, I, no. XIII, pp. 28-9.

violence became the distinguishing mark of an epoch and a social system may now be summarized in a few words.

'When, after the demise of the Roman Empire of the Franks, various kings shall seat themselves on the august throne, each man will put his trust only in the sword.' These words were uttered in the guise of a prophecy, about the middle of the ninth century, by a cleric from Ravenna who had seen and deplored the disappearance of the great Carolingian dream of empire.[1] Contemporaries were therefore clearly conscious of the evil; and the impotence of governments (which was itself in large measure the result of irrepressible habits of disorder) had helped to unleash it. So had the invasions, which brought murder and pillage to every part of the land, as well as effectively breaking down the old framework of government. But violence was also deep-rooted in the social structure and in the mentality of the age.

It played a part in the economy: at a time when trade was scarce and difficult, what surer means of becoming rich than plunder or oppression? A whole class of masters and warriors lived mainly by such means, and one monk could calmly make a petty lord say in a charter: I give this land 'free of all dues, of all exaction or tallage, of all compulsory services . . . and of all those things which by violence knights are wont to extort from the poor'.[2]

Violence entered into the sphere of law as well; partly on account of the principle of customary law which in the long run resulted in the legalization of almost every usurpation; and also in consequence of the firmly rooted tradition which recognized the right, or even made it the duty, of the individual or the small group to execute justice on its own account. The family feud was responsible for countless bloody tragedies; but there were other threats to public order as a result of people taking the law into their own hands. When the peace assemblies forbade the victim of a material wrong to indemnify himself by personally seizing one of the possessions of the offender, they knew that they were striking at one of the most frequent sources of trouble.

Finally, violence was an element in manners. Medieval men had little control over their immediate impulses; they were emotionally insensitive to the spectacle of pain, and they had small regard for human life, which they saw only as a transitory state before Eternity; moreover, they were very prone to make it a point of honour to display their physical strength in an almost animal way. 'Every day', wrote Bishop Burchard of Worms about 1024, 'murders in the manner of wild beasts are committed among the dependants of St. Peter's. They attack each other through drunkenness, through pride, or for no reason at all. In the course of one year

---

[1] *M.G.H., SS. rer. Langob. Saec. VI–IX*, p. 385, c. 166.
[2] *Cartulaire de Saint-Aubin d'Angers*, ed. B. de Broussillon, II, no. DCCX (17th September 1138).

thirty-five serfs of St. Peter's, completely innocent people, have been killed by other serfs of the church; and the murderers, far from repenting, glory in their crime.' Nearly a century later an English chronicle, praising the great peace which William the Conqueror had established in his kingdom, could think of no better way to express its plenitude than by naming those two characteristics: henceforth no man may put another to death for a wrong done to him, whatever its nature; and everyone may travel through England with his belt full of gold without danger.[1] This reveals the double root of the most common evils: the practice of private vengeance which, according to the ideas of the time, could plead a moral justification; and brigandage in all its nakedness.

Nevertheless, everyone suffered in the last resort from these brutalities and the chiefs, more than anyone, were aware of the disasters which they brought in their train. And so from the depths of this troubled epoch there arose with all the strength of man's yearning for the most precious and most unattainable of 'God's gifts' a long cry for peace—for internal peace, that is, above all. For a king, for a prince, there was no higher praise than the title of 'peacemaker'. The word must be understood in its most positive sense—not one who accepts peace, but one who imposes it. 'May there be peace in the realm'—this was the prayer on coronation day. 'Blessed are the peacemakers,' exclaimed St. Louis. This concern, common to all rulers, is sometimes expressed with a touching frankness. Listen to the wisdom of King Cnut—that same king of whom a court poet had sung: 'Thou wert still very young, O Prince, when the blazing dwellings of men lit the path of thy advance'. In his laws, he says: 'We require that every man above the age of twelve shall swear never to rob or become the accomplice of a robber.'[2] But precisely because the great temporal powers were ineffectual, there developed, outside the sphere of the regular authorities and at the instance of the Church, a spontaneous effort for the organization of the peace and order which were so much desired.

3 THE PEACE AND TRUCE OF GOD [3]

The peace associations had their origin in meetings of bishops. Among the clergy the sense of human solidarity derived sustenance from the conception

---

[1] *M.G.H.*, *Constitutiones*, I, p. 643, c. 30; *Two of the Saxon Chronicles*, ed. C. Plummer, I, p. 220; It is impossible to go on retailing anecdotes; but in order to convey the true colour of the period it would be necessary to do so. For example, we are not accustomed to think of Henry I of England as a wild beast. But read in Orderic Vitalis how, when the husband of one of his illegitimate daughters had the eyes of the young son of a royal castellan plucked out, the king in his turn ordered his own granddaughters to be blinded and mutilated.

[2] M. Ashdown, *English and Norse Documents relating to the Reign of Ethelred the Unready*, 1930, p. 137; Cnut, *Laws*, II, 21.

[3] Since works relating to the 'Peaces of God'—notably L. Huberti, *Studien zur Rechtsgeschichte der Gottesfrieden und Landesfrieden*, I, Ansbach, 1892, and G. C. W. Görris, *De denkbeelden over oorlog en de bemoeeiingen voor vrede in de elfde eeuw* (Ideas on

of Christianity as the mystical body of the Saviour. 'Let no Christian kill another Christian,' declared the bishops of the province of Narbonne in 1054; 'for no one doubts that to kill a Christian is to shed the blood of Christ.' In practice, the Church knew itself to be particularly vulnerable. It believed that it had a special duty to protect not only its own members but also all the weak, those *miserabiles personae* whose guardianship had been entrusted to it by canon law.

Nevertheless, despite the ecumenical character of the mother-institution and leaving out of account the tardy support given by the reformed papacy, the movement was in origin very specifically French, and more particularly Aquitanian. It seems to have started about 989 in the neighbourhood of Poitiers, at the council of Charroux, which was soon followed by numerous synods, from the Spanish March to Berry and the Rhône; but it was only in the second decade of the eleventh century that the peace movement spread to Burgundy and the northern parts of the kingdom. Some prelates from the kingdom of Arles and the abbot of Cluny tried, in 1040 and 1041, to win over the bishops of Italy, though apparently without much success.[1] Lorraine and Germany were not seriously affected till towards the end of the century, and England not at all. The peculiarities of this development are easily explained by differences of political structure. In 1023 the bishops of Soissons and Beauvais formed a peace association and invited their colleague the bishop of Cambrai to join them. But that prelate, who was, like them, a suffragan of the archbishopric of Rheims, but personally a subject of the Empire, refused: it was 'unfitting', he said, that a bishop should meddle in matters which pertained to kings. In the Empire, particularly among the imperial episcopate, the idea of the State was still very much alive and the State itself did not appear completely incapable of fulfilling its task. Similarly in Castile and Leon it was only after a disputed succession in 1124 had considerably weakened the monarchy that the great archbishop of Compostela, Diego Gelmirez, was able to introduce conciliar decisions modelled on those 'of the Romans and the Franks'. In France, on the contrary, the powerlessness of the monarchy was everywhere plain to see; but nowhere more than in the anarchic regions of the South and Centre, which had long been accustomed to an almost independent existence. There no principality as solidly constituted as for example Flanders or Normandy had succeeded in establishing itself, so that self-help was necessary if one was not to perish in the disorder.

To suppress violence completely was a vain dream, but at least one might

---

War and Efforts for Peace in the Eleventh Century), Nijmegen, 1912 (Diss. Leyden)— contain numerous references which are easy to follow up, it is hoped that the reader will understand why in the following pages there are a great number of citations without references.

[1] In the south of the peninsula, the truce of God was introduced by a French pope (Urban II) and the Norman barons (see Jamison in *Papers of the British School at Rome*, 1913, p. 240).

hope to keep it within bounds. At first these efforts took the form—and this was what was properly known as the 'Peace of God'—of extending a special protection to certain classes of persons or objects. The list drawn up by the council of Charroux was still very rudimentary: it was forbidden to enter churches by force or to plunder them; to carry off the peasants' livestock; to strike an unarmed cleric. Later the prohibitions were extended and more clearly defined. Merchants were included among those entitled to protection—for the first time, it seems, at the synod of Le Puy in 990. The list of forbidden acts became more and more detailed—one might not destroy a mill, uproot vines, or attack a man on his way to or from church. Yet certain exceptions were still provided for. Some seemed to be imposed by the necessities of war: the oath of Beauvais of 1023 sanctions the killing of peasants' livestock, if it is done to feed oneself or one's retinue. Other exceptions were explained by the respect for compulsion or even violence, when conceived as legally inseparable from any exercise of authority; 'I will not despoil the villeins,' promised the lords assembled at Anse on the Saône in 1025, 'I will not kill their beasts, except on my own land.' Others, finally, were rendered inevitable by universally respected legal or moral traditions. The right to prosecute the blood-feud after a murder is almost always reserved, either expressly or by pretermission. In fact to prevent the simple and the poor from becoming involved in the quarrels of the powerful; to avert the feud when its only justification, in the words of the council of Narbonne, was a dispute about a piece of land or a debt; above all, to check brigandage—these aims already seemed sufficiently ambitious.

But just as there were persons and things under special protection, so there were also days when violence was prohibited. A Carolingian capitulary had already forbidden the prosecution of the blood-feud on Sunday. This measure was revived—for the first time, apparently—in 1027 by a small diocesan synod held in Roussillon, 'in the Toulonges meadow'. (It is not necessary to assume a direct knowledge of an obscure capitulary, but at least the idea had survived.) Combined as a rule with prohibitions of the other type, it spread with great rapidity. Moreover, people soon began to be dissatisfied with a single day's respite; a similar ban for the Easter period had already made its appearance, in the north this time (at Beauvais in 1023). The 'truce of God', as this periodic armistice was called, was gradually extended, not only to the great feasts, but also to the three days of the week (from Wednesday evening) which preceded Sunday and were considered the preparation for it. Thus eventually there was less time for war than for peace. Virtually no exception was allowed in principle, and no law would have been more salutary—if it had not for the most part remained a dead letter because it asked too much.

The very first councils, like that of Charroux, had confined themselves to the most conventional form of legislation, enforced by religious sanctions. But in 990 Guy, bishop of Le Puy, assembled his diocesans, both knights and villeins, in a meadow and 'besought them to pledge themselves by oath to keep the peace, not to oppress the churches or the poor in their goods, to give back what they had carried off. . . . They refused.' Upon this, the prelate summoned troops whom he had secretly concentrated under cover of darkness. 'In the morning he set out to force the recalcitrants to take the oath of peace and give hostages: which, with the help of God, was done.' [1] This, according to local tradition, was the origin—and it could not be called purely voluntary—of the first 'peace pact'. Others followed, and soon there was scarcely an assembly concerned with limiting violence which was not concluded in this way by a great collective oath of reconciliation and good conduct. At the same time, the pledge inspired by the decisions of the councils became more and more precise in its terms. Sometimes it was accompanied by the handing over of hostages. It was in these sworn associations, which endeavoured to associate in the work of peace the entire population (represented naturally above all by its chiefs, great and small), that the real originality of the peace movement resided.

It remained either to coerce or to punish those who had not taken the oath or who, having done so, had broken their pledges. For to all appearance spiritual penalties were only intermittently effective. As for the temporal punishments which the assemblies also tried to introduce (particularly in the form of compensation for victims and fines), these could have some effect only where there was an authority capable of imposing them.

Reliance seems to have been placed on the existing powers at first. The violation of the peace continued to be subject to the jurisdiction of the local lord, duly bound by his oath and capable of being held to his responsibilities—as was seen at the council of Poitiers in the year 1000—by means of hostages. But this meant returning to the very system which had confessed its impotence. By an almost inevitable evolution the sworn associations, whose sole object had originally been to bind men together by a comprehensive pledge of good behaviour, tended to be transformed into executive organs. They may sometimes, at least in Languedoc, have appointed special judges with a responsibility, beyond the competence of the ordinary courts, for the punishment of offences against good order. It is in any case certain that many of them set up a genuine militia, thus simply regularizing the old principle which recognized the right of a threatened community to pursue brigands. At first this, too, was carried out with evident concern to respect the established authorities: the forces to which the council of Poitiers had entrusted the task of bringing the guilty man to book, if his own lord had not succeeded in doing so, were those of other lords participating in the common oath. But leagues of a new type were soon created which boldly went beyond the traditional limits. By chance we possess a text which has preserved the memory of the

[1] De Vic and Vaissète, *Histoire du Languedoc*, V, col. 15.

confederation instituted by Aimon, archbishop of Bourges, in 1038. All members of the diocese over fifteen years of age were required to take the oath, through the intermediary of their parish priests. The latter, displaying the banners of their churches, marched at the head of the parochial levies. More than one castle was destroyed and burned by this army of the people till at length, ill-armed and reduced, it is said, to using donkeys as mounts for its cavalry, it was massacred by the lord of Déols, on the banks of the Cher.

Unions of this sort were bound to arouse lively hostility, which was not confined to the circles most directly interested in prolonging disorder. For they unquestionably contained an element that conflicted with the social hierarchy; not only because they set up villeins against robber lords; but also and perhaps most of all because they committed men to defending themselves, instead of looking for protection to the regular powers. Not so very long before, in the heyday of the Carolingians, Charlemagne had prohibited the 'gilds' or 'brotherhoods', even when their object was to repress brigandage. The undoubted survival in these associations of practices inherited from German paganism was not the sole reason for their proscription at that time. A state which sought to base itself both on the idea of public office and on relationships of personal subordination pressed into the service of the monarchy could not allow police functions to be taken over by unauthorized groups, which even then, according to the capitularies, consisted in the main of peasants. The barons and lords of feudal times were no less jealous of their rights. Their attitude was displayed with remarkable clearness in an episode which took place in Aquitaine: the last spontaneous effort of a movement already nearly two centuries old.

In 1182, a carpenter of Le Puy, guided by visions, founded a peace brotherhood which spread rapidly in all the regions of Languedoc, in Berry, and even in the district of Auxerre. Its emblem was a white hood with a sort of scarf, the front band of which hung over the breast and bore an image of the Virgin surrounded by the inscription: 'Lamb of God, that takest away the sins of the world, give us peace.' Our Lady herself was supposed to have appeared to the artisan and handed him the emblem with the device. All blood-feuds were expressly prohibited by the group. If one of its members committed a murder the brother of the dead man, if he himself belonged to the *Capuchonnés*, would give the murderer the kiss of peace and take him to his own house where he would feed him, in token of forgiveness. These Peacemakers, as they liked to be called, had nothing Tolstoyan about them, and they fought one bitter and victorious war against the robber-nobles. But it was not long before their spontaneous efforts at law enforcement began to cause anxiety in seignorial circles. With a significant change of attitude we find the same monk who at Auxerre, in 1183, had heaped praises on these good servants of order, denouncing them the following year, as an unruly sect. In the words of another chronicler, they were accused of trying to bring about 'the ruin of the institutions that govern us by the will of God and the ministry of the powerful of this world'. Add to this that unverified revelations to a lay and therefore presumably an ignorant visionary—whether a carpenter Durand or a Joan of Arc—have always, and not without reason, appeared to the guardians of the faith to be fraught with dangers to orthodoxy. Crushed by the combined forces of the barons, the bishops, and the robber-nobles, the *Jurés* of Le Puy and their allies ended as miserably as the Berry militia in the previous century.

These catastrophes were only symptoms (though eloquent enough) of a general setback to the popular peace movement. Incapable of creating out of nothing the good policing and sound justice without which no peace was possible, neither the councils nor the leagues ever succeeded in permanently repressing disorder. 'The human race', wrote Ralph Glaber, 'was like a dog that returns to its vomit. The promise was made; but it was not fulfilled.' In other environments, however, and in diverse forms, the great vanished dream left deep traces.

Punitive expeditions, flying the banners of churches and directed against the castles of the robber lords, heralded the French communal movement at Le Mans in 1070. It all has a familiar ring to the historian of the peace movements—even the name 'holy institutions' by which the young commune of Le Mans described its decrees. Of course the needs which induced the burgesses to unite were many and various; but we should not forget that one of the principal motives of the urban 'friendship'—to use the fine name by which some groups liked to be known—was the repression or reconciliation of vendettas within its own body and the struggle against brigandage without. Above all, we can hardly fail to recall the link existing between the peace pact and the communal pact in the shape of a feature common to both—the oath of equals—whose revolutionary character we have already noted. But unlike the great confederations created under the auspices of councils and prelates, the commune confined itself to bringing together in a single city men bound by a strong class solidarity and already accustomed to living close together. This concentration was one of the main reasons for its strength.

Nevertheless, the king and the princes, from a sense of duty or from self-interest, also sought to establish internal order, and although the peace movement had arisen without their participation, it was inevitable that before long they should seek to turn it to advantage by setting themselves up, each in his own sphere, as 'great peacemakers'—the title expressly adopted by a count of Provence in 1226.[1] It appears that Archbishop Aimon had already planned to make the renowned Berry militia the means

---

[1] R. Busquet in *Les Bouches du Rhône, Encyclopédie départementale. Première partie*, II. *Antiquité et moyen âge*, 1924, p. 563.

of establishing an actual provincial sovereignty for his own benefit. In Catalonia the counts, who had at first confined themselves to taking part in the synods, soon began to incorporate the decisions of these councils in their own ordinances, giving them at the same time a twist which little by little transformed the peace of the Church into the peace of the prince. In Languedoc and particularly in the dioceses of the Massif Central, the progress of monetary circulation in the twelfth century had enabled the peace associations to put their finances on a regular basis: a subsidy, known as the 'common of peace' or *pezade*, was levied with the twofold object of indemnifying the victims of disturbances and financing expeditions. It was collected through the normal parish machinery and the bishop administered the fund. But this contribution very quickly lost its original character. The magnates—especially the counts of Toulouse, masters and feudal lords of many counties—compelled the bishops to give them a share of the revenues; and even the bishops came to forget the primary purpose of the fund. Thus in the long run—for the *pezade* was to last as long as the Ancien Régime—the most enduring result in France of the great effort of self-defence was to favour the creation of a territorial tax at a remarkably early date.

With the exception of Robert the Pious, who summoned great assemblies for the purpose of taking the oath of peace, the Capetians do not seem to have had much concern for a movement which they may have regarded as a challenge to their own judicial functions. The parochial levies which stormed the lords' strongholds in the reign of Louis VI were in the personal service of the king. As for the solemn ten years' peace which was promulgated by his successor, although it showed the influence of the usual conciliar decisions, it had in itself all the characteristics of an act of monarchic authority. On the other hand, in the strongest principalities of northern France—in Normandy and Flanders—the princes at first considered it advisable to co-operate in the work of the peace associations. In 1030, Baldwin IV of Flanders combined with the bishop of Noyon-Tournai to promote a great collective oath; and in 1047 a council at Caen, influenced perhaps by Flemish texts, proclaimed the Truce of God. But there were no armed leagues; they would not have been tolerated and would have seemed unnecessary. Very soon afterwards the count and the duke—the latter assisted, in Normandy, by certain traditions peculiar to Scandinavian law—assumed the place of the Church as legislators, judges, and guardians of good order.

It was in the Empire that the peace movement had the most far-reaching results and, at the same time, underwent the most curious deviations from its original purpose. We have already seen what opposition it encountered there at first. It is true that there also, from the beginning of the eleventh century, great assemblies were held, in which the various peoples were invited to general reconciliation and abstention from all violence; but these measures were effected in royal diets and through royal decrees, and this state of things continued until the great quarrel between Henry IV and Gregory VII. Then, for the first time in 1082, a Truce of God was proclaimed at Liége by the bishop with the collaboration of the barons of the diocese. The place and the date are equally deserving of attention: Lotharingia was more accessible than Germany proper to influences from the West; and it was barely five years since the first anti-king had been set up against Henry IV. Since it was due to the initiative of an imperialist bishop, the Truce was in no sense directed against the monarchy; Henry indeed confirmed it, though from far away, in the south of Italy. But about the same time, in the parts of Germany where the imperial authority was no longer recognized, the barons felt the necessity of combining to combat disorder. The Church and the local powers were plainly tending to take over the functions of the kings.

Nevertheless the imperial monarchy was still too strong to be forced to abandon this weapon. On his return from Italy Henry IV in his turn began to legislate against violence and henceforth, for several centuries, the emperors or kings from time to time promulgated great peace ordinances, some of them applicable to a particular province, others—and this was most often the case—to the Empire as a whole. This was not purely and simply a return to earlier practices. The influence of the French peace movements, transmitted through Lorraine, had encouraged the replacement of the older kind of very general peace ordinance by a great profusion of more and more detailed rules; and it became increasingly the practice to insert in these texts all sorts of orders which had only a remote relation to their original object. 'The *Friedensbriefe*', a Swabian chronicle of the beginning of the thirteenth century rightly says, 'are the only laws the Germans use.' [1] Among the results of the great effort made by the councils and the sworn associations not the least paradoxical was the fact that, while in Languedoc it helped to give rise to a tax for the benefit of the princes, in Germany it favoured the revival of royal legislation.

England in the tenth and eleventh centuries had its own type of peace association in its peace 'gilds'. The statutes of the London gild, set down in writing between 930 and 940, contain remarkable evidence of the prevailing state of insecurity and violence: rough justice, pursuers hot on the trail of cattle-thieves—we might easily believe we were among the pioneers of the Far West in the great days of the 'Frontier'. But what we have here are the completely secular police arrangements of a rude community, and a popular penal code whose sanguinary severity (as evidenced by an addition to the text) shocked the king and the bishops. The name gilds had been applied in Germanic law to associations of free men formed

---

[1] *M.G.H., SS.*, XXIII, p. 361. Cf. Frensdorff in *Nachr. von der Kgl. Gesellsch. zu Göttingen, Phil. hist. Kl.*, 1894. The same transformation took place in Catalonia and Aragon.

outside the bonds of kinship and intended in some measure to take their place. Their common characteristics were an oath, periodic drinking bouts, accompanied in pagan times by religious libations, occasionally a common fund, and above all an obligation of mutual aid: 'for friendship as well as for vengeance, we shall remain united, come what may,' say the London ordinances. In England, where relationships of personal dependence were much slower than on the continent to pervade the whole of life, these associations, far from being proscribed as in the Carolingian state, were freely recognized by the kings, who hoped to rely on them for the maintenance of order. Where the responsibility of the family or of the lord could not be enforced, it was replaced by the responsibility of the gild for its members. When after the Norman Conquest a very strong monarchy was set up, it borrowed from Anglo-Saxon tradition these practices of mutual surety-ship. But this was to make them in the end—under the name of 'frank-pledge', whose history we have already outlined[1]—one of the cogwheels of the new seignorial system. The original nature of English social development, which passed directly to a rigorous monarchy from a régime in which the collective action of the free man had never been completely effaced by the power of the lord, had precluded peace institutions of the French type.

On the continent itself the intensity and fervour of the longing for peace were manifested in the councils and the pacts, but it was the kingdoms and territorial principalities which, by bringing about the indispensable recon-centration of authority, finally gave them shape.

[1] p. 271.

XXXI

TOWARDS THE RECONSTRUCTION OF STATES: NATIONAL DEVELOPMENTS

1 REASONS FOR THE RECONCENTRATION OF AUTHORITY

IN the course of the second feudal age political authority, which up to that time was much subdivided, began everywhere to be concentrated in larger organisms. (These were not new, of course, but their effective powers were genuinely revived.) The apparent exceptions, like Germany, disappear as soon as one ceases to envisage the State exclusively in terms of kingship. So general a phenomenon could only have been the result of causes common to the entire West; and a list of these causes could almost be compiled by taking the opposites of those which earlier had led to disintegration.

The cessation of the invasions had relieved the royal and princely powers of a task which exhausted their strength. At the same time it made possible the enormous growth of population to which, from the eleventh century onwards, the progress of land clearance bore witness. The increased density of population not only facilitated the maintenance of order, but also favoured the revival of towns, of the artisan class, and of trade. As a result of a more active and abundant circulation of money taxation reappeared, and with it salaried officials; and the payment of troops began to be substituted for the inefficient system of hereditary contractual services. True, the small or medial lord also profited by the transformations of the economy; he had, as we have seen, his 'tallages'. But the king or the prince almost always possessed more lands and more vassals than anyone else. Moreover, the very nature of his authority provided him with many opportunities to levy taxes, particularly on the churches and the towns. The daily revenue of Philip Augustus at the time of his death was equal in amount to about half the annual revenue returned, a little later, by a monastic lordship which, while not accounted one of the richest, nevertheless owned very extensive properties in a particularly prosperous province.[1]

---

[1] The daily revenue of the French crown at the death of Philip Augustus, according to the testimony of Conon of Lausanne, was 1,200 *livres parisis* (*M.G.H., SS.*, XXIV, p. 782). The annual revenue of the abbey of Sainte-Geneviève in Paris, according to an assessment for the 'tenths' in 1246, was 1,810 *livres parisis* (Bibliothèque Sainte-Geneviève, MS. 356, p. 271). The first figure is probably too high, the second too low. But to restore the correct relation between the figures it should be added that there was apparently a rise in prices between the two dates. In any case, the contrast is striking.

Thus the State from this time onward began to acquire that essential element of its supremacy—financial resources incomparably greater than those of any private person or community.

Corresponding changes took place in the mentality of men. The cultural renaissance', from the end of the eleventh century, had made it easier for them to understand the social bond—always a somewhat abstract conception—which is implicit in the subordination of the individual to the government. It had also revived the memory of the great well-ordered monarchic states of the past: the Roman Empire, whose greatness and majesty under absolute rulers were proclaimed by its Codes and its books of history; the Carolingian Empire, embellished by legend. It is true that men sufficiently educated to be influenced by such memories continued to be relatively very few; but in an absolute sense this *élite* had become much more numerous. Above all, education had spread among the laity—not merely the greater aristocracy, but also the knightly class. At a time when every administrator had to be also a military leader, these noblemen of modest fortune were more useful than the clergy; they were also less liable to be diverted by interests alien to the temporal authorities, and they had long been experienced in the practice of law. Hence it was this class which, well in advance of the bourgeoisie, came to form the general staff of the revived monarchies—the England of Henry Plantagenet, the France of Philip Augustus and St. Louis. The practice of writing and the growing interest in its potentialities enabled states to form those archives without which there could be no real continuity of government. Lists of feudal services due from fiefs, periodic accounts, registers of documents dispatched or received—innumerable memoranda of various kinds made their appearance, from the middle of the twelfth century, in the Anglo-Norman state and the Norman kingdom of Sicily and, towards the end of the same century or in the course of the thirteenth, in the kingdom of France and most of its great principalities. Their emergence was the premonitory sign that there was arising a new power, or at least one that had hitherto been confined to the great churches and the papal court, namely the bureaucracy.

Although virtually universal in its fundamental features, this general development nevertheless followed very different lines from country to country. We shall confine ourselves here to considering briefly, and as it were by way of examples, three types of state.

2 A NEW MONARCHY: THE CAPETIANS

The relative strength of the Carolingian monarchy in its heyday had been based on a few general principles: the military service required of all its subjects; the supremacy of the royal court; the subordination of the counts, who at that time were genuine officials; the network of royal vassals, who were to be found everywhere; and finally, its power over the Church. Of all this almost nothing remained to the French monarchy towards the end of the tenth century. It is true that a fairly large number of medial and petty knights continued to do homage directly to the king, especially after the accession to the throne of the Robertian dukes, who brought with them their own retainers. But henceforth they were to be found almost exclusively in that rather restricted area of northern France where the dynasty itself exercised the rights of counts. Elsewhere, apart from the great barons, the crown had only sub-vassals—a serious handicap at a time when the local lord was the only one to whom men felt morally bound. The counts or the officials in control of several counties, who thus became the intermediate link of many vassal chains, did not deny that they held their dignities from the king. But the office had become a patrimony charged with obligations of a new type. Odo of Blois, who had tried to take the count's castle at Melun from another of Hugh Capet's vassals, is reported by a contemporary to have said: 'I did not act against the king; it does not matter to him whether one man or another holds the fief'[1]—meaning, when the relationship is one of lord and vassal. In the same way, a tenant-farmer might say: 'It does not matter who I am, provided the rent is paid.' Yet this rent of fealty and service was often, in cases of this kind, very unsatisfactorily discharged.

For his army the king was normally obliged to depend on his petty vassals, on the 'knights' of the churches over which he had retained some control, and on the rustic levies from the estates of those churches and his own villages. Occasionally one or two of the dukes or greater counts contributed their contingents, though as allies rather than as subjects. Among the litigants who continued to bring their cases to his court we find that it is almost exclusively the same circles which are represented— petty lords bound to the king by direct homage, and royal churches. When in 1023 one of the magnates, the count of Blois, pretended to submit to the judgment of the king's court, he made it a condition that the very fiefs which were the subject of litigation should first be made over to him. More than two-thirds of the bishoprics—along with four entire ecclesiastical provinces (Rouen, Dol, Bordeaux, and Narbonne)—had passed under the domination of the provincial dynasties and were completely outside the control of the crown. True, those that remained immediately subject to the king were still very numerous; and thanks to one or two of these the influence of the monarchy continued to be felt even in the heart of Aquitaine (through Le Puy) and, through Noyon-Tournai, in the very midst of the regions of Flemish domination. But the majority of these royal bishoprics were also concentrated between the Loire and the frontier of the Empire; and the same was true of the 'royal' abbeys, many of which had formed part of the heritage of the Robertians, who in their ducal period were cynical appropriators of monasteries. These churches were to be one of the

[1] Richer, IV, 80.

crown's greatest sources of strength. But the first Capetians seemed so weak that their own clergy attached little value to such privileges as they were able to distribute. Only a dozen charters of Hugh Capet are known to us, from the ten years of his reign; of his contemporary Otto III of Germany, in a reign of less than twenty years—during the earlier of which he was a minor—we know of more than four hundred.

This contrast between the weakness of the monarchy in the West Frankish kingdom and its relative strength in the great neighbouring state did not fail to impress contemporaries. In Lotharingia people were wont to speak of the 'undisciplined manners' of the *Kerlinger*, that is to say the inhabitants of the former kingdom of Charles the Bald.[1] It is easier to note the contrast than to explain it. Carolingian institutions had been originally no less strong in the one kingdom than in the other. Probably the explanation must be sought in fundamental facts of social structure. The great active principle of feudal disintegration was always the power of the local or personal chief over little groups who were thus removed from any wider authority. Now leaving out of account Aquitaine, traditionally insubordinate, the regions which formed in a true sense the heart of the French monarchy were precisely those regions between Loire and Meuse where the manor went back to remote ages and 'commendation' had found its favourite soil. In a country where the immense majority of landed properties were either tenements or fiefs and where, at an early date, the name 'free' came to be applied, not to the lordless man, but to him whose only privilege was the right to choose his master, there was no place for a genuine State.

Nevertheless the very decay of the old public law proved in the end an advantage to the Capetian monarchy. Not that the new dynasty ever contemplated a break with the Carolingian tradition, whence it derived the best part of its moral force. But it was of necessity compelled to replace the old, atrophied organs of the Frankish state with other instruments of power. The kings of the previous dynasty had looked on the counts as their representatives and had not believed it possible to govern any sizeable territory except through their agency. No county directly controlled by the crown seems to have been included in the heritage of the last Carolingians, as received by Hugh Capet. The Capetians, on the contrary, were descended from a family whose greatness was founded on an accumulation of county 'honours' and very naturally they continued the same policy when they were on the throne.

This policy, it is true, was not always very firmly pursued. The early Capetians have sometimes been compared to peasants patiently adding field to field. The picture is misleading in two ways. It expresses very poorly the mentality of these anointed kings who were also great warriors and at all times—like the knightly class whose temperament they shared—dan-

[1] *Gesta ep. Cameracensium*, III, 2, in *M.G.H., SS.*, XVII, p. 466; cf. III, 40, p. 481.

gerously susceptible to the glamour of adventure. It also assumes a continuity in their plans which the historian, if he takes a close look at them, seldom finds. If that Bouchard of Vendôme, whom Hugh Capet made count of Paris, Corbeil and Melun, had not lacked any direct heir save a son who had long ago entered a monastery, the most strongly situated of territorial principalities would have been established in the very heart of the Île-de-France. One of the charters of Henry I even envisages, as a not unlikely eventuality, the enfeoffment of Paris.[1] Plainly, it was not easy to break away from Carolingian practices.

Nevertheless from the beginning of the eleventh century the kings acquired one after another a series of counties without appointing any new counts to govern them. In other words the sovereigns, having with good reason ceased to regard these magnates as officials, were less and less reluctant to become their own counts; and so on the estates—inherited from ancestors or recently annexed—where there was now no intermediate power, the only representatives of the royal authority were persons of rather modest status, placed each at the head of a fairly small district. The very insignificance of these 'provosts' (*prévots*) prevented them from being a real danger, and though at first a few of them seem to have succeeded in making their posts hereditary, their masters had no great difficulty in the course of the twelfth century in limiting most of them to farming their offices for a specified term. Then from the time of Philip Augustus, at a higher level of the administrative hierarchy, genuine salaried officials made their appearance—the bailiffs (*baillis*) or seneschals. Because it had adapted itself to new social conditions and modestly based its power on the direct control of fairly restricted groups of men, the French monarchy benefited most by the eventual reconcentration of authority and was able to turn it to the advantage of the very ancient ideas and sentiments which it continued to embody.

But it was not the only power to benefit in this way, for the same phenomenon also occurred within the great territorial principalities which still subsisted. The mosaic of counties, ranging from Troyes to Meaux and Provins, which Odo of Blois about 1022 had succeeded in appropriating by an astute exploitation of family connections, was no less different from the county of Champagne at the beginning of the thirteenth century, with its law of succession based on primogeniture to the exclusion of partition, with its well-defined administrative districts, its officials and its archives, than was the kingdom of Robert the Pious from that of Louis VIII. The organisms thus formed were so strong that even their final absorption by the monarchy failed to disrupt them. Thus it might be said that the kings reassembled France rather than unified it. Observe the contrasts between France and England. In England there was the Great Charter; in France, in 1314–15, the Charters granted to the Normans, to the people of Languedoc, to the

[1] Tardif, *Cartons des rois*, no. 264.

Bretons, to the Burgundians, to the Picards, to the people of Champagne, of Auvergne, of the *Basses Marches* of the West, of Berry, and of Nevers. In England there was Parliament; in France, the provincial Estates, always much more frequently convoked and on the whole more active than the States-General. In England there was the common law, almost untouched by regional exceptions; in France the vast medley of regional 'customs'. All these contrasts were to hamper the national development of France. Indeed it seems as if the French monarchy, even when the State had been revived, continued permanently to bear the mark of that agglomeration of counties, castellanies and rights over churches which, in very 'feudal' fashion, it had made the foundation of its power.

3 AN ARCHAISTIC MONARCHY: GERMANY

Noting that 'the perpetuity of fiefs was established in France earlier than in Germany', Montesquieu attributed it to the 'phlegmatic humour and, if I may venture to say so, the mental immutability of the German nation'.[1] As psychological diagnosis this is certainly too sweeping, even when Montesquieu tones it down with a 'perhaps'. But it is a remarkably penetrating piece of intuition, especially if, instead of 'phlegmatic humour', we say simply 'archaism'; for this is the word which must occur to any student of medieval German society, compared period by period with French society. The remark certainly applies, as we have seen, to vassalage and the fief, to the manorial system, to the epic (so truly archaic in its legendary themes and the pagan atmosphere of its marvellous events); and it applies no less to the economic sphere (the 'urban renaissance' in Germany was a century or two later than in Italy, France and Flanders), and is equally valid when we pass to the evolution of the State. No example is more telling than the harmony between social structure and political structure. In Germany, far less profoundly and less uniformly 'feudalized' than France, the monarchy remained faithful much longer to the Carolingian model.

The king governs with the help of counts whose hereditary position is only slowly confirmed, and who, even when this has been established, continue to be regarded as the holders of an office rather than a fief. Even when they are not direct vassals of the king it is from him that in theory, like the advocates of immunist churches, they hold by special grant their power to give orders and to punish—their 'ban', as it was called. It is true that here also the monarchy came up against the rivalry of the territorial principalities—especially in the form of those duchies to whose original structure we have called attention. In spite of the suppressions or divisions carried out by the Saxon dynasty, the dukes continued to be dangerously powerful and insubordinate. But the kings were able to use

[1] *Esprit des Lois*, XXXI, 30.

the Church against them. For, unlike the Capetians, the German heirs of Charlemagne succeeded in retaining control of virtually all the bishoprics of the kingdom. The surrender of the Bavarian bishoprics by Henry I to the duke of Bavaria was only a measure of expediency and was soon revoked; the belated grant of sees beyond the Elbe made by Frederick Barbarossa to the duke of Saxony related only to a missionary field and did not last much longer, and the case of the small Alpine bishoprics, appointment to which was vested in their metropolitan at Salzburg, was an insignificant exception. The chapel royal was the seminary of the prelates of the Empire and it was this personnel of clerics, educated, ambitious, experienced in affairs of state, which more than anything maintained the continuity of the monarchic idea. Bishoprics and royal monasteries, from the Elbe to the Meuse, from the Alps to the North Sea, placed their 'services' at the disposition of the sovereign: contributions in money or in kind; lodging for the king or his followers; above all military service. The contingents of the churches formed the largest and most stable part of the royal army; but they were not the whole of it. For the king continued to demand aid from all his subjects, and although the general levy properly so called—'the call to the country' (*clamor patriae*)—applied in practice only to the frontier regions in the event of barbarian raids, the obligation to serve with their knights rested on the dukes and counts of the entire kingdom and was in fact fairly satisfactorily fulfilled.

This traditional system, however, never worked perfectly. True, it made possible the great projects of the 'Roman expeditions'; but in so doing—in favouring over-ambitious and anachronistic designs—it had already become dangerous. The internal structure of the country was not really strong enough to support such a load. It is really not surprising that this government which had no taxation other than the few financial 'services' of the churches, no salaried officials, no permanent army—this nomadic government, which possessed no convenient means of communication and which men felt to be physically and morally remote from them, should not always succeed in ensuring the obedience of its subjects. No reign in fact was free from rebellions.

With some delay and many differences, the process by which the powers of the State were broken up into small centres of personal authority triumphed in Germany as in France, The dissolution of the counties, for one thing, little by little deprived the edifice of its necessary basis. Now the German kings, since they were much more than territorial princes, had not provided themselves with anything resembling the restricted, but well-placed, domain of the Robertian dukes who had become kings of France. Even the duchy of Saxony, which Henry I had held before his accession, passed eventually—though reduced in size—out of the hands of the crown. This was one example of a usage which progressively acquired the force of law. Any *fief de dignité* provisionally falling in to the crown by confiscation or abeyance must be re-granted in fee without delay, and this characteristic principle of the imperial monarchy was especially fatal to its progress. Had it prevailed in France it would have prevented Philip Augustus from keeping Normandy, just as in Germany, some thirty years earlier, it did in fact prevent the annexation by Frederick Barbarossa of the duchies taken away from Henry the Lion. True, it was left to the twelfth century to formulate the principle in its full rigour, under pressure from the baronage. But without any doubt it took its origin from the character of a public office which in Germany was firmly attached to the 'honours' of counts and dukes. How could a sovereign appoint himself his own representative? Certainly, the German king was the direct lord of many villages; he had his own vassals, his *ministeriales*, his castles. But all these were very widely scattered. Belatedly, Henry IV realized the danger, and from 1070 he tried to create in Saxony a veritable Île-de-France, bristling with fortresses. The plan failed; for already the great crisis of the struggle with the popes was at hand, which was to reveal so many sources of weaknesses.

Here again we are faced with an anachronism. Henry IV and Gregory VII had been engaged for several years in an apparently commonplace conflict when in 1076 it suddenly developed into a relentless war. The cause was that dramatic event at Worms—the deposition of the pope pronounced, after consultation with a German council, by a king who had not even as yet been excommunicated. Now this act was only an echo of earlier events. Otto I had deposed one pope; Henry IV's own father and predecessor had deposed three at a single stroke. Since then, however, the world had changed. Reformed by the emperors themselves, the papacy had regained its moral prestige and a great movement of religious awakening was making it the highest symbol of spiritual values.

We have already seen how this long quarrel finally destroyed the hereditary principle in Germany. It ended by throwing the monarchs into the perpetual hornet's nest of Italy; it became a focal point for rebellion and its outcome profoundly affected the royal powers over the Church. Not, of course, that the kings ceased, even in the thirteenth century, to exercise an influence over the appointment of bishops and abbots—an influence which, though it varied greatly with the reign or the moment, continued to be on the whole very extensive. But the prelates, who were henceforth invested by a touch of the sceptre (symbolizing the grant of the fief), ceased to be regarded as holders of a public office, and appeared from now on as ordinary feudatories. Moreover, the development of religious consciousness weakened the idea of the sacred value hitherto attached to the royal dignity and rendered the clergy less willing to submit to attempts at domination which conflicted with their heightened sense of the pre-eminence of spiritual forces. At the same time social changes were in progress which finally transformed the former representatives of the monarchy in the provinces into hereditary lords of subdivided domains, reduced the number of free men (in the original sense of the word), and took away much of the public character of courts which were becoming progressively more subject to the local lords. In the twelfth century Frederick Barbarossa still gave the impression of being a very powerful monarch. The imperial idea, nourished by a richer and more self-conscious culture, had never been expressed more powerfully than during the reign and at the court of this prince. But badly buttressed and ill-adapted to contemporary forces, the monarchic structure was even then at the mercy of the slightest shock.

Meanwhile other powers were preparing to spring up on the ruins of both the monarchy and the old tribal duchies. From the end of the twelfth century territorial principalities, hitherto somewhat loosely held together, gradually emerged as bureaucratic states, relatively well-ordered, subject to State taxation, and possessing representative assemblies. In these states what survived of vassalage was turned to the advantage of their rulers and even the Church was obedient. Politically speaking, there was no longer a Germany; but, as they said in France, 'the Germanies'. On the one hand there was retarded social development, a specifically German characteristic; on the other, there was the advent, common to almost the whole of Europe, of conditions favourable to a concentration of public authority. The meeting of these two chains of causation meant that in Germany the reconcentration of forces was effected only at the cost of a long fragmentation of the ancient state.

4 THE ANGLO-NORMAN MONARCHY: CONQUEST AND GERMANIC SURVIVALS

The Anglo-Norman state was the fruit of a double conquest—the conquest of western Neustria by Rollo and of England by William the Bastard. It owed to this origin a structure much more regular than that of principalities built up piecemeal or of monarchies burdened with a long and sometimes confused tradition. What is more, the second conquest, that of England, had taken place at the very moment when the transformation of economic and intellectual conditions throughout the West began to favour the struggle against disintegration. It is significant that almost from the first this monarchy, born of a successful war, seems to have had at its disposal at an early date an educated personnel and bureaucratic machinery.

Anglo-Saxon England in its latest period had witnessed the creation under its earls of genuine territorial principalities formed, according to the classic pattern, from agglomerations of counties. The war of conquest and the harsh suppression of the subsequent rebellions removed from the scene the great native chiefs; and all danger to the unity of the State from that side might have seemed to be at an end. Nevertheless the idea that it was possible for a king to govern his whole realm directly was then so alien to men's minds that William believed it necessary to create regional commands of a similar type. Fortunately for the monarchy, the very faithlessness of the great barons to whom they were assigned quickly led—with only two exceptions, the earldom of Chester on the Welsh marches, and the ecclesiastical principality of Durham on the Scottish border—to the suppression of these formidable political units. The kings continued to create earls from time to time; but in the counties whose names they bore, they were thenceforth confined to receiving a part of the proceeds of justice. The actual exercise of judicial powers, the levying of troops, the collection of fiscal revenues, belonged to direct representatives of the king, called sheriffs. These men were not exactly officials in the usual sense. They farmed their office by paying a fixed sum to the royal treasury (at a time when economic conditions still precluded a salaried officialdom, this system was the only alternative to enfeoffment), and a fair number succeeded in making themselves hereditary. But this dangerous development was suddenly checked by the strong hand of the Angevin sovereigns. When in 1170 Henry II, at a single stroke, removed from office all the sheriffs in the kingdom, subjected their administration to an inquest, and reappointed only a few of them, it was plain to everyone that throughout England the king was master of those who governed in his name./ Because the public office was not completely identified with the fief, England was a truly unified state much earlier than any continental kingdom.

Although in certain respects, no state was more completely feudal, the feudalism was of such a kind as ultimately to enhance the prestige of the crown. In this country where every piece of land was a tenement, the king was literally the lord of all the lords. Nowhere was the system of military fiefs more methodically applied. With armies so recruited the essential problem was, as we know, to get the direct vassals of the king or prince to bring with them to the host a sufficient number of those subvassals of whom the bulk of the army was necessarily composed. Now in the Norman duchy and subsequently on a much larger scale in England this figure, instead of being left to be decided (as was so often the case elsewhere) by a varying custom, or individual agreements that were more or less ill observed, was fixed once for all for each barony—at least as to the required minimum—by the central power. And since it was a recognized principle that almost every obligation to do something might be replaced by its equivalent in cash, the kings, from the early years of the twelfth century, adopted the practice of occasionally demanding from their tenants-in-chief, instead of soldiers, a tax assessed on the basis of the number of knights or (to use the contemporary expression) 'shields' which they would have had to provide.

But this admirably planned feudal organization was linked with traditions derived from a more distant past. In the firm peace established, from the time of the occupation of the Neustrian counties, by the 'dukes of the pirates' we can surely recognize the code of an army in cantonment, like those laws which the Danish historian Saxo Grammaticus attributes to the legendary conqueror, King Frode. Above all, we must not underrate the part played by the Anglo-Saxon heritage. The oath of fealty which in 1086 William required of all those in authority in England, 'whose soever men they were', and which his first two successors caused to be renewed—that pledge which transcended and took precedence of all ties of vassalage—was it after all anything else than the ancient oath of the subject, familiar to all the barbarian monarchies and practised by the kings of the West Saxon dynasty, as well as by the Carolingians? Weak as the Anglo-Saxon monarchy in its final period may have seemed, it had none the less been able to maintain—alone among all its contemporaries—a general tax which, from having served at first to pay ransom to the Danish invaders and then to supply the means to fight them, had acquired the name of 'Danegeld'. In this extraordinary survival, which seems to presuppose in England a better monetary circulation than elsewhere, the Norman kings were to find a remarkably effective instrument. Finally, the persistence in England of the ancient courts of free men, associated in so many ways with the maintenance of public order—a Germanic institution if ever there was one—greatly favoured the maintenance and then the extension of royal justice and administrative authority.

Yet the strength of this complex monarchy was entirely relative, and here too the elements of disintegration were present. Service from the fiefs was more and more difficult to obtain because, while the royal government was capable of exercising some measure of coercion over its tenants-in-chief, it could not so easily reach down through them to the mass of often recalcitrant petty feudatories. The baronage was almost continually insubordinate, and from 1135 to 1154, during the long dynastic troubles of Stephen's reign, the building of innumerable 'adulterine' castles and the recognition of the hereditary position of the sheriffs, who sometimes united several counties under their domination and themselves bore the title of earls, seemed to proclaim the irresistible progress of disintegration. Nevertheless, after the recovery which marked the reign of Henry II, the aim of the magnates in their rebellions was henceforth much less to tear the kingdom asunder than to dominate it. The knightly class, for its part, found in the county courts the opportunity to consolidate itself as a group and appoint its own representatives. The powerful kingship of the conquerors had not destroyed all other powers; but it had forced them to act, even when in opposition to it, only within the framework of the State.

5 NATIONALITIES

To what extent were these states also nations or destined to become nations? Like every problem of group psychology, this question necessitates a careful distinction not only between periods but also between environments.

The growth of national sentiment was hardly possible among the most educated men. All that survived of culture worthy of the name took refuge till the twelfth century among a fraction of the clergy, and there was much in this legacy to alienate these intellectuals from what they would probably have treated as antiquated notions: for example the use of Latin, an international language, with the facilities for intellectual communication which flowed from it, and above all the cult of the great ideals of peace, piety, and unity, which in this world seemed to be embodied in the dual images of Christendom and Empire. Gerbert, although a native of Aquitaine and a former dignitary of the church of Rheims (and therefore in a double capacity a subject of the king of France), certainly did not believe that he was betraying any essential duty by becoming—at the time when the successor of Charlemagne was a Saxon—'a soldier in the camp of Caesar'.[1] In order to discover the obscure foreshadowings of nationalism we must turn to groups of men more simple-minded and more prone to live in the present; not so much, indeed, to the popular masses, of whose state of mind we have no documentary evidence, as to the knightly classes and that half-educated section of the clergy which confined itself, in its writings, to reflecting with sharper emphasis the public opinion of the time.

As a reaction against romantic historiography, it has been the fashion among some recent historians to deny that the early centuries of the Middle Ages had any group consciousness at all, either national or racial. This is to forget that in the crude and naive form of antagonism to the stranger, the 'outsider' (horsin), such sentiments did not require a very great refinement of mind. We know today that they manifested themselves in the period of the Germanic invasions with much more strength than Fustel de Coulanges, for example, believed. In the greatest example of conquest offered by the feudal era—that of Norman England—we see them clearly at work. When the youngest son of William, Henry I, had by a characteristic gesture, judged it a shrewd move to marry a princess of the ancient dynasty of Wessex—of the 'direct' line of England, as it was called by a monk of Canterbury—the Norman knights took a derisive pleasure in loading the royal couple with Saxon nicknames. But singing the praises of this marriage, about half a century later, in the reign of the grandson of Henry and Edith, a hagiographer wrote: 'Now England has a king of English race; it finds among the same race bishops, abbots, barons, brave knights, born of both seeds.'[2] The history of this assimilation, which is the history of English nationality, cannot be recounted here even in outline, owing to limitations of space. Leaving aside acts of con-

---

[1] *Lettres*, ed. Havet, nos. 12 and 13.

[2] Marc Bloch, *La vie de S. Edouard le Confesseur par Osbert* in *Analecta Bollandiana*, XLI, 1923, pp. 22 and 38.

quest, it is within the boundaries of the former Frankish Empire, to the north of the Alps, that we must be content to examine the formation of national entities—the birth, so to speak, of France and Germany.[1]

Here, of course, the tradition was unity—a relatively recent tradition, it is true, and to some extent an artificial one, as regards the Carolingian Empire as a whole; but within the narrower limits of the old *regnum Francorum*, many centuries old and based on a real community of civilization. However palpable the differences of manners and language at the lower levels of the population, it was the same aristocracy and the same clergy which had helped the Carolingians to govern the vast state from the Elbe to the Atlantic Ocean. Moreover it was these great families, linked by ties of kinship, which after 888 had provided the kingdoms and principalities resulting from the dismemberment with their rulers, who were only superficially national. Franks disputed the crown of Italy; a Bavarian had assumed that of Burgundy; the successor to the West Frankish throne (Odo) was perhaps of Saxon origin. In the wanderings to which they were committed either by the policy of the kings (to whom they looked for rewards) or by their own ambitions, the magnates took with them a whole body of dependants; with the result that the vassal class itself shared this—so to speak—supra-provincial character. To contemporaries the laceration of the Empire in 840–843 naturally had the appearance of civil war.

Nevertheless, beneath this unity there survived the memory of older groups; and in a divided Europe it was these that first reasserted themselves, in mutual expressions of contempt or hatred. The Neustrians, exalted by their pride in coming from 'the noblest region in the world', are quick to describe the Aquitanians as 'perfidious' and the Burgundians as 'poltroons'; the 'perversity' of the 'Franks' is denounced in its turn by the Aquitanians, and Swabian 'deceit' by the people of the Meuse; a dark picture of Thuringian cowardice, Alemannian rapine, and Bavarian avarice is painted by the Saxons, all of course fine fellows who never run away. It would not be difficult to augment this anthology of abuse with examples drawn from writers ranging from the end of the ninth century to the beginning of the eleventh.[2] For reasons already known to us, antagonisms of this type were particularly deep-rooted in Germany. Far from helping the monarchic states, they were a threat to their unity. The patriotism of the chronicler-monk Widukind, in the reign of Otto I, was

---

[1] Besides the Bibliography, Section XVII, see F. Lot, *Les derniers carolingiens*, p. 308 *et seq.;* Lapôtre, *L'Europe et le Saint-Siège*, 1895, p. 330 *et seq.;* F. Kern, *Die Anfänge der französischen Ausdehnungspolitik*, 1910, p. 124 *et. seq.;* M. L. Bulst-Thiele, *Kaiserin Agnes*, 1933, p. 3, n. 3.

[2] Abbo, *De bello Parisiaco*, ed. Pertz, I, v. 618; II, vv. 344 and 452; Adhemar of Chabannes, *Chronique*, ed. Chabanon, p. 151; *Gesta ep. Leodensium*, II, 26, in *M.G.H., SS.*, VII, p. 204; Widukind, ed. P. Hirsch, I, 9 and 11; II, 3; Thietmar of Merseburg, ed. R. Holtzmann, V, 12 and 19.

certainly not wanting in fervour or intransigence; but it was a Saxon, not a German, patriotism. What effected the transition from this attitude to a consciousness of nationality adjusted to the new political framework?

It is not easy to form a clear picture of a fatherland without a name. Nothing is more instructive than the difficulty which men so long experienced in giving names to the two principal states carved out of the *regnum Francorum* by the partitions. Both were 'Frances'; but the adjectives East and West by which they were long distinguished were not well fitted to evoke national consciousness. As for the labels Gaul and Germania, which a few writers at an early date sought to revive, they meant little except to the learned. Moreover, they did not correspond to the new frontiers. Recalling that Caesar had made the Rhine the frontier of Gaul, the German chroniclers frequently applied this name to their own provinces on the left bank.[1] Sometimes, unconsciously emphasizing the original artificiality of the boundaries, men fastened on the memory of the first sovereign for whose benefit the kingdom had been carved out: to their neighbours in Lorraine and adjoining territories the Franks of the West remained the men of Charles the Bald (*Kerlinger, Carlenses*), just as the Lorrainers themselves were the men of the obscure Lothar II. German literature long remained faithful to this terminology, probably because it was reluctant to acknowledge the western people's monopoly of the name of Franks or French—the *Chanson de Roland* still employs the two terms indifferently—to which all the successor states seemed to have a legal right.

As everyone knows, however, this restriction of meaning did take place; even at the time of the *Chanson de Roland* the Lorraine chronicler Sigebert of Gembloux regarded it as generally accepted.[2] How did it come about? This great riddle of the French national name has not yet been adequately studied. The usage seems to have been implanted at the time when—in face of an East Frankish kingdom ruled by Saxons—the western kingdom returned to the authentic Frankish dynasty, the Carolingian line. It found support in the royal title itself. By contrast with his rivals who in their charters called themselves simply kings, Charles the Simple, after his conquest of Lorraine, had resumed the old title of *rex Francorum* in order to proclaim his dignity as the heir of Charlemagne. His successors, although they now reigned only over France as we know it today, continued to parade the title more and more generally, even when they had ceased to belong to the ancient line of kings. What is more, in Germany the name 'Franks', as against other tribal groups, preserved almost of necessity a particularist character; it served in current usage to describe the people of the riparian dioceses and the valley of the Main—the region we call today Franconia—and a Saxon, for example, would scarcely have agreed to let himself be so described. On the other side of the frontier, however, there was nothing to prevent the term from being applied, if not to the entire

[1] Cf. Plate XII.　　[2] *M.G.H., SS*, VI, p. 339, 1, 41–2.

population of the kingdom, at least to the inhabitants of the region between Loire and Meuse whose customs and institutions continued to be profoundly marked with the imprint of the Franks. Finally, the name was the more easily restricted to the France of the west, because the other France was by a natural process coming to be known by a very different name.

There was a striking contrast between 'Charles's men' and the people of the eastern kingdom—a linguistic contrast, overriding the differences of dialect within each group—in that the language of the former was Romance and that of the latter *diutisc*. This adjective is the word from which the modern German *deutsch* is derived, but at that time in the Latin of the clergy, which abounded with classical memories, it was frequently rendered, in defiance of etymology, by 'Teutonic'. There is no doubt as to its origin. The *theotisca lingua* mentioned by the missionaries of the Carolingian age was none other, in the literal sense, than the speech of the people (*thiuda*), as opposed to the Latin of the Church; perhaps it was also the language of the pagans, the 'Gentiles'. Now since the term 'German', a learned rather than a popular one, had never been deeply rooted in the general consciousness, the label thus devised to describe a mode of speech very soon rose to the dignity of an ethnic name—'the people speaking *diutisc*' is a phrase used already in the reign of Louis the Pious in the prologue to one of the oldest poems written in that language. From this it was an easy step to its employment as the name of a political entity. Usage probably settled the matter long before writers ventured to give recognition to a development so little in accordance with traditional historiography. As early as 920, however, the Salzburg annals mention the kingdom of the Theotisci (or Teutons).[1]

These facts will perhaps surprise those who are inclined to regard emphasis on language factors as a recent symptom of national consciousness. But the linguistic argument in the hands of politicians is not confined to the present day. In the tenth century a Lombard bishop, indignant at the claims—historically well founded—of the Byzantines to Apulia, wrote: 'that this region belongs to the kingdom of Italy is proved by the speech of its inhabitants'.[2]

The use of the same language draws men closer together; it brings out the common factors in their mental traditions and creates new ones. But a difference of language makes an even greater impact on untutored minds; it produces a sense of separation which is a source of antagonism in itself. In the ninth century a Swabian monk noted that the 'Latins' made fun of Germanic words, and it was from gibes about their respective languages

---

[1] Prologue of the *Heliand*, ed. Sievers, p. 3. The distinction between the royal vassals *Teutisci quam et Langobardi* is made in an Italian deed of 845 (Muratori, *Ann.*, II, col. 971); *Annales Juvavenses maximi*, in *M.G.H.*, *SS.*, XXX, 2, p. 738.

[2] Liutprand, *Legatio*, c. 7.

that there arose, in 920, an affray between the escorts of Charles the Simple and Henry I so bloody that it put an end to the meeting of the two sovereigns.[1] Moreover, within the West Frankish kingdom, the curious course of development (not yet adequately explained) which had led to the formation within the Gallo-Romanic tongue of two distinct language groups meant that for long centuries the 'Provençaux' or people of Languedoc, though without any sort of political unity, had a clear sense of belonging to a separate community. Similarly, at the time of the Second Crusade, the knights of Lorraine, who were subjects of the Empire, drew near to the French, whose language they understood and spoke.[2] Nothing is more absurd than to confuse language with nationality; but it would be no less foolish to deny its rôle in the crystallization of national consciousness.

The texts make it plain that so far as France and Germany were concerned this consciousness was already highly developed about the year 1100. During the First Crusade Godfrey of Bouillon who, as a great Lotharingian noble, was fortunate enough to speak both languages, was hard put to it to control the hostility which, we are told, was already traditional between the French and German knights.[3] The 'sweet France' of the *Chanson de Roland* was present in all memories—a France whose frontiers were still a little uncertain, so that it was easily confused with the vast Empire of the Charlemagne of legend, but whose centre was unmistakably situated in the Capetian kingdom. Moreover, among men easily elated by conquests, national pride drew greater strength from being as it were gilded by the memory of the Carolingians; the use of the name 'France' favoured the assimilation, and the legend in its turn helped to fix the name. (The Germans for their part took great pride in the fact that they were still the imperial people.) Loyalty to the crown helped to keep these sentiments alive: it is significant that they are almost completely absent from the epic poems of purely baronial inspiration, like the cycle of Lorraine. We must not suppose, however, that the identification was complete. The monk Guibert de Nogent who, in the reign of Louis VI, wrote a history of the Crusade under the famous title of *Gesta Dei per Francos* was an ardent patriot, but only a very lukewarm admirer of the Capetians. Nationality was nourished by more complex factors—community of language, of tradition, of historical memories more or less well understood; and the sense of a common destiny imposed by political boundaries each of which, though fixed largely by accident, corresponded as a whole to far-reaching and long-established affinities.

All this had not been created by patriotism; but in the course of the

---

[1] Walafrid Strabo, *De exordiis*, c. 7, in *Capitularia reg. Francorum*, II, p. 481; Richer, I, 20.

[2] Odo of Deuil, in *M.G.H., SS.*, XXVI, p. 65.

[3] Ekkehard of Aura, in *M.G.H., SS.*, VI, p. 218.

second feudal age, which was characterized both by men's need to group themselves in larger communities and by the clearer general consciousness of itself which society had acquired, patriotism became as it were the outward manifestation of these latent realities, and so in its turn the creator of new realities. Already, in a poem a little later than the *Chanson de Roland*, 'no Frenchman is worth more than he' is the praise accorded to a knight particularly worthy of esteem.[1] The age whose deeper history we are endeavouring to trace not only witnessed the formation of states; it also saw true fatherlands confirmed or established—though these were destined still to undergo many vicissitudes.

[1] *Girart de Roussillon*, trans. P. Meyer, §631; ed. Foerster (*Romanische Studien*, V) v. 9324.

PART VIII

Feudalism as a Type of Society and its Influence

XXXII

FEUDALISM AS A TYPE OF
SOCIETY

1 HAS THERE BEEN MORE THAN ONE FEUDALISM?

IN the eyes of Montesquieu, the establishment of 'feudal laws' was a phenomenon *sui generis*, 'an event which happened once in the world and which will perhaps never happen again'. Voltaire, less experienced, no doubt, in the precise formulation of legal definitions, but a man of wider outlook, demurred. 'Feudalism', he wrote, 'is not an event; it is a very old form which, with differences in its working, subsists in three-quarters of our hemisphere.'[1] Modern scholarship has in general rallied to the side of Voltaire. Egyptian feudalism, Achaean feudalism, Chinese feudalism, Japanese feudalism—all these forms and more are now familiar concepts. The historian of the West must sometimes regard them with a certain amount of misgiving. For he cannot be unaware of the different definitions which have been given of this famous term, even on its native soil. The basis of feudal society, Benjamin Guérard has said, is land. No, it is the personal group, rejoins Jacques Flach. Do the various exotic versions of feudalism, which seem to abound in universal history today, conform to Guérard's definition or to Flach's? The only remedy for these uncertainties is to go back to the origins of the problem. Since it is obvious that all these societies, separated by time and space, have received the name 'feudal' only on account of their similarities, real or supposed, to Western feudalism, it is the characteristics of this basic type, to which all the others must be referred, that it is of primary importance to define. But first it is necessary to dispose of some obvious instances of the misuse of a term which has made too much noise in the world not to have undergone many perversions.

In the system which they christened 'feudalism' its first godfathers, as we know, were primarily conscious of those aspects of it which conflicted with the idea of a centralized state. Thence it was a short step to describing as feudal every fragmentation of political authority; so that a value judgment was normally combined with the simple statement of a fact. Because sovereignty was generally associated in the minds of these writers

---

[1] *Esprit des Lois*, XXX, I; Voltaire, *Fragments sur quelques révolutions dans l'Inde*, II (ed. Garnier, XXIX, p. 91).

with fairly large states, every exception to the rule seemed to fall into the category of the abnormal. This alone would suffice to condemn a usage which, moreover, could scarcely fail to give rise to intolerable confusion. Occasionally, indeed, there are indications of a more precise notion. In 1783 a minor municipal official, the market-watchman of Valenciennes, denounced as responsible for the increase in the price of foodstuffs 'a feudality of great country landlords'.[1] How many polemists since then have held up to public obloquy the 'feudalism' of bankers or industrialists! Charged with more or less vague historical associations, the word with certain writers seems to suggest no more than the brutal exercise of authority, though frequently it also conveys the slightly less elementary notion of an encroachment of economic powers on public life. It is in fact very true that the identification of wealth—then consisting mainly of land —with authority was one of the outstanding features of medieval feudalism. But this was less on account of the strictly feudal character of that society than because it was, at the same time, based on the manor.

Feudalism, manorial system—the identification here goes back much farther. It had first occurred in the use of the word 'vassal'. The aristocratic stamp which this term had received from what was, after all, a secondary development, was not strong enough to prevent it from being occasionally applied, even in the Middle Ages, to serfs (originally closely akin to vassals properly so called because of the personal nature of their dependence) and even to ordinary tenants. What was then only a kind of linguistic aberration, especially frequent in somewhat incompletely feudalized regions like Gascony or Leon, became a more and more widespread usage, as familiarity with genuine vassalage faded. 'Everyone knows', wrote Perreciot in 1786, 'that in France the subjects of lords are commonly called their vassals.'[2] Similarly it became customary, in spite of etymology, to describe as 'feudal rights' the burdens to which peasant holdings were subject. Thus when the men of the Revolution announced their intention to destroy feudalism, it was above all the manorial system that they meant to attack. But here again the historian must interpose. Though an essential element in feudal society, the manor was in itself an older institution, and was destined to last much longer. In the interests of sound terminology it is important that the two ideas should be kept clearly separate.

Let us therefore try to bring together in broad outline what we have learned about European feudalism, in the strict sense of the word, from its history.

[1] G. Lefebvre, *Les paysans du Nord*, 1924, p. 309.

[2] For example, E. Lodge, 'Serfdom in the Pyrenees', in *Vierteljahrschr. für Soz. und W. G.*, 1905, p. 31; Sanchez-Albornoz, *Estampas de la vida en Leon*, 2nd ed., p. 86, n. 37; Perreciot, *De l'état-civil des personnes*, II, 1786, p. 193, n. 9.

FEUDALISM AS A TYPE OF SOCIETY

2 THE FUNDAMENTAL CHARACTERISTICS OF EUROPEAN FEUDALISM

The simplest way will be to begin by saying what feudal society was not. Although the obligations arising from blood-relationship played a very active part in it, it did not rely on kinship alone. More precisely, feudal ties proper were developed when those of kinship proved inadequate. Again, despite the persistence of the idea of a public authority superimposed on the multitude of petty powers, feudalism coincided with a profound weakening of the State, particularly in its protective capacity. But much as feudal society differed from societies based on kinship as well as from those dominated by the power of the State, it was their successor and bore their imprint. For while the characteristic relationships of personal subjection retained something of the quasi-family character of the original companionage, a considerable part of the political authority exercised by innumerable petty chiefs had the appearance of a usurpation of 'regalian' rights.

European feudalism should therefore be seen as the outcome of the violent dissolution of older societies. It would in fact be unintelligible without the great upheaval of the Germanic invasions which, by forcibly uniting two societies originally at very different stages of development, disrupted both of them and brought to the surface a great many modes of thought and social practices of an extremely primitive character. It finally developed in the atmosphere of the last barbarian raids. It involved a far-reaching restriction of social intercourse, a circulation of money too sluggish to admit of a salaried officialdom, and a mentality attached to things tangible and local. When these conditions began to change, feudalism began to wane.

It was an unequal society, rather than a hierarchical one—with chiefs rather than nobles; and with serfs, not slaves. If slavery had not played so small a part, there would have been no need for the characteristically feudal forms of dependence, as applied to the lower orders of society. In an age of disorder, the place of the adventurer was too important, the memory of men too short, the regularity of social classifications too uncertain, to admit of the strict formation of regular castes.

Nevertheless the feudal system meant the rigorous economic subjection of a host of humble folk to a few powerful men. Having received from earlier ages the Roman *villa* (which in some respects anticipated the manor) and the German village chiefdom, it extended and consolidated these methods whereby men exploited men, and combining inextricably the right to the revenues from the land with the right to exercise authority, it fashioned from all this the true manor of medieval times. And this it did partly for the benefit of an oligarchy of priests and monks whose task it was to propitiate Heaven, but chiefly for the benefit of an oligarchy of warriors.

As even the most perfunctory comparative study will show, one of the most distinctive characteristics of feudal societies was the virtual identity of the class of chiefs with the class of professional warriors serving in the only way that then seemed effective, that is as heavily armed horsemen. As we have seen, of the societies where an armed peasantry survived, some knew neither vassalage nor the manor, while others knew them only in very imperfect forms—as in Scandinavia for example, or the kingdoms of north-western Spain. The case of the Byzantine Empire is perhaps even more significant because its institutions bore the stamp of a much more conscious directing thought. There, after the anti-aristocratic reaction of the eighth century, a government which had preserved the great administrative traditions of the Roman period, and which was furthermore concerned to provide itself with a strong army, created tenements charged with military obligations to the State—true fiefs in one sense, but differing from those of the West in that they were peasant fiefs, each consisting of a small farm. Thenceforth it was a paramount concern of the imperial government to protect these 'soldiers' properties', as well as small-holdings in general, against the encroachments of the rich and powerful. Nevertheless there came a time towards the end of the eleventh century when the Empire, overwhelmed by economic conditions which made independence more and more difficult for a peasantry constantly in debt, and further weakened by internal discords, ceased to extend any useful protection to the free farmers. In this way it not only lost precious fiscal resources, but found itself at the mercy of the magnates, who alone were capable thereafter of raising the necessary troops from among their own dependants.

In feudal society the characteristic human bond was the subordinate's link with a nearby chief. From one level to another the ties thus formed—like so many chains branching out indefinitely—joined the smallest to the greatest. Land itself was valued above all because it enabled a lord to provide himself with 'men' by supplying the remuneration for them. We want lands, said in effect the Norman lords who refused the gifts of jewels, arms, and horses offered by their duke. And they added among themselves: 'It will thus be possible for us to maintain many knights, and the duke will no longer be able to do so.'[1]

It remained to devise a form of real property right suitable for the remuneration of services and coinciding in duration with the personal tie itself. From the solution which it found for this problem, Western feudalism derived one of its most original features. While the 'men of service' who surrounded the Slav princes continued to receive their estates as outright gifts, the fief of the Frankish vassal, after some fluctuations of policy, was in theory conceded to him only for the term of his life. For among the highest classes, distinguished by the honourable profession of arms,

[1] Dudo of Saint-Quentin, ed. Lair (*Mém. Soc. Antiquaires Normandie*, XXIII), III 43–4 (933).

relationships of dependence had assumed, at the outset, the form of contracts freely entered into between two living men confronting one another. From this necessary personal contact the relationship derived the best part of its moral value. Nevertheless at an early date various factors tarnished the purity of the obligation: hereditary succession, natural in a society where the family remained so strong; the practice of enfeoffment which was imposed by economic conditions and ended by burdening the land with services rather than the man with fealty; finally and above all, the plurality of vassal engagements. The loyalty of the commended man remained, in many cases, a potent factor. But as a paramount social bond designed to unite the various groups at all levels, to prevent fragmentation and to arrest disorder, it showed itself decidedly ineffective.

Indeed in the immense range of these ties there had been from the first something artificial. Their general diffusion in feudal times was the legacy of a moribund State—that of the Carolingians—which had conceived the idea of combating social disintegration by means of one of the institutions born of that very condition. The system of superposed protective relationships was certainly not incapable of contributing to the cohesion of the State: witness, the Anglo-Norman monarchy. But for this it was necessary that there should be a central authority favoured, as in England, not only by the fact of conquest itself but even more by the circumstance that it coincided with new material and moral conditions. In the ninth century the forces making for disintegration were too strong.

In the area of Western civilization the map of feudalism reveals some large blank spaces—the Scandinavian peninsula, Frisia, Ireland. Perhaps it is more important still to note that feudal Europe was not all feudalized in the same degree or according to the same rhythm and, above all, that it was nowhere feudalized completely. In no country did the whole of the rural population fall into the bonds of personal and hereditary dependence. Almost everywhere—though the number varied greatly from region to region—there survived large or small allodial properties. The concept of the State never absolutely disappeared, and where it retained the most vitality men continued to call themselves 'free', in the old sense of the word, because they were dependent only on the head of the people or his representatives. Groups of peasant warriors remained in Normandy, in the Danelaw, and in Spain. The mutual oath, strongly contrasting with the oaths of subordination, survived in the peace associations and triumphed in the communes. No doubt it is the fate of every system of human institutions never to be more than imperfectly realized. Capitalism was unquestionably the dominant influence on the European economy at the beginning of the twentieth century; yet more than one undertaking continued to exist outside it.

Returning to our feudal map, we find between the Loire and the Rhine, and in Burgundy on both banks of the Saône, a heavily shaded area which, in the eleventh century, is suddenly enlarged by the Norman conquests of England and southern Italy. All round this central nucleus there is an almost regular shading-off till, in Saxony and especially in Leon and Castile, the stippling becomes very sparse indeed. Finally the entire shaded area is surrounded by blank spaces. In the most heavily shaded zone it is not difficult to recognize the regions where the regularizing influence of the Carolingians had been most far-reaching and where also the mingling of Romanized elements and Germanic elements—more pronounced here than elsewhere—had most completely disrupted the structure of the two societies and made possible the growth of very old seeds of territorial lordship and personal dependence.

3 A CROSS-SECTION OF COMPARATIVE HISTORY

A subject peasantry; widespread use of the service tenement (i.e. the fief) instead of a salary, which was out of the question; the supremacy of a class of specialized warriors; ties of obedience and protection which bind man to man and, within the warrior class, assume the distinctive form called vassalage; fragmentation of authority—leading inevitably to disorder; and, in the midst of all this, the survival of other forms of association, family and State, of which the latter, during the second feudal age, was to acquire renewed strength—such then seem to be the fundamental features of European feudalism. Like all the phenomena revealed by that science of eternal change which is history, the social structure thus characterized certainly bore the peculiar stamp of an age and an environment. Yet just as the matrilineal or agnatic clan or even certain types of economic enterprise are found in much the same forms in very different societies, it is by no means impossible that societies different from our own should have passed through a phase closely resembling that which has just been defined. If so, it is legitimate to call them feudal during that phase. But the work of comparison thus involved is clearly beyond the powers of one man, and I shall therefore confine myself to an example which will at least give an idea of what such research, conducted by surer hands, might yield. The task is facilitated by the existence of excellent studies which already bear the hall-mark of the soundest comparative method.

In the dark ages of Japanese history we dimly perceive a society based on kinship groups, real or fictitious. Then towards the end of the seventh century of our era, under Chinese influence a system of government is founded which strives (exactly as the Carolingians did) to maintain a kind of moral control over its subjects. Finally, about the eleventh century, the period begins which it has become customary to call feudal and whose advent seems (in accordance with a pattern with which we are now familiar) to have coincided with a certain slackening of commercial activity. Here, therefore, as in Europe, 'feudalism' seems to have been preceded by two very different forms of social organization; and, as with us, it was profoundly influenced by both. The monarchy, though it had less connection than in Europe with the feudal structure proper—since the chains of vassalage terminated before reaching the Emperor—subsisted, in law, as the theoretical source of all power; and there also the fragmentation of political authority, which was fostered by very old habits, was held to be a consequence of encroachments on the State.

Above the peasantry a class of professional warriors had arisen. It was in these circles that ties of personal dependence developed, on the model furnished by the relations of the armed retainer with his chief; they were thus, it appears, marked by a much more pronounced class character than European 'commendation'. They were hierarchically organized, just as in Europe; but Japanese vassalage was much more an act of submission than was European vassalage and much less a contract. It was also more strict, since it did not allow plurality of lords. As these warriors had to be supported they were granted tenements closely resembling the fiefs of the West. Sometimes even, on the pattern of our *fiefs de reprises*, the grant was purely fictitious and involved in fact lands which had originally belonged to the patrimony of the pretended recipient. These fighting-men were naturally less and less willing to cultivate the soil, though as in Europe there were to the end exceptional cases of peasant 'vavasours'. The vassals therefore lived mainly on the rents from their own tenants. There were too many of them, however—far more, apparently, than in Europe—to admit of the establishment for their benefit of real manors, with extensive powers over the people. Few manors were created, except by the baronage and the temples, and being widely scattered and having no demesne, they recalled the embryonic manors of Anglo-Saxon England rather than those of the really manorialized regions of the West. Furthermore, on this soil where irrigated rice-fields represented the prevailing form of agriculture, the technical conditions were so different from European practice that the subjection of the peasantry assumed correspondingly different forms.

Although far too brief, of course, and too absolute in its appraisal of the contrasts between the two societies, it seems to me that this outline nevertheless enables us to reach a fairly firm conclusion. Feudalism was not 'an event which happened once in the world'. Like Europe—though with inevitable and deep-seated differences—Japan went through this phase. Have other societies also passed through it? And if so, what were the causes, and were they perhaps common to all such societies? It is for future works to provide the answers. I should be happy if.this book, by suggesting questions to students, were to prepare the way for an inquiry going far beyond it.

XXXIII

THE PERSISTENCE OF EUROPEAN
FEUDALISM

1 SURVIVALS AND REVIVALS

FROM the middle of the thirteenth century onwards European societies diverged decisively from the feudal pattern. But a social system, which is simply a phase of a continuous evolution within human groups possessed of memory, cannot perish outright or at a single stroke. Feudalism had its continuations.

The manorial system, on which feudalism had left its mark, long survived it, undergoing many changes, which do not concern us here. It is plain, however, that when manorialism had ceased to form part of a closely related system of political institutions, it was bound to appear more and more pointless in the eyes of the subject populations, and consequently more odious. Of all forms of dependence within the manor, the most genuinely feudal was serfdom, and although it had undergone profound changes and become territorial rather than personal, it nevertheless survived in France till the eve of the Revolution. Who at that time remembered that among those subject to *mainmorte* there were undoubtedly some whose ancestors had voluntarily 'commended' themselves to a protector? And even supposing this remote circumstance had been known, would that knowledge have made an anachronistic state of affairs any easier to bear?

With the exception of England, where the first of the seventeenth-century Revolutions abolished all distinctions between tenure by knight-service and other forms of tenure, the obligations arising from vassalage and the fief were rooted in the soil, and they lasted, as in France, as long as the manorial system or, as in Prussia (which in the eighteenth century proceeded to a general 'allodification' of fiefs), very nearly as long. The State, which alone was capable henceforth of utilizing the hierarchy of dependence, only very slowly abandoned recourse to it for the supply of military forces. Louis XIV summoned the whole body of vassals on more than one occasion. But this was now only an exceptional measure on the part of governments in need of troops; or it might even be a mere fiscal expedient to raise funds through the medium of fines and exemptions. After the end of the Middle Ages the only characteristics of the fief which really retained practical importance were the pecuniary burdens to which it was subject and the special rules which regulated its inheritance. Since there were no more household warriors, homage was henceforth invariably attached to the possession of an estate. Its ceremonial aspect, 'empty' though it might seem in the eyes of jurists nurtured in the rationalism of the new age,[1] was not a matter of indifference to a noble class with a natural concern for etiquette. But the ceremony itself, formerly charged with such profound human significance, now only served—apart from the monetary levies of which it was sometimes the occasion—to establish the ownership of the property, a source of rights which were more or less lucrative, according to the 'custom'. 'Feudal matters' were essentially contentious and a preoccupation of jurisprudence. They supplied a prolific literature of legal theorists and practitioners with splendid themes for dissertations. But that in France the edifice was very decayed, and the profits which its beneficiaries expected from it mostly rather poor, is clearly demonstrated by the ease with which it was overthrown. The disappearance of the manorial system was effected only at the cost of much resistance and not without seriously upsetting the distribution of wealth; that of the fief and of vassalage seemed the inevitable and almost insignificant termination of a long death-agony.

Nevertheless, in a society which continued to be beset with many disorders, the needs which had given rise to the ancient practice of companionage, and then to vassalage, had not ceased to be felt. Among the various reasons which led to the creation of the orders of chivalry which were founded in such great number in the fourteenth and fifteenth centuries, one of the most decisive was undoubtedly the desire of the princes to attach to themselves a group of highly-placed retainers by an especially compelling bond. The knights of Saint-Michel, according to the statutes drawn up by Louis XI, promised the king *bonne et vraye amour* and pledged themselves to serve him loyally in his just wars. The attempt was to prove as vain as that of the Carolingians in an earlier day: in the oldest list of persons honoured by the famous collar, the third place was occupied by the Constable of St. Pol, who was so basely to betray his master.

More effective—and more dangerous—was the reconstitution, during the disorders of the closing years of the Middle Ages, of bands of private warriors, very much akin to the 'satellite' vassals whose brigandage had been denounced by the writers of the Merovingian age. Frequently their dependence was expressed by the wearing of a costume displaying the colours of their chieftain or emblazoned with his arms. This practice was condemned in Flanders by Philip the Bold,[2] but it seems to have been especially widespread in the England of the last Plantagenets, of the

---

[1] P. Hévin, *Consultations et observations sur la coutume de Bretagne*, 1724, p. 343.
[2] P. Thomas, *Textes historiques sur Lille et le Nord*, II, 1936, p. 285 (1385 and 1397); cf. p. 218 (no. 68).

Lancastrians and the Yorkists—so much so that the groups thus formed round the great barons received the name of 'liveries'. Like the household vassals of former days they did not consist exclusively of low-born adventurers, and in fact, the majority were probably recruited from the 'gentry'. When one of these men was involved in a law-suit, the lord extended his protection to him in court. Although illegal, this practice of 'maintenance' was extraordinarily tenacious, as is attested by repeated Parliamentary prohibitions; it reproduced practically feature for feature the ancient *mithium* which the powerful man in Frankish Gaul had extended over his retainer. And since it was also to the advantage of the sovereigns to make use of the personal bond in its new form, we find Richard II seeking to spread through the kingdom—like so many *vassi dominici*—his personal followers, distinguished by the 'white hart' with which their uniform was emblazoned.[1]

Even in the France of the early Bourbons the nobleman who in order to make his way in the world became the servant of a great man assumed a status remarkably akin to primitive vassalage. In a phrase that recalled the vigour of the old feudal language, one said of so-and-so that he 'belonged' to Monsieur le Prince or to the Cardinal. True, the ceremony of homage was no longer performed, though it was often replaced by a written agreement. For, from the end of the Middle Ages, the 'promise of friendship' was substituted for the dying practice of homage. See, for example, this 'letter' addressed to Fouquet on the 2nd June, 1658, by a certain Captain Deslandes. 'I promise and give my fealty to My Lord the Procurator-General . . . never to belong to any but him, to whom I give myself and attach myself with the greatest attachment of which I am capable; and I promise to serve him generally against all persons without exception and to obey none but him, nor even to have any dealings with those whom he forbids me to deal with . . . I promise him to sacrifice my life against all whom he pleases . . . without any exception whatsoever.' It is as though we were hearing, across the ages, the echoes of the most absolute of the formulas of commendation: 'thy friends shall be my friends, thy enemies shall be my enemies'[2]—without even a reservation in favour of the king!

2 THE WARRIOR IDEA AND THE IDEA OF CONTRACT

To the societies which succeeded it the feudal era had bequeathed knighthood, which had become crystallized as nobility. From this origin the dominant class retained pride in its military calling, symbolized by the right to wear the sword, and clung to it with particular tenacity where, as

---

[1] T. F. Tout, *Chapters in the Administrative History of Mediaeval England*, IV, 1928, p. 62.
[2] Colbert, *Lettres*, ed. P. Clément, II, p. xxx. For an old example of a promise of friendship see J. Quicherat, *Rodrigue de Villandrando*, 1879, Documents, no. XIX.

in France, it derived from this calling the justification for valuable fiscal privileges. Nobles need not pay *taille*, explain two squires of Varennes-en-Argonne about 1380; for 'by their noble status, nobles are obliged to expose their bodies and belongings in wars'.[1] Under the Ancien Régime, the nobility of ancient lineage, in contrast with the aristocracy of office, continued to call itself the nobility 'of the sword'. Even today, when to die for one's country has altogether ceased to be the monopoly of one class or one profession, the persistence of the feeling that a sort of moral supremacy attaches to the function of professional warrior—an attitude quite foreign to other societies, such as the Chinese—is a continual reminder of the separation which took place, towards the beginning of feudal times, between the peasant and the knight.

Vassal homage was a genuine contract and a bilateral one. If the lord failed to fulfil his engagements he lost his rights. Transferred, as was inevitable, to the political sphere—since the principal subjects of the king were at the same time his vassals—this idea was to have a far-reaching influence, all the more so because on this ground it was reinforced by the very ancient notions which held the king responsible in a mystical way for the welfare of his subjects and deserving of punishment in the event of public calamity. These old currents happened to unite on this point with another stream of thought which arose in the Church out of the Gregorian protest against the myth of sacred and supernatural kingship. It was the writers of this clerical group who first expressed, with a force long unequalled, the notion of a contract binding the sovereign to his people—'like the swineherd to the master who employs him', wrote an Alsatian monk about 1080. The remark seems even more full of meaning when taken in the context of the indignant protest of a (moderate) partisan of monarchy: 'the Lord's anointed cannot be dismissed like a village reeve!' But these clerical theorists themselves did not fail to invoke, among the justifications for the deposition to which they condemned the bad prince, the universally recognized right of the vassal to abandon the bad lord.[2]

It was above all the circles of the vassals which translated these ideas into practice, under the influence of the institutions which had formed their mentality. In this sense, there was a fruitful principle underlying many revolts which on a superficial view might appear as mere random uprisings: 'A man may resist his king and judge when he acts contrary to law and may even help to make war on him. . . . Thereby, he does not violate the duty of fealty.' These are the words of the *Sachsenspiegel*.[3] This

---

[1] C. Aimond, *Histoire de la ville de Varennes*, 1925, p. 50.

[2] Manegold of Lautenbach, in *Libelli de lite* (M.G.H.), I, p. 365; Wenrich, *ibid.*, p. 289; Paul of Bernried, *Vita Gregorii*, c. 97 in Watterich, *Pontificum Romanorum vitae*, I, p. 532.

[3] *Landr.*, III, 78, 2. The meaning of this passage is disputed by Zeumer in *Zeitschrift der Savigny-Stiftung*, G.A., 1914, pp. 68–75, but is fully confirmed by F. Kern, *Gottesgnadentum und Widerstandsrecht im früheren Mittelalter*, Leipzig, 1914.

famous 'right of resistance', the germ of which was already present in the Oaths of Strasbourg (843) and in the pact between Charles the Bald and his vassals (856), resounded in the thirteenth and fourteenth centuries from one end of the Western world to the other, in a multitude of texts. Though most of these documents were inspired by reactionary tendencies among the nobility, or by the egoism of the bourgeoisie, they were of great significance for the future. They included the English Great Charter of 1215; the Hungarian 'Golden Bull' of 1222; the Assizes of the kingdom of Jerusalem; the Privilege of the Brandenburg nobles; the Aragonese Act of Union of 1287; the Brabantine charter of Cortenberg; the statute of Dauphiné of 1341; the declaration of the communes of Languedoc (1356). It was assuredly no accident that the representative system, in the very aristocratic form of the English Parliament, the French 'Estates', the *Stände* of Germany, and the Spanish *Cortés*, originated in states which were only just emerging from the feudal stage and still bore its imprint. Nor was it an accident that in Japan, where the vassal's submission was much more unilateral and where, moreover, the divine power of the Emperor remained outside the structure of vassal engagements, nothing of the kind emerged from a regime which was nevertheless in many respects closely akin to the feudalism of the West. The originality of the latter system consisted in the emphasis it placed on the idea of an agreement capable of binding the rulers; and in this way, oppressive as it may have been to the poor, it has in truth bequeathed to our Western civilization something with which we still desire to live.

BIBLIOGRAPHY

WHEN the English edition of *Feudal Society* was in preparation, we had to consider what was to be done with the bibliography, which was compiled in 1938-9.

One of two courses seemed open to us: either to attempt to bring it up to date by the inclusion of more recent material, or to print it as it stood, with a supplementary list of titles. There was a strong argument against the first of these alternatives. Bloch's bibliography is a work of personal selection and classification, intended to serve not only as a guide for students, but also as an acknowledgement of his debt to other scholars.[1] To have introduced additional titles into this framework would have been, it seemed to us, an unwarranted interference with Bloch's design, especially as he had made it a principle not to include works of which he had no personal knowledge. We have therefore adopted the second course and reproduced his bibliography as he left it, with the omission of one section only: a list of general histories, the majority of which, we believed, would already be familiar to students of medieval history. A supplement lists more recent publications.[2]

Although this book is based on a profound study of original sources, many of which are referred to in the footnotes, the author in his bibliography has confined himself to listing the standard guides to such material except in the case of the legal sources, which he has enumerated separately. Again, for the intellectual and social 'climate' which he has discussed from a particular point of view in Part II, his list of secondary authorities is limited to a few special questions. The bibliography is much fuller, however, on the subject of the last invasions and, as might be expected, on the special aspects of social and political development which form the central theme of the book.

Except where otherwise indicated, the place of publication is Paris for a book in French, or London for a book in English.

L. A. Manyon

PLAN OF BIBLIOGRAPHY

I THE EVIDENCE
(1) Standard Guides to Sources.[3] (2) The Linguistic Evidence. (3) Historiography. (4) The Literary Evidence.

II MENTAL ATTITUDES
(1) Modes of Feeling and Thought. (2) 'Terrors' of the Year 1000.

III THE LAST INVASIONS
(1) General. (2) The Saracens in the Alps and the Italian Peninsula. (3) The Hungarians. (4) The Scandinavians. (5) The Conversion of the North. (6) Effects of the Scandinavian Invasions.

IV LEGAL AND POLITICAL STRUCTURE
(1) Original Sources. (2) Modern Works on the History of Law and Institutions. (3) The Legal Mind and the Teaching of Law. (4) Political Ideas.

V TIES OF KINSHIP
(1) The Family and the Vendetta. (2) Economic Solidarity.

VI FEUDAL INSTITUTIONS PROPER
(1) Feudalism in General; Frankish Origins. (2) Feudalism by Countries and Regions. (3) 'Companionage', Vassalage and Homage. (4) *Precaria*, 'Benefit', Fief, and Allod. (5) The Law of the Fief. (6) Plurality of Lords and Liege Homage.

---

[1] See p. xxi, n.   [2] Pp. 478-81.   [3] Excluding literary sources in the vernacular.

BIBLIOGRAPHY

I. THE EVIDENCE

(1) STANDARD GUIDES TO SOURCES

BALLESTER (Rafael), *Fuentes narrativas de la historia de España durante la edad media*, Palma, 1912.
—— *Bibliografía de la historia de España*, Gerona, 1921.
Bibliotheca hagiographica latina antiquae et mediae aetatis, 2 vols. and supplementary vol., Brussels, 1898–1911.
DAHLMANN-WAITZ, *Quellenkunde der deutschen Geschichte*, 9th edn., Leipzig. 2 vols., 1931–2.
EGIDI (Pietro), *La storia medievale*, Rome, 1922.
GROSS (Charles), *The Sources and Literature of English History from the Earliest Times to about 1485*, 2nd edn., London, 1915.
JACOB (Karl), *Quellenkunde der deutschen Geschichte im Mittelalter*, Berlin, 1917 (*Sammlung Göschen*).
JANSEN (M.) and SCHMITZ-KALLENBERG (L.), *Historiographie und Quellen der deutschen Geschichte bis 1500*, 2nd edn., Leipzig, 1914 (A. MEISTER, *Grundriss*, I, 7).
MANITIUS (M.), *Geschichte der lateinischen Literatur des Mittelalters*, 3 vols., Munich, 1911–31 (*Handbuch der klassischen Altertumswissenschaft*, ed. I. MÜLLER).
MOLINIER (Auguste), *Les Sources de l'histoire de France des origines aux guerres d'Italie*, 6 vols., 1901–6.
OESTERLEY (H.), *Wegweiser durch die Literatur der Urkunden-Sammlung*, 2 vols., Berlin, 1886.
PIRENNE (Henri), *Bibliographie de l'histoire de Belgique*, 3rd edn., Brussels, 1931.
POTTHAST (August), *Bibliotheca historica medii aevi*, 2 vols., Berlin, 1875–96.
STEIN (Henri), *Bibliographie générale des cartulaires français ou relatifs à l'histoire de France*, 1907.
UEBERWEG (Friedrich), *Grundriss der Geschichte der Philosophie*, II, 11th edn., Berlin, 1928.
VILDHAUT (H.), *Handbuch der Quellenkunde zur deutschen Geschichte bis zum Ausgange der Staufer*, 2nd edn., 2 vols., Werl, 1906–9.
WATTENBACH (W.), *Deutschlands Geschichtsquellen im Mittelalter bis zur Mitte des dreizehnten Jahrhunderts*, I, 7th edn., Berlin, 1904; II, 6th edn., Berlin, 1894.

BIBLIOGRAPHY

WATTENBACH (W.) and HOLTZMANN (R.), *Deutschlands Geschichtsquellen im Mittelalter. Deutsche Kaiserzeit*, I, Part 1, Berlin, 1938.

(2) THE LINGUISTIC EVIDENCE

ARNALDI (F.), 'Latinitatis italicae medii aevi inde ab anno CDLXXVI usque ad annum MDXXII lexicon imperfectum' in *Archivum latinitatis medii aevi*, X, 1936.

BAXTER (J. H.) *et al.*, *Medieval Latin Word-List from British and Irish Sources*, Oxford, 1934.

BLOCH (Oscar), with the collaboration of W. VON WARTBURG, *Dictionnaire étymologique de la langue française*, 1932.

BRUNEL (C.), 'Le Latin des chartes', *Revue des études latines*, 1925.

—— 'Les Premiers Exemples de l'emploi du provençal', *Romania*, 1922.

DIEFENBACH (L.), *Glossarium latino-germanicum mediae et infimae latinitatis*, Frankfurt, 1857. *Novum glossarium*, Frankfurt, 1867.

DU CANGE, *Glossarium mediae et infimae latinitatis*, ed. HENSCHEL, 7 vols., 1830–50. New impression, Niort, 1883–7. Further impression, 10 vols. in 5, Graz, 1954.

GAMILLSCHEG (E.), *Etymologisches Wörterbuch der französischen Sprache*, Heidelberg, 1928.

HABEL (E.), *Mittellateinisches Glossar*, Paderborn, 1931.

HECK (Philippe), *Übersetzungsprobleme im früheren Mittelalter*, Tübingen, 1931.

HEGEL (Karl), 'Lateinische Wörter und deutsche Begriffe', in *Neues Archiv der Gesellschaft für ältere deutsche Geschichtskunde*, 1893.

KLUGE (Friedrich), *Etymologisches Wörterbuch der deutschen Sprache*, 11th edn., Berlin, 1934.

MERKEL (Felix), *Das Aufkommen der deutschen Sprache in den städtischen Kanzleien des ausgehenden Mittelalters*, Leipzig, 1930 (*Beiträge zur Kulturgeschichte des Mittelalters*, 45).

MEYER-LÜBKE (W.), *Romanisches Etymologisches Wörterbuch*, 3rd edn., Heidelberg, 1935.

MURRAY (J. A. H.) (ed.), *The Oxford English Dictionary*, 12 vols. and supplement, Oxford, 1888–1928.

NÉLIS (H.), 'Les Plus Anciennes Chartes en flamand', *Mélanges d'histoire offerts à H. Pirenne*, Brussels, 1926, I.

OBREEN (H), 'Introduction de la langue vulgaire dans les documents diplomatiques en Belgique et dans les Pays-Bas', *Revue belge de philologie*, 1935.

OGLE (M. B.), 'Some Aspects of Mediaeval Latin Style', *Speculum*, 1926.

STRECKER (Karl), *Introduction à l'étude du latin médiéval*, translated (into French) by P. VAN DE WOESTIJNE, Ghent, 1933.

TRAUBE (L.), 'Die lateinische Sprache des Mittelalters', in TRAUBE, *Vorlesungen und Abhandlungen*, II, Munich, 1911.

VANCSA (Max), *Das erste Auftreten der deutschen Sprache in den Urkunden*, Leipzig, 1895 (*Preisschriften gekrönt . . . von der fürstlich Jablonowskischen Gesellschaft, histor.-nationalökonom. Section*, XXX).

WARTBURG (W. von), *Französisches etymologisches Wörterbuch*, 1928 ff. (in course of publication).

(3) HISTORIOGRAPHY

BALZANI (Ugo), *Le cronache italiane nel medio evo*, 2nd edn., Milan, 1900.

GILSON (E.), 'Le Moyen-âge et l'histoire', in GILSON, *L'Esprit de la philosophie médiévale*, II, 1932.

HEISIG (Karl), 'Die Geschichtsmetaphysik des Rolandliedes und ihre Vergeschichte', *Zeitschrift für romanische Philologie*, LV, 1935.

LEHMANN (Paul), 'Das literarische Bild Karls des Grossen, vornehmlich im lateinischen Schrifttum des Mittelalters', *Sitzungsberichte der bayerischen Akademie, Phil.-hist. Kl.*, 1934.

POOLE (R. L.), *Chronicles and Annals: a Brief Outline of their Origin and Growth*, Oxford, 1926.

BIBLIOGRAPHY

SCHMIDLIN (Joseph), *Die geschichtsphilosophische und kirchenpolitische Weltanschauung Ottos von Freising. Ein Beitrag zur mittelalterlichen Geistesgeschichte*. Freiburg im Breisgau, 1906 (*Studien und Darstellungen aus dem Gebiete der Geschichte*, ed. H. GRAUERT, IV, 2-3).
SPÖRL (Johannes), *Grundformen hochmittelalterlicher Geschichtsanschauung*, Munich, 1935.

(4) THE LITERARY EVIDENCE

ACHER (Jean), 'Les Archaïsmes apparents dans la chanson de "Raoul de Cambrai"', *Revue des langues romanes*, 1907.
FALK (J.), *Étude sociale sur les chansons de geste*, Nyköping, 1879.
KALBFLEISCH, Die Realien im altfranzösischen Epos "Raoul de Cambrai", Giessen, 1897 (*Wissenschaftliche Beilage zum Jahresbericht des Grh. Realgymnasiums*).
MEYER (Fritz), *Die Stände, ihr Leben und Treiben dargestellt nach den altfranzösischen Artus- und Abenteuerromanen*, Marburg, 1892 (*Ausgabe und Abhandlungen aus dem Gebiete der roman. Philologie*, 89).
TAMASSIA (G.), 'Il diritto nell' epica francese dei secoli XII e XIII', *Rivista italiana per le scienze giuridiche*, I, 1886.

II. MENTAL ATTITUDES

(1) MODES OF FEELING AND THOUGHT

BESZARD (L.), *Les Larmes dans l'épopée*, Halle, 1903.
BILFINGER, *Die mittelalterlichen Horen und die modernen Stunden*, Stuttgart, 1892.
DORIACHE-RODJESVENSKY, *Les Poésies des Goliards*, 1931.
DRESDNER (Albert), *Kultur- und Sittengeschichte der italienischen Geistlichkeit im 10. und 11. Jahrhundert*, Breslau, 1910.
EICKEN (Heinrich von), *Geschichte und System der mittelalterlichen Weltanschauung*, Stuttgart, 1887.
GALBRAITH (V. H.), 'The Literacy of the Medieval English Kings', *Proceedings of the British Academy*, 1935.
GHELLINCK (J. de), *Le Mouvement théologique du XII⁰ siècle*, 1914.
GLORY (A.) and UNGERER (T.), 'L'Adolescent au cadran solaire de la cathédrale de Strasbourg', *Archives alsaciennes d'histoire de l'art*, 1932.
HASKINS (Charles H.), *The Renaissance of the Twelfth Century*, Cambridge (Mass.), 1927.
HOFMEISTER (A.), 'Puer, juvenis, senex: zum Verständnis der mittelalterlichen Altersbezeichnungen', *Papsttum und Kaisertum: Forschungen P. Kehr dargebracht*, 1926.
IRSAY (S. d'), *Histoire des universités françaises et étrangères*, I, 1933.
JACOBIUS (Helene), *Die Erziehung des Edelfräuleins im alten Frankreich nach Dichtungen des XII., XIII. und XIV. Jahrhunderts*, Halle, 1908 (*Beihefte zur Zeitschrift für romanische Philologie*, XVI).
LIMMER (R.), *Bildungszustände und Bildungsideen des 13. Jahrhunderts*, Munich, 1928.
PARÉ (G.), BRUNET (A.), TREMBLAY (P.), *La Renaissance du XII⁰ siècle: les Écoles et l'enseignement*, 1938 (*Publications de l'Institut d'études médiévales d'Ottawa*, 3).
RASHDALL (H.), *The Universities of Europe in the Middle Ages*, 2nd edn. by F. M. POWICKE and A. B. EMDEN, 3 vols., Oxford, 1936.
SASS (Johann), *Zur Kultur- und Sittengeschichte der sächsischen Kaiserzeit*, Berlin, 1892.
SÜSSMILCH (Hans), *Die lateinische Vagantenpoesie des 12. und 13. Jahrhunderts als Kulturerscheinung*, Leipzig, 1917 (*Beiträge zur Kulturgeschichte des Mittelalters und der Renaissance*, 25).

(2) 'TERRORS' OF THE YEAR 1000

BURR (G. L.), 'The Year 1000', *American Historical Review*, 1900-1.
EICKEN (H. von), 'Die Legende von der Erwartung des Weltuntergangs und der Wiederkehr Christi im Jahre 1000', *Forschungen zur deutschen Geschichte*, XXIII, 1883.

BIBLIOGRAPHY

ERMINI (Filippo), 'La fine del mondo nell' anno mille e il pensiero di Odone di Cluny', *Studien zur lateinischen Dichtung des Mittelalters, Ehrengabe für K. Strecker*, Dresden, 1931 (*Schriftenreihe der Historischen Vierteljahrschrift*, 1).

GRUND (Karl), *Die Anschauungen des Radulfus Glaber in seinen Historien*, Greifswald, 1910.

ORSI (P.), 'L'anno mille', *Rivista storica italiana*, IV, 1887.

PLAINE (Dom François), 'Les Prétendues Terreurs de l'an mille', *Revue des questions historiques*, XIII, 1873.

WADSTEIN (Ernst), *Die eschatologische Ideengruppe: Antichrist-Weltsabbat-Weltende und Weltgericht*, Leipzig, 1896.

III. THE LAST INVASIONS

(1) GENERAL

LOT (Ferdinand), *Les Invasions barbares et le peuplement de l'Europe; introduction à l'intelligence des derniers traités de paix*, 2 vols., 1937.

(2) THE SARACENS IN THE ALPS AND THE ITALIAN PENINSULA

DUPRAT (E.), 'Les Sarrasins en Provence', *Les Bouches-du-Rhône, Encyclopédie départementale*, 1924.

LATOUCHE (R.), 'Les Idées actuelles sur les Sarrasins dans les Alpes', *Revue de géographie alpine*, 1931.

PATRUCCO (Carlo E.), 'I Saraceni nelle Alpi Occidentali', *Biblioteca della Società storica subalpina*, XXXII, 1908.

POUPARDIN (René), *Le Royaume de Bourgogne (888–1038)*, 1907 (*Bibliothèque de l'École des Hautes Études, Sc. histor.*, 163).

—— *Le Royaume de Provence sous les Carolingiens*, 1901 (*ibid.*, 131).

VEHSE (O.), 'Das Bündnis gegen die Sarazenen vom Jahre 915', *Quellen und Forschungen aus italienischen Archiven*, XIX, 1927.

(3) THE HUNGARIANS

BÜDINGER (Max), *Österreichische Geschichte bis zum Ausgange des dreizehnten Jahrhunderts*, I, Leipzig, 1858.

CARO (G.), 'Der Ungarntribut unter Heinrich I.', *Mitteilungen des Instituts für österreichische Geschichtsforschung*, XX, 1899.

DARKO (E.), 'Influences touraniennes sur l'évolution de l'art militaire des Grecs, des Romains et des Byzantins', *Byzantion*, 1935 and 1937.

JOKAY (Z.), 'Die ungarische Ortsnamenforschung', *Zeitschrift für Ortsnamenforschung*, 1935.

KAINDL (R. F.), *Beiträge zur älteren ungarischen Geschichte*, Vienna, 1893.

LÜTTICH (Rudolf), *Ungarnzüge in Europa im 10. Jahrhundert*, Berlin, 1910 (*Ebering's Histor. Studien*, 74).

MACARTNEY (C. A.), *The Magyars in the Ninth Century*, Cambridge, 1930 (reviewed by G. MORAVSIK, *Byzantinische Zeitschrift*, 1933).

MARCZALI (Heinrich), *Ungarns Geschichtsquellen im Zeitalter der Arpaden*, Berlin, 1882.

MARQUART (J.), *Osteuropäische und ostasiatische Streifzüge*, Leipzig, 1903.

SAUVAGEOT (A.), 'L'Origine du peuple hongrois', *Revue des études hongroises*, II, 1924.

SCHÖNEBAUM (Herbert), *Die Kenntnis der byzantinischen Geschichtsschreiber von der ältesten Geschichte der Ungarn vor der Landnahme*, Berlin, 1922.

SEBESTYEN (Charles C. S.), 'L'Arc et la flèche des Hongrois', *Nouvelle Revue de Hongrie*, LI, 1934.

STEINACKER (Harold), 'Über Stand und Aufgabe der ungarischen Verfassungsgeschichte', *Mitteilungen des Instituts für Oesterreichische Geschichtsforschung*, XVIII, 1907.

SZINNYEI, *Die Herkunft der Ungarn, ihre Sprache und Urkultur*, 2nd edn., Berlin, 1923.

ZICHY (Étienne), 'L'Origine du peuple hongrois', *Revue des études hongroises*, I, 1923.

BIBLIOGRAPHY

(4) THE SCANDINAVIANS

ARBMAN (Holger) and STENBERGER (Mårten), *Vikingar i Västerled* (The Vikings on the Western routes), Stockholm, 1935.

BUGGE (Alexander), *Die Wikinger: Bilder aus der nordischen Vergangenheit*, Halle, 1906.

—— 'The Norse Settlements in the British Islands', *Transactions of the Royal Historical Society*, 1921.

CLAPHAM (J. H.), 'The Horsing of the Danes', *English Historical Review*, 1910.

COLLINGWOOD (W. G.), *Scandinavian Britain*, 1908.

CURTIS (E.), 'The English and Ostmen in Ireland', *English Historical Review*, 1908.

DARLINGTON (R. R.), 'The Last Phase of Anglo-Saxon History', *History*, 1937.

FALK (H.), 'Altnordisches Seewesen', *Wörter und Sachen*, IV, 1912.

GARAUD (Marcel), 'Les Invasions des Normands en Poitou et leurs conséquences', *Revue historique*, CLXXX, 1937.

GOSSES (I. H.), 'Deensche Heerschappijen in Friesland gedurende den Noormannentijd', *Mededeelingen der koninklijke Akademie van Wetenschappen, Afd. Letterkunde*, 56, Series B, 1923.

HOFMEISTER (A.), 'Ein angeblicher Normannenzug ins Mittelmeer um 825', *Historische Aufsätze K. Zeumer dargebracht*, Weimar, 1909.

JACOBSEN (Lis), 'Les Vikings suivant les inscriptions runniques du Danemark', *Revue Historique*, CLVIII, 1938.

JORANSON (Einar), *The Danegeld in France*, Rock Island, 1923 (*Augustana Library Publ.*, 10).

KENDRICK (T. D.), *A History of the Vikings*, 1930.

LOT (F.), 'La Grande Invasion normande de 856–862', *Bibliothèque de l'École des Chartes*, 1908.

—— 'La Loire, l'Aquitaine et la Seine de 862 à 866', *ibid.*, 1908.

—— 'Le Monastère inconnu pillé par les Normands en 845', *ibid.*, 1909.

MONTELIUS (Oskar), *Kulturgeschichte Schwedens von der ältesten Zeiten bis zum elften Jahrhundert*, Leipzig, 1906.

—— 'Sverige och Vikingafäderna västernt' (Sweden and the Viking Expeditions to the West), *Antikvarisk Tidskrift*, XXI, 2.

NORDENSTRENG (Rolf), *Die Züge der Wikinger*, trans. L. MEYN, Leipzig, 1925.

OLRIK (Axel), *Viking Civilization*, 1930.

OMAN (Charles W. C.), 'The Danish Kingdom of York', *Archaeological Journal*, XCI, 1934.

PAULSEN (P.), *Studien zur Wikingerkultur*, Neumünster, 1933.

PRENTOUT (Henri), *Étude critique sur Dudon de Saint-Quentin*, 1916.

—— *Essai sur les origines et la formation du duché de Normandie*, Caen, 1911.

SHETELIG (Haakon), *Les Origines des invasions des Normands* (*Bergens Museums Årbog Historisk-antikvarisk rekke*, no. 1).

—— *Préhistoire de la Norvège*, Oslo, 1926. (*Instituttet for sammenlignende Kulturforskning*, Series A, V.

STEENSTRUP (J.), 'Normandiets Historie under de syo fürste Hertuger 911–1066' (with a summary in French), *Mémoires de l'Académie royale des sciences et des lettres de Danemark*, 7th Series, Section des Lettres, V, 1, 1925.

—— *Normannerne*, 4 vols., Copenhagen, 1876–1882. (Part of vol. I has been translated into French as *Études préliminaires pour servir à l'histoire des Normands*, *Bulletin Soc. Antiquaires Normandie*, vol. V, and separately, 1881.)

VAN DER LINDEN, 'Les Normands à Louvain', *Revue historique*, CXXIV, 1917.

VOGEL (W.), *Die Normannen und das fränkische Reich bis zur Gründung der Normandie (799–911)*, Heidelberg, 1906.

—— 'Handelsverkehr, Städtewesen und Staatenbildung in Nordeuropa im früheren Mittelalter', *Zeitschrift der Gesellschaft für Erdkunde zu Berlin*, 1931.

—— 'Wik-Orte und Wikinger: eine Studie zu den Anfängen des germanischen Städtewesens', *Hansische Geschichtsblätter*, 1935.

WADSTEIN, 'Le Mot viking', *Mélanges de philologie offerts à M. Johan Vising*, 1925.

BIBLIOGRAPHY

(5) THE CONVERSION OF THE NORTH

JOHNSON (E. N.), 'Adalbert of Hamburg-Bremen', *Speculum*, 1934.
MAURER (Konrad), *Die Bekehrung des norwegischen Stammes zum Christentume*, 2 vols., Munich, 1855–6.
MOREAU (E. de), *Saint Anschaire*, Louvain, 1930.
SCHMEIDLER (B.), *Hamburg-Bremen und Nordost-Europa vom 9. bis zum 11. Jahrhundert*, Leipzig, 1918.

(6) EFFECTS OF THE SCANDINAVIAN INVASIONS

ANDERSON (Olaf S.), *The English Hundred-Names*, Lund, 1934.
BRÖNDAL (Viggo), 'Le Normand et la langue des Vikings', *Normannia*, 1930.
EKWALL (E.), 'How Long did the Scandinavian Language Survive in England?', *A Grammatical Miscellany Offered to O. Jespersen*, Copenhagen, 1930.
—— *Scandinavians and Celts in the North-West of England*, Lund, 1918 (Lunds Universitets Årsskrift, New Series, Afd. I, vol. 14).
—— 'The Scandinavian Element', in A. MAWER and F. W. STENTON, *Introduction to the Survey of English Place-Names*, I, Cambridge, 1929.
—— 'The Scandinavian Element', in H. C. DARBY, *An Historical Geography of England*, Cambridge, 1936.
EMANUELLI, 'La Colonisation normande dans le département de la Manche', *Revue de Cherbourg*, 1907 ff.
JESPERSEN (O.), *Growth and Structure of the English Language*, 7th edn., Leipzig, 1913.
JORET (C.), 'Les Noms de lieu d'origine non-romane et la colonisation germanique et scandinave en Normandie', *Congrès du millénaire de la Normandie*, Rouen, 1912, II (enlarged edn., separately published, 1913).
LINDKVIST, *Middle-English Place Names of Scandinavian Origin*, Upsala, 1912.
LOT (Ferdinand), 'De l'origine et de la signification historique des noms de lieux en-ville et en-court', *Romania*, 1933 (cf. Marc BLOCH, 'Réflexions d'un historien sur quelques travaux de toponymie', *Annales d'histoire économique*, VI, 1934).
MAWER (A.), *Problems of Place-Name Study*, Cambridge, 1929.
—— 'The Scandinavian Settlements in England as Reflected in English Place-Names', *Acta Philologica*, VII, 1932–3.
PRENTOUT (H.), 'Le Rôle de Normandie dans l'histoire', *Revue historique*, CLX, 1929.
SHETELIG (H.), *Vikingeminner i Vest Europa* (Archaeological Remains of the Vikings in Western Europe), Oslo, 1933 (*Instituttet for sammenlignende kulturforskning*, A, XVI).
SION (Jules), *Les Paysans de la Normandie orientale*, 1908.
SJÖGREN (A.), 'Le Genre des mots d'emprunt norrois en normand', *Romania*, 1928.
STENTON (F. M.), 'The Danes in England', *History*, 1920–1.
—— 'The Danes in England', *Proceedings of the British Academy*, XIII, 1927.

IV. LEGAL AND POLITICAL STRUCTURE

(1) ORIGINAL SOURCES

ACHER (Jean), 'Notes sur le droit savant au moyen âge', *Nouvelle revue historique de droit*, 1906 (Treatise on homage by J. DE BLANOT).
ATTENBOROUGH (F. L.), *The Laws of the Earliest English Kings*, Cambridge, 1922.
BRACTON, *De legibus et consuetudinibus Angliae*. Edited by G. E. WOODBINE, 2 vols., New Haven, 1932 (*Yale Historical Publications*, MS. III); edited by TWISS, 6 vols., London, 1878–83 (*Rolls Series*).
Capitularia Regum Francorum. Edited by A. BORETIUS and V. KRAUSE, Hanover, 1883–97 (*MGH*, quarto).
Formulae Merovingici et Karolini Aevi. Edited by K. ZEUMER, Hanover, 1886 (*MGH*, quarto).
FOURGOUS (J.) and BEZIN (G. de), *Les Fors de Bigorre*, Bagnères-de-Bigorre, 1901. (*Travaux sur l'histoire du droit méridional*, fasc. 1)

459

BIBLIOGRAPHY

GLANVILL, *De legibus et consuetudinibus regni Angliae*. Edited by G. E. WOODBINE, New Haven, 1932 (*Yale Historical Publications, MS*. XIII).

GULIELMUS DURANDUS, *Speculum judiciale* (written between 1271 and 1276; several times printed).

Le Conseil de Pierre de Fontaines. Edited by A. J. MARNIER, 1886.

LEHMANN (Karl), *Das Langobardische Lehnrecht (Handschriften, Textentwicklung, ältester Text und Vulgattext nebst den capitula extraordinaria)*, Göttingen, 1896.

Les Établissements de Saint-Louis. Edited by P. VIOLLET, 4 vols., 1881-6 (*Soc. de l'Histoire de France*).

LIEBERMANN (F.), *Die Gesetze der Angelsachsen*, 3 vols., Halle, 1903-16 (includes both the Customaries of the Norman period and a valuable historical index).

MUÑOZ ROMERO (T.), *Colección de fueros municipales y cartas pueblas de los reinos de Castilla, León, Corona de Aragón y Navarra*, I, Madrid, 1847.

PHILIPPE DE BEAUMANOIR, *Coutumes de Beauvaisis*. Edited by A. SALMON, 2 vols., 1899-1900 (*Collection des textes pour servir à l'étude . . . de l'histoire*).

ROBERTSON (A. J.), *The Laws of the Kings of England from Edmund to Henry I*, Cambridge, 1925.

Sachsenspiegel. Edited by K. A. ECKHARDT, Hanover, 1933 (*MGH, Fontes juris germanici*, New Series).

SECKEL (E.), 'Über neuere Editionen juristischer Schriften des Mittelalters', *Zeitschrift der Savigny Stiftung, G.A.*, 1909 (on the *Summae feudorum* of the thirteenth century).

TARDIF (Joseph), *Coutumiers de Normandie*, 2 vols., Rouen, 1881-1903.

Usatges de Barcelona, editats amb una introduccio per R. D'ABADAL I VINYALS and F. VALLS TABERNER, Barcelona, 1913 (*Textes de dret catala*, I).

(2) WORKS ON THE HISTORY OF LAW AND INSTITUTIONS

BELOW (Georg von), *Der deutsche Staat des Mittelalters*, I, Leipzig, 1914.

—— *Vom Mittelalter zur Neuzeit*, Leipzig, 1924 (*Wissenschaft und Bildung*, 198).

BESNIER (Robert), *La Coutume de Normandie: Histoire externe*, 1935.

BESTA (E.), *Fonti, legislazione e scienza giuridica della caduta dell' impero romano al, secolo XV°*, Milan, 1923 (*Storia del diritto italiano . . . di* P. GIUDICE).

BRUNNER (Heinrich), *Deutsche Rechtsgeschichte*, 2nd edn., 2 vols., Leipzig, 1926-8.

CHADWICK (H. M.), *The Origin of the English Nation*, Cambridge, 1924.

—— *Studies in Anglo-Saxon Institutions*, Cambridge, 1905.

CHÉNON (Émile), *Histoire générale du droit français public et privé*, 2 vols., 1926-9.

ESMEIN (A.), *Cours élémentaire d'histoire du droit français*, 14th edn., 1921.

FICKER (J.), *Forschungen zur Reichs- und Rechtsgeschichte Italiens*, 4 vols., Innsbruck, 1868-74.

FLACH (J.), *Les Origines de l'ancienne France*, 4 vols., 1886-1917.

FUSTEL DE COULANGES, *Histoire des institutions politiques de l'ancienne France*, 6 vols. 1888-92.

GAMA-BARROS (H. da), *Historia de la administraçao publica em Portugal nos seculos XII a XV*, 2 vols., Lisbon, 1885-96 (also contains much information on Leon and Castile).

HASKINS (C. H.), *Norman Institutions*, Cambridge (Mass.), 1918 (*Harvard Historical Studies*, XXIV).

HOLDSWORTH (W. S.), *A History of English Law*, vols. I-III, 3rd edn., London, 1923.

JAMISON (E.), 'The Norman Administration of Apulia and Capua', *Papers of the British School at Rome*, VI, 1913.

JOLLIFFE (J. E. A.), *The Constitutional History of Medieval England*, 1937.

KEUTGEN (F.), *Der deutsche Staat des Mittelalters*, Jena, 1918.

KIENER (Fritz), *Verfassungsgeschichte der Provence seit der Ostgothenherrschaft bis zur Errichtung der Konsulate (510-1200)*, Leipzig, 1900.

LEICHT (P. S.), *Ricerche sul diritto privato nei documenti preirneriani*, 2 vols., Rome, 1914-22.

LUCHAIRE (Achille), *Manuel des institutions françaises. Période des Capétiens directs*, 1892.

MAITLAND (F. W.), *Domesday Book and Beyond*, Cambridge, 1921.

460

BIBLIOGRAPHY

MAYER (Ernst), *Mittelalterliche Verfassungsgeschichte: deutsche und französische Geschichte vom 9. bis zum 14. Jahrhundert*, 2 vols., Leipzig, 1899.

—— *Historia de las instituciones sociales y políticas de España y Portugal durante los siglos V a XIV*, 2 vols., Madrid, 1925–6.

—— *Italienische Verfassungsgeschichte von der Gothenzeit zur Zunftherrschaft*, 2 vols., Leipzig, 1900.

MEYER (Walter), *Das Werk des Kanzlers Gislebert von Mons besonders als verfassungsgeschichtliche Quelle betrachtet*, Königsberg, 1888.

NIESE (Hans), *Die Gesetzgebung der normannischen Dynastie in regnum Siciliae*, Halle, 1910.

OLIVIER-MARTIN, *Histoire de la coutume de la prévôté et vicomté de Paris*, 3 vols., 1922–30.

POLLOCK (F.), *The Land Laws*, 3rd edn., 1896.

POLLOCK (F.) and MAITLAND (F. W.), *The History of English Law before the Time of Edward I*, 2 vols., Cambridge, 1898.

RIAZA (Román) and GALLO (Alfonso García), *Manual de historia del derecho español*, Madrid, 1935.

ROGÉ (Pierre), *Les Anciens Fors de Béarn*, Toulouse, 1907.

SALVIOLI (G.), *Storia del diritto italiano*, 8th edn., Turin, 1921.

SANCHEZ-ALBORNOZ (C.), 'Conferencias en la Argentina', *Anuario de historia del derecho español*, 1933.

—— 'La potestad real y los señorios en Asturias, León y Castilla', *Revista de Archivos*, 3rd series, XXXI, 1914.

SCHRÖDER (R.), *Lehrbuch der deutschen Rechtsgeschichte*, 6th edn., Leipzig, 1919–22.

SOLMI (A.), *Storia del diritto italiano*, 3rd edn., Milan, 1930.

STUBBS (William), *Constitutional History of England*, 3 vols., Oxford, 1895–7 (French translation, with additional notes, by C. PETIT-DUTAILLIS and G. LEFEBVRE, 3 vols., 1907–27).

VIOLLET (Paul), *Histoire des institutions politiques et administratives de la France*, 3 vols., 1890–1903.

VINOGRADOFF (P.), *English Society in the Eleventh Century*, Oxford, 1908.

WAITZ (G.), *Deutsche Verfassungsgeschichte*, vols. I to VI, 2nd edn., Berlin, 1880–96; vols. 7 and 8, Kiel, 1876–8.

(3) THE LEGAL MIND AND THE TEACHING OF LAW

BESTA (E.), *L'opera d'Irnerio*, Turin, 1910.

BRIE (S.), *Die Lehre vom Gewohnheitsrecht, I: Geschichtliche Grundlegung*, Breslau, 1899.

CHÉNON (E.), 'Le Droit romain à la Curia Regis', *Mélanges Fitting*, vol. I, Montpellier, 1907 (reviewed by J. ACHER, *Revue générale de droit*, XXXII, 1908).

CHIAPPELLI (L.), 'Recherches sur l'état des études de droit romain en Toscane au XIᵉ siècle', in *Nouvelle revue historique de droit*, 1896.

CONRAT (Max), *Die Quellen und Literatur des Römischen Rechts im früheren Mittelalter*, Leipzig, 1891.

FLACH (J.), *Études critiques sur l'histoire du droit romain au moyen âge*, 1890.

FOURNIER (P.), 'L'Église et le droit romain au XIIIᵉ siècle', *Nouvelle revue historique de droit*, 1890.

GARAUD (Marcel), 'Le Droit romain dans les chartes poitevines du IXᵉ au XIᵉ siècle', *Bull. de la Société des Antiquaires de l'Ouest*, 1925.

GOETZ (W.), 'Das Wiederaufleben des römischen Rechts im 12. Jahrhundert', *Archiv für Kulturgeschichte*, 1912.

MEYNIAL (E.), 'Note sur la formation de la théorie du domaine divisé . . . du XIIᵉ au XIVᵉ siècle', *Mélanges Fitting*, vol. II, Montpellier, 1908.

—— 'Remarques sur la réaction populaire contre l'invasion du droit romain en France au XIIᵉ et XIIIᵉ siècles', *Mélanges Chabaneau*, Erlangen, 1907.

OLIVIER-MARTIN (F.), 'Le Roi de France et les mauvaises coutumes', *Zeitschrift der Savigny Stiftung*, G.A., 1938.

VINOGRADOFF (P.), *Roman Law in Medieval Europe*, 2nd edn., Oxford, 1929.

WEHRLÉ (R.), *De la coutume dans le droit canonique*, 1928.

BIBLIOGRAPHY

(4) POLITICAL IDEAS

CARLYLE (R. W. and A. J.), *A History of Medieval Political Theory in the West*, vols. I to III, 1903–15.

DEMPF (Alois), *Sacrum imperium: Geschichts- und Staatsphilosophie des Mittelalters und der politischen Renaissance*, Munich, 1929.

KERN (Fritz), 'Recht und Verfassung im Mittelalter', *Historische Zeitschrift*, 1919.

V. TIES OF KINSHIP

(1) THE FAMILY AND THE VENDETTA

BRUNNER (Heinrich), 'Sippe und Wergeld in den niederdeutschen Rechten', in BRUNNER, *Abhandlungen der Rechtsgeschichte*, vol. I, Weimar, 1931 (previously *Zeitschrift der, Savigny Stiftung, G.A.*, III).

CATTIER (F.), 'La Guerre privée dans le comté de Hainaut', *Annales de la Faculté de philosophie de Bruxelles*, I, 1889–90.

DUBOIS (Pierre), *Les asseurements au XIIIᵉ siècle dans nos villes de Nord*, 1900.

ESPINAS (G.), 'Les Guerres familiales dans la commune de Douai aux XIIᵉ et XIIIᵉ siècles', *Nouvelle revue historique de droit*, 1900.

FRAUENSTÄDT (Paul), *Blutrache und Todtschlagsühne im deutschen Mittelalter*, Leipzig, 1881.

HINOJOSA (Eduardo de), 'Das germanische Element im spanischen Rechte', *Zeitschrift der Savigny Stiftung, G.A.*, 1910.

HIS (R.), 'Gelobter und gebotener Friede im deutschen Mittelalter', *Zeitschrift der Savigny-Stiftung, G.A.*, 1912.

PETIT-DUTAILLIS (C.), *Documents nouveaux sur les mœurs populaires et le droit de vengeance dans les Pays-Bas au XVᵉ siècle*, 1908 (with bibliography).

PHILLPOTTS (Bertha Surtees), *Kindred and Clan in the Middle Ages and After: A Study in the Sociology of the Teutonic Races*, Cambridge, 1913 (*Cambridge Archaeological and Ethnological Series*).

ROEDER (Fritz), *Die Familie bei den Angelsachsen*, Part I, Halle, 1899 (*Studien zur englischen Philologie*, IV).

VALAT (G.), *Poursuite privée et composition pécuniaire dans l'ancienne Bourgogne*, Dijon, 1907.

VAN KEMPEN (Georges), *De la composition pour homicide d'après la Loi Salique. Son maintien dans les Coutumes de Saint-Omer jusqu'à la fin du XVIᵉ siècle*, Saint-Omer, 1902.

WILKE (Carl), *Das Friedegebot: ein Beitrag zur Geschichte des deutschen Strafrechts*, Heidelberg, 1911 (*Deutschrechtliche Beiträge*, VI, 4).

YVER (J.), *L'Interdiction de la guerre privée dans le très ancien droit normand* (*Extrait des travaux de la semaine d'histoire du droit normand*), Caen, 1928.

(2) ECONOMIC SOLIDARITY

BRUNNER (H.), 'Der Totenteil in germanischen Rechten', in BRUNNER, *Abhandlungen zur Rechtsgeschichte*, II, Weimar, 1937 (previously *Zeitschrift der Savigny Stiftung, G.A.*, XIX).

CAILLEMER (Robert), 'Les Idées coutumières et la renaissance du droit romain dans le Sud-Est de la France: I, "Laudatio" des héritiers', in *Essays in Legal History*, edited by P. VINOGRADOFF, Oxford, 1913.

—— 'Le Retrait lignager dans le droit provençal', in *Studi giuridici in onore di Carlo Fadda*, IV, Naples, 1906.

FALLETTI (Louis), *Le Retrait lignager en droit coutumier français*, 1923.

FORMENTINI (Ubaldo), 'Sulle origini e sulla costituzione d'un grande gentilizio feodale', *Atti della Società ligure di storia patria*, LIII, 1926.

GÉNESTAL (Robert), 'Le Retrait lignager en droit normand', *Travaux de la semaine d'histoire du droit normand . . . 1923*, Caen, 1925.

LAPLANCHE (Jean de), *La Réserve coutumière dans l'ancien droit français*, 1925.

BIBLIOGRAPHY

PLUCKNETT (Theodore F. T.), 'Bookland and Folkland', *Economic History Review*, VI, 1935–6 (with bibliography).

PORÉE (Charles), 'Les Statuts de la communauté des seigneurs pariers de La Garde-Guérin (1238–1313)', in *Bibliothèque de l'École des Chartes*, 1907, and *Études historiques sur le Gévaudan*, 1919.

SCHULTZE (A.), 'Augustin und der Seelteil des germanischen Erbrechts', *Abhandlungen der sächsischen Akademie der Wissenschaften, Phil-hist. Kl.*, 28.

TAMASSIO (G.), 'Il diritto di prelazione e l'espropriazione forzata negli statuti dei comuni italiani', *Archivio giuridico*, 1885.

VI. FEUDAL INSTITUTIONS PROPER

(1) FEUDALISM IN GENERAL: FRANKISH ORIGINS

BLOCH (Marc), 'Feudalism (European)', in *Encyclopaedia of the Social Sciences*, VI, 1931.

BOURGEOIS (Emile), *Le Capitulaire de Kiersy-sur-Oise: étude sur l'état et le régime politique de la société carolingienne à la fin du IX⁰ siècle d'après la législation de Charles le Chauve*, 1885.

CALMETTE (J.), *La Société féodale*, 1923 (*Collection A. Colin*).

DOPSCH (A.), 'Benefizialwesen und Feudalität', *Mitteilungen des österreichischen Instituts für Geschichtsforschung*, 1932.

—— 'Die Leudes und das Lehnwesen', *ibid.*, 1926.

—— *Die Wirtschaftsentwicklung der Karolingerzeit*, 2nd edn., Vienna, 1921–2.

DUMAS (Auguste), 'Le Serment de fidélité et la conception du pouvoir du Iᵉʳ au IXᵉ siècle', *Revue historique de droit*, 1931; cf. LOT (F.), 'Le Serment de fidélité à l'époque franque', *Revue belge de philologie*, 1933; DUMAS (A.), 'Le Serment de fidélité à l'époque franque', *ibid.*, 1935.

GANSHOF (F. L.), 'Note sur les origines de l'union du bénéfice avec la vassalité', *Études d'histoire dédiées à la mémoire de Henri Pirenne*, Brussels, 1937.

GUILHIERMOZ (A.), *Essai sur les origines de la noblesse en France au moyen âge*, 1902.

HALPHEN (L.), 'À propos du capitulaire de Quierzy', *Revue historique*, CVI, 1911.

KIENAST (W.), *Die deutschen Fürsten im Dienste der Westmächte bis zum Tode Philipps des Schönen von Frankreich*, 2 vols., Utrecht, 1924–31.

KRAWINKEL (H.), *Zur Entstehung des Lehnwesens*, Weimar, 1936.

LESNE (E.), *Histoire de la propriété ecclésiastique en France*, 4 vols., Lille, 1910–36.

MAYER (Ernst), 'Die Entstehung der Vasallität und des Lehnwesens', *Festgabe für R. Sohm*, Munich, 1914.

MENZEL (Viktor), *Die Entstehung des Lehnwesens*, Berlin, 1890.

MITTEIS (H.), *Lehnrecht und Staatsgewalt*, Weimar, 1933.

—— 'Politische Prozesse des früheren Mittelalters in Deutschland und Frankreich', *Sitzungsberichte der Heidelberger Akademie der Wissenschaften*, 1926.

ROTH (P.), *Feudalität und Unterthanenverband*, Weimar, 1863.

SOCIÉTÉ JEAN BODIN, *Les Liens de vassalité et les immunités*, Brussels, 1936 (and *Revue de l'Institut de Sociologie*, 1936).

VINOGRADOFF (P.), 'Foundations of Society' and 'Feudalism' in *Cambridge Medieval History*, 1911–36, vols. II and III.

WAITZ (G.), 'Die Anfänge des Lehnwesens', in WAITZ, *Gesammelte Abhandlungen*, I, Göttingen, 1896.

(2) STUDIES OF FEUDALISM BY COUNTRIES AND REGIONS

ADAMS (G. B.), 'Anglo-Saxon Feudalism', *American Historical Review*, VII, 1901–2.

BESELER (Georg), *System des gemeinen deutschen Privatrechts*, vol. II, Berlin, 1885.

BROOKE (Z. N.), 'Pope Gregory VII's Demand of Fealty from William the Conqueror', *English Historical Review*, XXVI, 1911.

BRUTAILS (J.-A.), 'Les Fiefs du roi et les alleux en Guienne', *Annales du Midi*, 1917.

CAPASSO (B.), 'Sul catalogo dei feudi e dei feudatari delle provincie napoletane sotto la dominazione normanna', *Atti della reale Accademia di archeologia*, IV, 1868–9.

BIBLIOGRAPHY

CECI (C.), 'Normanni di Inghilterra e Normanni d'Italia', *Archivio scientifico del Reale Istituto superiore di Scienze Economiche . . . di Bari*, VII, 1932–3.

CHEW (H. M.), *The English Ecclesiastical Tenants-in-Chief and Knight Service, especially in the Thirteenth and Fourteenth Century*, Oxford, 1932.

DEL GIUDICE (P.) and CALISSE (C.), 'Feudo' in *Il digesto italiano*, XI, 2, 1892–8.

DILLAY (Madeleine), 'Le "Service" annuel en deniers des fiefs de la région angevine', *Mélanges Paul Fournier*, 1929.

DOUGLAS (D. C.), *Feudal Documents from the Abbey of Bury St Edmunds*, London, 1932 (*Records of the Social and Economic History of England*, VIII); important introduction.

ERDMANN (Karl), 'Das Papsttum und Portugal im ersten Jahrhunderte der portugiesischen Geschichte', *Abhandlungen der Preussischen Akademie, Phil.-hist. Kl.*, 1938.

ESPINAY (G. d'), 'La Féodalité et le droit civil français', Saumur, 1862 (*Rec. de l'Académie de Législation de Toulouse*, Livraison supplémentaire).

HOMEYER (C. G.), 'System des Lehnrechts der sächsischen Rechtsbücher' in *Sachsenspiegel*, ed. HOMEYER, vol. II, 2, Berlin, 1844.

JOLLIFFE (J. E. A.), 'Northumbrian Institutions', *English Historical Review*, XLI, 1926.

JORDAN (Karl), 'Das Eindringen des Lehnwesens in das Rechtsleben der römischen Kurie', *Archiv für Urkundenforschung*, 1931.

KEHR (P.), 'Die Belehnungen der süditalienischen Normannenfürsten durch die Päpste', *Abhandlungen der preussischen Akademie, Phil.-hist. Kl.*, 1934.

—— 'Das Papsttum und der katalanische Prinzipat bis zur Vereinigung mit Aragon', *ibid.*, 1926.

—— 'Das Papsttum und die Königreiche Navarra und Aragon bis zur Mitte des XII. Jahrhunderts', *ibid.*, 1928.

—— 'Wie und wann wurde das Reich Aragon ein Lehen der römischen Kirche', *Sitzungsberichte der preussischen Akademie, Phil.-hist. Kl.*, 1928.

KÖLMEL (W.), *Rom und der Kirchenstaat im 10. und 11. Jahrhundert bis in die Anfänge der Reform*, Berlin, 1935 (*Abhandlungen zur mittleren und neueren Geschichte*, 78).

LAGOUELLE (Henri), *Essai sur la conception féodale de la propriété foncière dans le très ancien droit normand*, 1902.

LA MONTE (J. L.), *Feudal Monarchy in the Latin Kingdom of Jerusalem*, Cambridge (Mass.), 1932 (*Monographs of the Medieval Academy*, 4).

LIPPERT (Waldemar), *Die deutschen Lehnsbücher*, Leipzig, 1903.

MACKECHNIE (W. S.), *Magna Carta: A Commentary*, 2nd edn., Glasgow, 1914.

MENENDEZ PIDAL, *La España del Cid*, 2 vols., Madrid, 1929; English trans. (abridged), *The Cid and His Spain*, 1934.

MONTI (G. M.), 'Ancora sulla feudalità e i grandi domani feudali del regno di Sicilia', *Rivista di storia del diritto italiano*, IV, 1921.

MUNOZ-ROMERO (T.), 'Del estado de las personas en los reinos de Asturias y León', *Revista de Archivos*, 1883.

PAZ (Ramon), 'Un nuevo feudo castellano', *Anuario de historia de derecho español*, 1928.

RABASSE (Maurice), *Du régime des fiefs en Normandie au moyen âge*, 1905.

RICHARDOT (Hubert), 'Le Fief roturier à Toulouse aux XIIe et XIIIe siècles', *Revue historique de droit français*, 1935.

ROUND (J. H.), *Feudal England*, London, 1907.

—— 'Military Tenure before the Conquest', *English Historical Review*, XII, 1897.

SANCHEZ-ALBORNOZ (C.), 'Las behetrias' and 'Muchas páginas más sobre las behetrias', *ibid.*, 1924 and 1927.

—— 'Un feudo castellano del XIII', *ibid.*, 1926.

SECRÉTAN (E.), 'De la féodalité en Espagne', *Revue historique de droit*, 1863.

SCHNEIDER (F.), *Die Entstehung von Burg und Landgemeinde in Italien*, Berlin, 1924 (*Abhandlungen zur mittleren und neueren Geschichte*, 68).

STENTON (F. M.), 'The Changing Feudalism of the Middle Ages', *History*, XIX, 1934–5.

—— *The First Century of English Feudalism (1066–1166)*, Oxford, 1932.

STRAYER (J. R.), 'Knight-Service in Normandy', in *Anniversary Essays by Students of Charles H. Haskins*, 1929.

BIBLIOGRAPHY

Tomassetti (G.), 'Feudalismo romano', *Rivista internazionale di scienze sociale*, V, 1894.

Wunderlich (Erich), *Aribert von Antemiano, Erzbischof von Mailand*, Halle, 1914.

Yver (Jean), *Les Contrats dans le très ancien droit normand*, 1926.

(3) 'COMPANIONAGE', VASSALAGE, AND HOMAGE

Bloch (Marc), 'Les Formes de la rupture de l'hommage dans l'ancien droit féodal', *Nouvelle revue historique de droit*, 1912.

Brunner (H.), 'Zur Geschichte des fränkischen Gefolgswesens', in *Forschungen zur Geschichte des d. und fr. Rechtes*, Stuttgart, 1894 (previously *Zeitschrift der Savigny Stiftung, G.A.*, IX).

Calmette (Joseph), 'Le "Comitatus" germanique et la vassalité', *Nouvelle revue historique de droit*, 1904.

Chénon (E.), 'Le Rôle juridique de l'osculum dans l'ancien droit français', *Mémoires de la Société nationale des Antiquaires*, 8th series, VI, 1919-23.

Doublier (Othmar), 'Formalakte beim Eintritt in die altnorwegische Gefolgschaft' in *Mitteilungen des Instituts für österreichische Geschichtsforschung*, Ergänzungsband VI, 1901.

Ehrenberg (V.), *Commendation und Huldigung nach fränkischem Recht*, 1877.

Ehrismann (G.), 'Die Wörter für "Herr" im Althochdeutschen', *Zeitschrift für deutsche Wortforschung*, VII, 1905-6.

Grosse (Robert), *Römische Militärgeschichte von Gallienus bis zum Beginn der byzantinischen Themenverfassung*, Berlin, 1920.

His (Rudolf), 'Todschlagsühne und Mannschaft', in *Festgabe für K. Güterbock*, Berlin, 1910.

Jud (J.), 'Zur Geschichte und Herkunft von frz. "dru" ', *Archivum romanicum*, 1926.

Larson (L. M.), *The King's Household in England before the Conquest*, Madison, 1904.

Lécrivain (C.), 'Les Soldats privés au Bas-Empire', *Mélanges d'archéologie et d'histoire*, 1890.

Leicht (P. S.), 'Gasindi e vassalli', *Rendiconti della reale Accademia nazionale dei Lincei, Scienze morali*, 6th series, III, 1927.

Little (A. G.), 'Gesiths and thegns', *English Historical Review*, IV, 1887.

Meyer-Lübke (W.), 'Senyor, "Herr" ', *Wörter und Sachen*, VIII, 1923.

Mirot (Léon), 'Les Ordonnances de Charles VII relatives à la prestation des hommages', *Mémoires de la Société pour l'Histoire du droit et des institutions des anciens pays bourguignons*, fasc. 2, 1935.

Müller (Martin), *Minne und Dienst in der altfranzösischen Lyrik*, Marburg, 1907.

Myrick (Arthur B.), 'Feudal Terminology in Medieval Religious Poetry', *Romanic Review*, XI, 1920.

Petot (Pierre), 'La Capacité testimonial du vassal', *Revue historique de droit*, 1931.

Platon (G.), 'L'Hommage féodal comme moyen de contracter des obligations privées', *Revue générale de droit*, XXVI, 1902.

Ramos y Loscertales, 'La "devotio iberica" ', *Anuario de Historia del derecho español*, 1924.

Richter (Elise), 'Senior, Sire', *Wörter und Sachen*, XII, 1929.

Schubert (Carl), *Der Pflegesohn im französischen Heldenepos*, Marburg, 1906.

Seeck (Otto), 'Buccellarii', in Pauly-Wissowa, *Realencyclopädie der klassischen Altertumswissenschaft*, III, 1899.

—— 'Das deutsche Gefolgswesen auf römischem Boden', *Zeitschrift der Savigny Stiftung, G.A.*, 1896.

Waitz (G.), 'Über die Anfänge der Vasallität', in Waitz, *Gesammelte Abhandlungen*, I, Göttingen, 1896.

Wechssler (Eduard), 'Frauendienst und Vasallität', *Zeitschrift für französische Sprache*, XXIV, 1902.

—— *Das Kulturproblem des Minnesangs*, I, Halle, 1907.

Windisch, 'Vassus und vassallus', *Berichte über die Verhandlungen der königlichen sächsischen Gesellschaft der Wissenschaften*, 1892.

BIBLIOGRAPHY

(4) 'PRECARIA', 'BENEFIT', FIEF, AND ALLOD

BLOCH (Marc), 'Un Problème d'histoire comparée: la ministérialité en France et en Allemagne', *Revue historique de droit*, 1928.

BONDROIT, 'Les "Precariae verbo regis" devant le concile de Leptinnes', *Revue d'histoire ecclésiastique*, 1900.

BRUNNER (H.), 'Die Landschenkungen der Merowinger und Agilolfinger', *Forschungen zur Geschichte des d. und fr. Rechtes*, Stuttgart, 1877 (previously *Sitzungsberichte der preussischen Akademie, Phil.-hist. Kl.*, 1885).

CHÉNON (E.), *Étude sur l'histoire des alleux*, 1888.

CLOTET (L.), 'Le Bénéfice sous les deux premières races', *Comptes rendus du Congrès scientifique international des catholiques*, 1891.

GIERKE (O.), 'Allod', in *Beiträge zum Wörterbuch der deutschen Rechtssprache*, Weimar, 1908.

GLADISS (D. von), 'Die Schenkungen der deutschen Könige zu privatem Eigen', *Archiv für Geschichte des Mittelalters*, 1937.

JOLLIFFE (J. E. A.), 'Alod and fee', *Cambridge Historical Journal*, 1937.

KERN (H.), 'Feodum, fief', *Mémoires de la Société Linguistique de Paris*, II, 1872.

KRAWINKEL (H.), *Feudum*, Weimar, 1938 (*Forschungen zum deutschen Recht*, III, 2).

—— *Untersuchungen zum fränkischen Benefizialrecht*, Weimar, 1936 (*Forsehungen zum deutschen Recht*, II, 2).

LESNE (E.), 'Les Bénéficiers de Saint-Germain des Près au temps de l'abbé Irminon', *Revue Mabillon*, 1922.

—— 'Les Diverses Acceptions du mot "beneficium" du VIIIᵉ au IXᵉ siècle', *Revue historique de droit*, 1921.

LOT (Ferdinand), 'Origine et nature du bénéfice', *Anuario de historia del derecho español*, 1933.

PÖSCHL (A.), 'Die Entstehung des geistlichen Beneficiums', *Archiv für katholisches Kirchenrecht*, 1926.

ROTH (P.), *Geschichte des Benefizialwesens von den ältesten Zeiten bis ins zehnte Jahrhundert*, Erlangen, 1850.

SCHÄFER (D.), 'Honor . . . im mittelalterlichen Latein', *Sitzungsberichte der preussischen Akademie, Phil.-hist. Kl.*, 1921.

STUTZ (U.), 'Lehen und Pfründe', *Zeitschrift der Savigny Stiftung, G.A.*, 1899.

WIART (René), *Le Régime des terres du fisc sous le Bas-Empire, Essai sur la precaria*, 1894.

(5) THE LAW OF THE FIEF

ACHER (Jean), 'Les Archaïsmes apparents dans la Chanson de "Raoul de Cambrai"'', *Revue des langues romanes*, 1907.

ARBOIS DE JUBAINVILLE, D', 'Recherches sur la minorité et ses effets dans le droit féodal français', *Bibliothèque de l'École des Chartes*, 1851 and 1852.

BELLETTE (E.), *La Succession aux fiefs dans les coutumes flamandes*, 1927.

BLUM (Edgar), 'La Commise féodale', *Tijdschrift voor Rechtsgeschiedenis*, IV, 1922–3.

ERMOLAEF, *Die Sonderstellung der Frau im französischen Lehnrecht*, Ostermundingen, 1930.

GÉNESTAL (R.), 'La Formation du droit d'aînesse dans la coutume de Normandie', *Normannia*, 1928.

—— *Le Parage normand*, Caen, 1911 (*Bibliothèque d'histoire du droit normand*, 2nd series, I, 2).

—— *Études de droit privé normand. I. La tutelle*, 1930 (*Bibliothèque d'histoire du droit normand*, 2nd series, III).

KLATT (Kurt), *Das Heergewäte*, Heidelberg, 1908 (*Deutschrechtliche Beiträge*, II, fasc. 2).

MEYNIAL (E.), 'Les Particularités des successions féodales dans les Assises de Jérusalem', *Nouvelle Revue historique de droit*, 1892.

MITTEIS (Heinrich), 'Zur Geschichte der Lehnsvormundschaft', *Alfred Schulze Festschrift*, Weimar, 1934.

BIBLIOGRAPHY

SCHULZE (H. J. F.), *Das Recht der Erstgeburt in den deutschen Fürstenhäusern und seine Bedeutung für die deutsche Staatsentwicklung*, Leipzig, 1851.

STUTZ (U.), ' "Römerwergeld" und "Herrenfall" ', *Abhandlungen der preussischen Akademie, Phil.-hist. Kl.*, 1934.

(6) PLURALITY OF LORDS AND LIEGE HOMAGE

BAIST (G.), 'Lige, liege', *Zeitschrift für romanische Philologie*, XXVIII, 1904, p. 112.

BEAUDOIN (A.) 'Homme lige', *Nouvelle Revue historique de droit*, VII, 1883.

BLOOMFIELD, 'Salic "Litus" ', *Studies in Honor of H. Collitz*, Baltimore, 1930.

BRÜCH (Joseph), 'Zu Meyer-Lübke's Etymologischem Wörterbuch', *Zeitschrift für romanische Philologie*, XXXVIII, 1917, pp. 701-2.

GANSHOF (F. L.), 'Depuis quand a-t-on pu en France être vassal de plusieurs seigneurs?', *Mélanges Paul Fournier*, 1929 (review by W. KIENAST, *Historische Zeitschrift*, CXLI, 1929-30).

PIRENNE (Henri), 'Qu-est-ce qu'un homme lige?', *Académie royale de Belgique, Bulletin de la classe des lettres*, 1909.

PÖHLMANN (Carl), *Das ligische Lehensverhältnis*, Heidelberg, 1931.

ZEGLIN (Dorothea), *Der 'homo ligius' und die französische Ministerialität*, Leipzig, 1917 (*Leipziger Historische Abhandlungen*, XXXIX).

VII. FEUDAL WARFARE

(1) THE ART OF WAR

BALTZER (Martin), *Zur Geschichte des deutschen Kriegswesens in der Zeit von den letzten Karolingern bis auf Kaiser Friedrich II*, Leipzig, 1877.

BOUTARIC (Edgar), *Institutions militaires de la France*, 1863.

DELBRÜCK (Hans), *Geschichte der Kriegskunst im Rahmen der politischen Geschichte*, III, Berlin, 1907.

DELPECH (H.), *La Tactique au XIIIᵉ siècle*, 2 vols., 1886.

FRAUENHOLZ (Eugen von), *Entwicklungsgeschichte des deutschen Heerwesens*, I, *Das Heerwesen der germanischen Frühzeit, des Frankenreiches und des ritterlichen Zeitalters*, Munich, 1935.

KÖHLER (G.), *Entwicklung des Kriegswesens und der Kriegsführung in der Ritterzeit*, 3 vols., Breslau, 1886-93.

OMAN (Charles), *A History of the Art of War: The Middle Ages from the Fourth to the Fourteenth Century*, 2nd edn., 1924.

(2) CAVALRY TACTICS AND EQUIPMENT

BACH (Volkmar), *Die Verteidigungswaffen in den altfranzösischen Artus- und Abenteuerroman*, Marburg, 1887 (*Ausgabe und Abhandlungen aus dem Gebiete der roman. Philologie*, 70).

BRUNNER (Heinrich), 'Der Reiterdienst und die Anfänge des Lehnwesens', *Forschungen zum d. und fr. Recht*, Stuttgart, 1874 (previously *Zeitschrift der Savigny Stiftung*, G.A., VIII).

DEMAY (G.), *Le Costume au moyen âge d'après les sceaux*, 1880.

GESSLER (E. A.), *Die Trutzwaffen der Karolingerzeit vom VIII. bis zum XI. Jahrhundert*, Basel, 1908.

GIESSE (W.), 'Waffen nach den provenzialischen Epen und Chroniken des XII. und XIII. Jahrhunderts', *Zeitschrift für romanische Philologie*, LII, 1932.

LEFEBVRE DES NOËTTES, *L'Attelage et le cheval de selle à travers les âges*, 2 vols., 1931 (cf. Marc Bloch, 'Les Inventions médiévales', *Annales d'histoire économique*, 1935).

MANGOLDT-GAUDLITZ (Hans von), *Die Reiterei in den germanischen und fränkischen Heeren bis zum Ausgang der deutschen Karolinger*, Berlin, 1922 (*Arbeiten zur deutschen Rechts- und Verfassungsgeschichte*, IV).

ROLOFF (Gustav), 'Die Umwandlung des fränkischen Heeres von Chlodwig bis Karl den Grossen', *Neue Jahrbücher für das klassische Altertum*, IX, 1902.

467

BIBLIOGRAPHY

Sanchez-Albornoz (C.), 'Los Arabes y los origines del feudalismo', *Anuario de historia del derecho español*, 1929; 'Les Arabes et les origines de la féodalité', *Revue historique de droit*, 1933.

—— 'La caballeria visigoda' in *Wirtschaft und Kultur: Festschrift zum 70. Geburtstag von A. Dopsch*, Vienna, 1938.

Schirling (V.), *Die Verteidigungswaffen im altfranzösischen Epos*, Marburg, 1887 (*Ausgabe und Abhandlungen aus dem Gebiete der roman. Philologie*, 69).

Schwietering (Julius), 'Zur Geschichte vom Speer und Schwert im 12. Jahrhundert', *Mitteilungen aus dem Museum für Hamburgische Geschichte*, 3 (Suppl. 8, Part 2, of *Jahrbuch der Hamburgischen wissenschaftlichen Anstalten*, XXIX, 1911).

Sternberg (A.), *Die Angriffswaffen im altfranzösischen Epos*, Marburg, 1886 (*Ausgabe und Abhandlungen aus dem Gebiete der roman. Philologie*, 48).

(3) THE MILITARY OBLIGATION

Fehr (Hans), 'Landfolge und Gerichtsfolge im fränkischen Recht', *Festgabe für R. Sohm*, Munich, 1914.

Noyes (A. G.), *The Military Obligation in Mediaeval England*, Columbus (Ohio), 1931.

Rosenhagen (Gustav), *Zur Geschichte der Reichsheerfahrt von Heinrich VI. bis Rudolf von Habsburg*, Meissen, 1885.

Schmitthenner (Paul), 'Lehnkriegswesen und Söldnertum im abendländischen Imperium des Mittelalters', *Historische Zeitschrift*, 1934.

Weiland (L.), 'Die Reichsheerfahrt von Heinrich V. bis Heinrich VI., nach ihrer staatsrechtlichen Seite', *Forschungen zur deutschen Geschichte*, VII, 1867.

(4) CASTLES

Armitage (E. S.), *Early Norman Castles of the British Isles*, 1913 (cf. Round, *English Historical Review*, 1912, p. 544).

Coulin (Alexander), *Befestigungshoheit und Befestigungsrecht*, Leipzig, 1911.

Desmarez (G.), 'Fortifications de la frontière du Hainaut et du Brabant au XIIᵉ siècle', *Annales de la Société royale d'archéologie de Bruxelles*, 1914.

Enlart (C.), *Manuel d'archéologie française, Deuxième partie. II. Architecture militaire et navale*, 1932.

Painter (Sidney), 'English Castles in the Middle Ages', *Speculum*, 1935.

Round (J. H.), 'Castle-guard', *Archaeological Journal*, LIX, 1902.

Schrader (Erich), *Das Befestigungsrecht in Deutschland*, Göttingen, 1909.

Schuchardt (C.), *Die Burg im Wandel der Geschichte*, Potsdam, 1931.

Thompson (A. Hamilton), *Military Architecture in England During the Middle Ages*, Oxford, 1912.

VIII. TIES OF DEPENDENCE AMONG THE LOWER ORDERS OF SOCIETY

(Cf. Part VI, sec. 2, p. 464: Sanchez-Albornoz, 'Las behetrias . . .')

Below (G. von), *Geschichte der deutschen Landwirtschaft des Mittelalters*, Jena, 1937.

Bloch (Marc), *Les Caractères originaux de l'histoire rurale française*, 1931.

—— 'Les "Colliberti", étude sur la formation de la classe servile', *Revue historique*, CLVII, 1928.

—— 'De la cour royale à la cour de Rome: le procès des serfs de Rosny-sous-Bois', *Studi di storia e diritto in onore di E. Besta*, Milan, 1938.

—— 'Liberté et servitude personnelles au moyen âge', *Anuario de historia del derecho español*, 1933.

—— 'Les Transformations du servage', *Mélanges d'histoire du moyen âge offerts à M. F. Lot*, 1925.

Boeren (P.-C.), *Étude sur les tributaires d'église dans le comté de Flandre du IXᵉ au XIVᵉ siècle*, Amsterdam, 1936 (*Uitgaven van het Instituut voor middeleeuwsche Geschiedenis der . . . Universitet te Nijmegen*, 3).

BIBLIOGRAPHY

CATO (G.), *Beiträge zur älteren deutschen Wirtschafts- und Verfassungsgeschichte*, Leipzig, 1905.

—— *Neue Beiträge zur deutschen Wirtschafts- und Verfassungsgeschichte*, Leipzig, 1911.

COULTON (G. G.), *The Medieval Village*, Cambridge, 1925.

HINOJOSA (E. de), *El regimen señorial y la cuestion agraria en Cataluña*, Madrid, 1905.

KELLER (Robert von), *Freiheitsgarantien für Person und Eigentum im Mittelalter*, Heidelberg, 1933 (*Deutschrechtliche Beiträge*, XIV, 1).

KIELMEYER (O. A.), *Die Dorfbefreiung auf deutschem Sprachgebiet*, Bonn, 1931.

LUZZATO (G.), *I servi nelle grande proprietà ecclesiastiche italiane nei secoli IX e X*, Pisa, 1910.

MINNIGERODE (H. von), 'Wachzinsrecht', *Vierteljahrschrift für Sozial- und Wirtschaftsgeschichte*, 1916.

PERRIN (C.-Edmond), *Essai sur la fortune immobilière de l'abbaye alsacienne de Marmoutier*, Strasbourg, 1935.

—— *Recherches sur la seigneurie rurale en Lorraine d'après les plus anciens censiers*, Strasbourg, 1935.

PETIT (A.), *Coliberti ou culverts: essai d'interprétation des textes qui les concernent, IXᵉ-XIIᵉ siècles*), Limoges, 1926.

—— *Coliberti ou culverts: réponse à diverses objections*, Limoges, 1930.

PETOT (P.), 'L'Hommage servile', *Revue historique de droit*, 1927 (cf. the same writer's contribution to Société Jean Bodin, *Le Servage*, see below).

—— 'La Commendise personnelle', *Mélanges Paul Fournier*, 1929 (cf. Marc Bloch, *Annales d'histoire économique*, 1931, pp. 234 ff.).

PIRENNE (Henri), 'Liberté et propriété en Flandre du VIIᵉ au IXᵉ siècle', *Bulletin Académie royale de Belgique, Cl. Lettres*, 1911.

PUIGARNAU (Jaime M. Mans), *Las clases serviles bajo la monarquia visigoda y en los estados cristianos de la reconquista española*, Barcelona, 1928.

SÉE (Henri), *Les Classes rurales et le régime domanial en France au moyen-âge*, 1901.

SEELIGER (G.), 'Die soziale und politische Bedeutung der Grundherrschaft im früheren Mittelalter', *Abhandlungen der sächsischen Gesellschaft der Wissenschaften*, XX, 1903.

SOCIÉTÉ JEAN BODIN, *Le Servage*, Brussels, 1937 (and *Revue de l'Institut de Sociologie*, 1937).

—— *La Tenure*, Brussels, 1938.

THIBAULT (Fabien), 'La Condition des personnes en France du IXᵉ siècle au mouvement communal', *Revue historique de droit*, 1933.

VACCARI (P.), 'L'affrancazione dei servi della gleba nell' Emilia e nella Toscana', Bologna, 1925 (*Reale Accademia dei Lincei. Commissione per gli atti delle assemblee costituzionali*).

VANDERKINDERE, 'Liberté et propriété en Flandre du IXᵉ au XIIᵉ siècle', *Bulletin Académie royale de Belgique, Cl. Lettres*, 1906.

VERRIEST (L.), 'Le Servage dans le comté de Hainaut', *Académie royale de Belgique, Cl. Lettres*, Mémoires in-8º, 2nd series, VI, 1910.

VINOGRADOFF (P.), *Villeinage in England*, Oxford, 1892.

WELLER (K.), 'Die freien Bauern in Schwaben', *Zeitschrift der Savigny Stiftung, G.A.*, 1934.

—— 'Die Frage der Freibauern', *ibid.*

IX. COUNTRIES WITHOUT FEUDALISM

(1) SARDINIA

BESTA (E.), *La Sardegna medioevale*, 2 vols., Palermo, 1909.

RASPI (R. C.), *Le classi sociali nella Sardegna medioevale*, Cagliari, 1938.

SOLMI (A.), *Studi storici sulle istituzione della Sardegna nel medio evo*, Cagliari, 1917.

(2) FRISIA AND DITHMARSCHEN

GOSSE (J. H.), 'De Friesche Hoofdeling', *Mededeelingen der Kl. Akademie van Wetenschappen, Afd. Letterk.*, 1933.

BIBLIOGRAPHY

KÖHLER (Johannes), *Die Struktur der Dithmarscher Geschlechter*, Heide, 1915.
MARTEN (G.) and MÄCKELMANN (K.), *Dithmarschen*, Heide, 1927.
SIEBS (B. E.), *Grundlagen und Aufbau der altfriesischen Verfassung*, Breslau, 1933 (*Untersuchungen zur deutschen Staats- und Rechtsgeschichte*, 144).

X. SOCIAL CLASSES IN GENERAL AND THE NOBILITY

(1) ORIGINS AND HISTORY

BLOCH (Marc), 'Sur le passé de la noblesse française; quelques jalons de recherche', *Annales d'histoire économique et sociale*, 1936.
DENHOLM-YOUNG (N.), 'En remontant le passé de l'aristocratie anglaise: le moyen-âge', *ibid.*, 1937.
DESBROUSSES (X.), *Condition personnelle de la noblesse au moyen-âge*, Bordeaux, 1901.
DU CANGE, 'Des chevaliers bannerets. Des gentilshommes de nom et d'armes' (*Dissertations sur l'histoire de saint Louis*, IX and X), in *Glossarium*, ed. Henschel, vol. VII.
DUNGERN (O. VON), 'Comes, liber, nobilis in Urkunden des 11. bis 13. Jahrhundert', *Archiv für Urkundenforschung*, 1932.
—— *Der Herrenstand im Mittelalter*, I. Papiermühle, 1908.
—— *Die Entstehung der Landeshoheit in Österreich*, Vienna, 1930.
ERNST (Viktor), *Die Entstehung des niederen Adels*, Stuttgart, 1916.
—— *Mittelfreie, ein Beitrag zur schwäbischen Standesgeschichte*, 1920.
FEHR (Hans), 'Das Waffenrecht der Bauern im Mittelalter', *Zeitschrift der Savigny Stiftung, G.A.*, 1914 and 1917.
FICKER (Julius), *Vom Heerschilde*, Innsbruck, 1862.
FORST-BATTAGLIA (O.), *Vom Herrenstande*, Leipzig, 1916.
FRENSDORFF (F.), 'Die Lehnsfähigkeit der Bürger', *Nachrichten der königlichen Gesellschaft der Wissenschaften zu Göttingen, Phil.-hist. K.*, 1894.
GARCÍA RIVES (A.), 'Clases sociales en León y Castilla (Siglos X–XIII)', *Revista de Archivos*, XLI and XLII, 1921 and 1922.
GUILHIERMOZ (P.), *Essai sur les origines de la noblesse en France au moyen-âge*, 1902.
HECK (Philipp), *Beiträge zur Geschichte der Stände im Mittelalter*, 2 vols., Halle, 1900–5.
—— *Die Standesgliederung der Sachsen im frühen Mittelalter*, Tubingen, 1927.
—— *Übersetzungsprobleme im früheren Mittelalter*, Tübingen, 1931.
LANGLOIS (Charles V.), 'Les Origines de la noblesse en France', *Revue de Paris*, 1904, V (in relation to GUILHIERMOZ, *Essai* . . . , *q.v. supra*).
LA ROQUE (DE), *Traité de la noblesse*, 1761.
LINTZEL (M.), 'Die ständischen Ehehindernisse in Sachsen', *Zeitschrift der Savigny-Stiftung, G.A.*, 1932.
MARSAY (DE), *De l'âge des privilèges au temps des vanités*, 1934, and *Supplement*, 1933.
MINNIGERODE (H. VON), *Ebenburt und Echtheit. Untersuchungen zur Lehre von der adeligen Heiratsebenburt vor dem 13. Jahrhundert*, Heidelberg, 1932 (*Deutschrechtliche Beiträge*, VIII, 1).
NECKEL (Gustav), 'Adel und Gefolgschaft', *Beiträge zur Geschichte der deutschen Sprache*, XLVI, 1916.
NEUFBOURG (DE), 'Les Origines de la noblesse', in DE MARSAY, *Supplement* (*q.v. supra*).
OTTO (Eberhard F.), *Adel und Freiheit im deutschen Staat des frühen Mittelalters*, Berlin, 1937.
PLOTHO (V.), 'Die Stände des deutschen Reiches im 12. Jahrhundert und ihre Fortentwicklung', *Vierteljahrschrift für Wappen- Siegel- und Familienkunde*, XLV, 1917.
REID (R. R.), 'Barony and Thanage', *English Historical Review*, XXXV, 1920.
ROUND (J. H.), ' "Barons" and "Knights" in the Great Charter', in *Magna Carta: Commemoration Essays*, 1917.
—— 'Barons and Peers', *English Historical Review*, 1918.
SANTIFALLER (Leo), 'Über die Nobiles', in SANTIFALLER, *Das Brixner Domkapitel in seiner persönlichen Zusammensetzung*, I, pp. 59–64, Innsbruck, 1924 (*Schleiern-Schriften*, 7).
SCHNETTLER (Otto), *Westfalens Adel und seine Führerrolle in der Geschichte*, Dortmund, 1926.

BIBLIOGRAPHY

SCHNETTLER (Otto), *Westfalens alter Adel*, Dortmund, 1928.
SCHULTE (Aloys), *Der Adel und die deutsche Kirche im Mittelalter*, 2nd edn., Stuttgart.
VOGT (Friedrich), *Der Bedeutungswandel des Wortes edel*, Marburg, 1909 (*Marburger Akademische Reden*, 20).
WERMINGHOFF (Albert), 'Ständische Probleme in der Geschichte der deutschen Kirche des Mittelalters', *Zeitschrift der Savigny Stiftung, K.A.*, 1911.
WESTERBLAD (C. A.), *Baro et ses dérivés dans les langues romanes*, Upsala, 1910.

(2) DUBBING TO KNIGHTHOOD: THE LITURGIES

ANDRIEU (Michel), *Les Ordines Romani du haut moyen âge: I. Les manuscrits*, Louvain, 1931 (*Spicilegium sacrum lovaniense*, 11).
Benedictio ensis noviter succincti. Pontifical of Mainz: Ms. and ed. cf. ANDRIEU (*Les Ordines . . . , supra*), p. 178, and index, *s.v.* 'ensis'; facsimile, MONACI, *Archivio paleografico*, II, n. 73.
Blessing of the sword: Besançon Pontifical, cf. ANDRIEU, p. 445. Ed. MARTÈNE, *De antiquis ecclesiae ritibus*, II, 1788, p. 239; FRANZ, II, p. 294.
FRANZ (A.), *Die kirchlichen Benediktionen des Mittelalters*, 2 vols. Freiburg im Breisgau, 1909.
Liturgy for the dubbing: Reims Pontifical, cf. ANDRIEU, p. 112. Ed. HITTORP, *De divinis catholicae ecclesiae officiis*, 1719, col. 178; FRANZ, II, p. 295.
Liturgy for the dubbing: Pontifical of Gulielmus Durandus, ed. J. CATALANI, *Pontificale romanum*, I, 1738, p. 424.
Liturgy for the dubbing: *Pontificale romanum*, ed. by (among others) CATALANI, I, p. 419.

(3) MEDIEVAL TREATISES ON CHIVALRY

BONIZO, *Liber de vita christiana*, ed. PERELS, 1930 (*Texte zur Geschichte des römischen und kanonischen Rechts*, I), VII, 28.
CHRÉTIEN DE TROYES, *Perceval le Gallois*, ed. POTVIN, vol. II, vv. 2831 ff.
DER MEISSNER, 'Swer ritters name wil empfan . . .', in F. H. VON DER HAGEN, *Minnesinger*, III, p. 107, no. 10.
Lancelot, in H. O. SOMMER, *The Vulgate Version of the Arthurian Romances*, III, 1, pp. 113–15.
L'Ordene de Chevalerie in BARBAZAN, *Fabliaux*, 2nd edn. by MÉON, I, 1808, pp. 59–79.
NAVONE (G.), *Le rime di Folgore da San Gemignano*, Bologna, 1880, pp. 45–9 (*Scelta di curiosità letterarie*, CLXXII).
RAIMON LULL, *Libro de la orden de Caballería*, ed. by J. R. DE LUANCO, Barcelona, R. Academia de Buenos Letras, 1901. English trans., *The Book of the Ordre of Chivalry, translated and printed by W. Caxton*, ed BYLE;, 1926 (*Early English Text Society*, CLXVIII).

(4) MODERN WORKS ON CHIVALRY AND KNIGHTHOOD

BARTHÉLEMY (Anatole de), 'De la qualification de chevalier', *Revue nobiliaire*, 1868.
ERBEN (Wilhelm), 'Schwertleite und Ritterschlag: Beiträge zu einer Rechtsgeschichte der Waffen', *Zeitschrift für historische Waffenkunde*, VIII, 1918–20.
GAUTIER (Léon), *La Chevalerie*, 3rd edn., s.d.
MASSMANN (Ernst Heinrich), *Schwertleite und Ritterschlag, dargestellt auf Grund der mittelhochdeutschen literarischen Quellen*, Hamburg, 1932.
PIVANO (Silvio), 'Lineamenti storici e giuridici della cavalleria medioevale', *Memorie della reale Accademia delle scienze di Torino*, Series II, LV, 1905, *Scienze Morali*.
PRESTAGE (Edgar) (ed.), *Chivalry: A Series of Studies to Illustrate its Historical Significance and Civilizing Influence*, London, 1928.
ROTH VON SCHRECKENSTEIN (K. H.), *Die Ritterwürde und der Ritterstand. Historisch-politische Studien über deutsch-mittelalterliche Standesverhältnisse auf dem Lande und in der Stadt*, Freiburg im Breisgau, 1886.
SALVEMINI (Gaetano), *La dignità cavalleresca nel Comune di Firenze*, Florence, 1896.
TREIS (K.), *Die Formalitäten des Ritterschlags in der altfranzösischen Epik*, Berlin, 1887.

BIBLIOGRAPHY

(5) ENNOBLEMENT

ARBAUMONT (J.), 'Des anoblissements en Bourgogne', *Revue nobiliaire*, 1866.
BARTHÉLEMY (Anatole de) 'Étude sur les lettres d'anoblissement', *Revue nobiliaire*, 1869.
KLÜBER (J. L.), 'De nobilitate codicillari', in KLUBER, *Kleine juristische Bibliothek*, VII, Erlangen, 1793.
THOMAS (Paul), 'Comment Guy de Dampierre, comte de Flandre, anoblissait les roturiers', *Commission historique du Nord*, 1933; cf. P. THOMAS, *Textes historiques sur Lille et le Nord*, II, 1936, p. 229.

(6) LIFE OF THE NOBLES

APPEL (Carl), *Bertran von Born*, Halle, 1931.
BORMANN (Ernst), *Die Jagd in den altfranzösischen Artus- und Abenteuerroman*, Marburg, 1887 (*Ausgabe und Abhandlungen aus dem Gebiete der roman. Philologie*, 68).
DU CANGE, 'De l'origine et de l'usage des tournois. Des armes à outrance, des joustes, de la Table Ronde, des behourds et de la quintaine' (*Dissertations sur l'histoire de Saint Louis*, VI and VII), in *Glossarium*, ed. HENSCHEL, VII.
DUPIN (Henri), *La Courtoisie au moyen âge (d'après les textes du XIIe et XIIIe siècle)*, [1931].
EHRISMANN (G.), 'Die Grundlagen des ritterlichen Tugendsystems', *Zeitschrift für deutsches Altertum*, LVI, 1919.
ERDMANN (Carl), *Die Entstehung des Kreuzzugsgedankens*, Stuttgart, 1935 (*Forschungen zur Kirchen- und Geistesgeschichte*, VI).
GEORGE (Robert H.), 'The Contribution of Flanders to the Conquest of England', *Revue belge de philologie*, 1926.
GILSON (Étienne), 'L'Amour courtois', in GILSON, *La Théologie mystique de saint Bernard*, 1934, pp. 192–215.
JANIN (R.), 'Les "Francs" au service des Byzantins', *Échos d'Orient*, XXXIX, 1930.
JEANROY (Alfred), *La Poésie lyrique des troubadours*, 2 vols., 1934.
LANGLOIS (Charles-V.), 'Un Mémoire inédit de Pierre du Bois, 1313; De torneamentis et justis', *Revue historique*, XLI, 1889.
NAUMANN (Hans), 'Ritterliche Standeskultur um 1200' in NAUMANN (H.) and MÜLLER (Gunther), *Höfische Kultur*, Halle, 1929 (*Deutsche Vierteljahrschrift für Literaturwissenschaft und Geistesgeschichte*, Buchreihe, XVII).
—— *Der staufische Ritter*, Leipzig, 1936.
NIEDNER (Felix), *Das deutsche Turnier im XII. und XIII. Jahrhundert*, Berlin, 1881.
PAINTER (Sidney), *William Marshal, Knight-Errant, Baron and Regent of England*, Baltimore, 1933 (*Johns Hopkins Historical Publications*).
RUST (Ernst), *Die Erziehung des Ritters in der altfranzösischen Epik*, Berlin, 1888.
SCHRADER (Werner), *Studien über das Wort "höfisch" in der mittelhochdeutschen Dichtung*, Bonn, 1935.
SCHULTE (Aloys), 'Die Standesverhältnisse der Minnesänger', *Zeitschrift für deutsches Altertum*, XXXIX, 1895.
SCHULTZ (Alwin), *Das höfische Leben zur Zeit der Minnesinger*, 2nd edn., 2 vols., 1889.
SEILER (Friedrich), *Die Entwicklung der deutschen Kultur im Spiegel des deutschen Lehnworts*, II. *Von der Einführung des Christentums bis zum Beginn der neueren Zeit*, 2nd edn., Halle, 1907.
WHITNEY (Maria P.), 'Queen of Mediaeval Virtues: Largesse' in FISKE, C. F. (ed.), *Vassar Mediaeval Studies*, New Haven, 1923.

(7) HERALDRY

BARTHÉLEMY (A. de), 'Essai sur l'origine des armoiries féodales', *Mémoires de la Société des antiquaires de l'Ouest*, XXXV, 1870–1.
ILGEN (T.), 'Zur Entstehung und Entwicklungsgeschichte der Wappen', *Korrespondenzblatt des Gesamtvereins der deutschen Geschichts- und Altertumsvereine*, LXIX, 1921.
ULMENSTEIN (C. U. VON), *Über Ursprung und Entstehung des Wappenwesens*, Weimar, 1935 (*Forschungen zum deutschen Recht*, I, 2).

BIBLIOGRAPHY

(8) SERJEANTS AND SERJEANTIES

(For the German and French literature on this subject earlier than 1925, see the work of Ganshof listed below)

BLOCH (Marc), 'Un Problème d'histoire comparée: la ministérialité en France et en Allemagne', *Revue historique de droit*, 1928.

BLUM (E.), 'De la patrimonialité des sergenteries fieffées dans l'ancienne Normandie', *Revue générale de droit*, 1926.

GANSHOF (F. L.), 'Étude sur les ministeriales en Flandre et en Lotharingie', *Mémoires Acad. royale Belgique, Cl. Lettres*, in-8°, 2nd series, XX, 1926.

GLADISS (D. VON), *Beiträge zur Geschichte der staufischen Ministerialität*, Berlin, 1934 (*Ebering's Histor. Studien*, 249).

HAENDLE (Otto), *Die Dienstmannen Heinrichs des Löwen*, Stuttgart, 1930 (*Arbeiten zur deutschen Rechts- und Verfassungsgeschichte*, 8).

KIMBALL (E. G.), *Serjeanty Tenure in Mediaeval England*, New York, 1936 (*Yale Historical Publications, Miscellany*, XXX).

LE FOYER (Jean), *L'Office héréditaire de Focarius regis Angliae*, 1931 (*Bibliothèque d'histoire du droit normand*, 2nd series, 4).

STENGEL (Edmund E.), 'Über den Ursprung der Ministerialität', in *Papsttum und Kaisertum: Forschungen P. Kehr dargebracht*, Munich, 1925.

XI. THE CHURCH IN THE FEUDAL WORLD: THE 'ADVOCATESHIP'

It has not been considered necessary to include in the following list either general histories of the Church or works dealing with the various problems of ecclesiastical history proper. But the reader may be reminded of the value to the student of feudal society of A. HAUCK's great work (*Kirchengeschichte Deutschlands*, 5 vols., Leipzig, 1914–20) and the fine book of P. FOURNIER and G. LE BRAS (*Histoire des collections canoniques en Occident depuis les Fausses Decrétales jusqu'au Décret de Gratien*, 2 vols., 1931–2).

As many works—particularly German works—do not distinguish clearly between the closely related problems of the 'advocateship' and of judicial institutions in general, the bibliography in Section XII below should also be consulted.

GÉNESTAL (R.), 'La Patrimonialité de l'archidiaconat dans la province ecclésiastique de Rouen', *Mélanges Paul Fournier*, 1929.

LAPRAT (R), 'Avoué', in *Dictionnaire d'histoire et de géographie ecclésiastique*, V, 1931.

LESNE (E.), *Histoire de la propriété ecclésiastique en France*, 4 vols., Lille, 1910–38.

MERK (C. J.), *Anschauungen über die Lehre und das Leben der Kirche im altfranzösischen Heldenepos*, Halle, 1914 (*Zeitschrift für romanische Philologie*, Beiheft 41).

OTTO (Eberhard F.), *Die Entwicklung der deutschen Kirchenvogtei im 10. Jahrhundert*, Berlin, 1933 (*Abhandlungen zur mittleren und neueren Geschichte*, 72).

PERGAMENI (C.), *L'Avouerie ecclésiastique belge*, Gand, 1907. Cf. BONENFANT (P.), 'Notice sur le faux diplome d'Otton Ier' in *Bulletin—Commission royale histoire*, 1936.

SENN (Félix), *L'Institution des avoueries ecclésiastiques en France*, 1903. Cf. review by W. SICKEL, *Göttingsche Gelehrte Anzeigen*, CLVI, 1904.

—— *L'Institution des vidamies en France*, 1907.

WAAS (A.), *Vogtei und Bede im deutschen Kaiserzeit*, 2 vols., Berlin, 1919–23.

XII. JUDICIAL INSTITUTIONS

AULT (W. O.), *Private Jurisdiction in England*, New Haven, 1923 (*Yale Historical Publications, Miscellany*, X).

BEAUDOIN (A.), 'Étude sur les origines du régime féodal: la recommandation et la justice seigneuriale', *Annales de l'enseignement supérieur de Grenoble*, I, 1889.

BEAUTEMPS-BEAUPRÉ, *Recherches sur les juridictions de l'Anjou et du Maine*, 1890.

CAM (Helen M.), 'Suitors and Scabini', *Speculum*, 1935.

BIBLIOGRAPHY

CHAMPEAUX (Ernest), 'Nouvelles théories sur les justices du moyen âge', *Revue historique de droit*, 1935, pp. 101–11.

ESMEIN (A.), 'Quelques renseignements sur l'origine des juridictions privées', *Mélanges d'archéologie et d'histoire*, 1886.

FERRAND (N.), 'Origines des justices féodales', *Le Moyen Âge*, 1921.

FRÉVILLE (R. DE), 'L'Organisation judiciaire en Normandie aux XIIᵉ et XIIIᵉ siècles', *Nouvelle revue historique de droit*, 1912.

GANSHOF (François L.), 'Notes sur la compétence des cours féodales en France', *Mélanges d'histoire offerts à Henri Pirenne*, 1926.

—— 'Contribution à l'étude des origines des cours féodales en France', *Revue historique de droit*, 1928.

—— 'La Juridiction du seigneur sur son vassal à l'époque carolingienne', *Revue de l'Université de Bruxelles*, XXVIII, 1921–2.

—— 'Recherches sur les tribunaux de châtellenie en Flandre, avant le milieu du XIIIᵉ siècle', 1932 (*Universiteit de Gent, Werken uitgg. door de Faculteit der Wijsbegeerte en Letteren*, 68).

—— 'Die Rechtssprechung des gräflichen Hofgerichtes in Flandern', *Zeitschrift der Savigny Stiftung, G.A.*, 1938.

GARAUD (Marcel), *Essai sur les institutions judiciaires du Poitou sous le gouvernement des comtes indépendants: 902–1137*, Poitiers, 1910.

GARCIA DE DIEGO (Vicenze), 'Historia judicial de Aragon en los siglos VIII al XII', *Anuario de historia del derecho español*, XI, 1934.

GLITSCH (Heinrich), 'Der alemannische Zentenar und sein Gericht', *Berichte über die Verhandlungen der k. sächsischen Gesellschaft der Wissenschaften, Phil.-histor. Kl.*, LXIX, 1917.

—— *Untersuchungen zur Mittelalterlichen Vogtgerichtsbarkeit*, Bonn, 1912.

HALPHEN (L.), 'Les Institutions judiciaires en France au XIᵉ siècle: région angevine', *Revue historique*, LXXVII, 1901.

—— 'Prévots et voyers au XIᵉ siècle: région angevine', *Le Moyen Âge*, 1902.

HIRSCH (Hans), *Die hohe Gerichtsbarkeit im deutschen Mittelalter*, Prag, 1922.

—— *Die Klosterimmunität seit dem Investiturstreit*, Weimar, 1913.

KROELL (Maurice), *L'Immunité franque*, 1910.

LOT (Ferdinand), 'La "Vicaria" et le "vicarius" ', *Nouvelle revue historique de droit*, 1893

MASSIET DU BIEST (J.), 'A propos des plaids généraux', *Revue du Nord*, 1923.

MORRIS (W. A.), *The Frankpledge System*, New Haven, 1910 (*Harvard Historical Studies*, XIV).

PERRIN (Charles-Edmond), 'Sur le sens du mot "centena" dans les chartes lorraines du moyen âge', *Bulletin du Cange*, V, 1929–30.

SALVIOLI (Giuseppe), 'L'immunità e le giustizie delle chiese in Italia', *Atti e memorie delle R. R. Deputazioni di Storia Patria per le provincie Modenesi e Parmensi*, Series III, V and VI, 1888–90.

—— *Storia della procedura civile e criminale*, Milan, 1925 (*Storia del diritto italiano pubblicata sotto la direzione di Pasquale del Giudice*, III, Part I).

STENGEL (Edmund E.), *Die Immunität in Deutschland bis zum Ende des 11. Jahrhunderts*, I, *Diplomatik der deutschen Immunitäts-Privilegien*, Innsbruck, 1910.

THIRION (Paul), 'Les Échevinages ruraux aux XIIᵉ et XIIIᵉ siècles dans les possessions des églises de Reims', *Études d'histoire du moyen âge dédiées à G. Monod*, 1896.

XIII. THE PEACE MOVEMENTS

ERDMANN (C.), *Zur Überlieferung der Gottesfrieden-Konzilien*, in ERDMANN, *Die Entstehung . . .* (see part VIII, sect. 6 above).

GÖRRIS (G. C. W.), *De denkbeelden over oorlog en de bemoeeiingen voor vrede in de elfde eeuw* (Ideas on War and Efforts for Peace in the Eleventh Century), Nijmegen, 1912 (Leiden dissertation).

HERTZBERG-FRANKEL (S.), 'Die ältesten Land- und Gottesfrieden in Deutschland', *Forschungen zur deutschen Geschichte*, XXIII, 1883.

BIBLIOGRAPHY

HUBERTI (Ludwig), *Studien zur Rechtsgeschichte der Gottesfrieden und Landesfrieden:* I, *Die Friedensordnungen in Frankreich*, Ansbach, 1892.

KLUCKHOHN (A.), *Geschichte des Gottesfriedens*, Leipzig, 1857.

MANTEYER (G. DE), 'Les Origines de la maison de Savoie . . . La paix en Viennois (Anse, 17? juin 1025)', *Bulletin de la Société de statistique de l'Isère*, 4th series, VII, 1904.

MOLINIÉ (Georges), *L'Organisation judiciaire, militaire et financière des associations de la paix: étude sur la Paix et la Trève de Dieu dans le Midi et le Centre de la France*, Toulouse, 1912.

PRENTOUT (H.), 'La Trêve de Dieu en Normandie', *Mémoires de l'Académie de Caen*, New series, VI, 1931.

QUIDDE (L.), *Histoire de la paix publique en Allemagne au moyen âge*, 1929.

SCHNELBÖGL (Wolfgang), *Die innere Entwicklung des bayerischen Landfriedens des 13. Jahrhunderts*, Heidelberg, 1932 (*Deutschrechtliche Beiträge*, XIII, 2).

SÉMICHON (E.), *La Paix et la Trève de Dieu*, 2nd edn., 2 vols., 1869.

WOHLHAUPTER (Eugen), *Studien zur Rechtsgeschichte der Gottes- und Landfrieden in Spanien*, Heidelberg, 1933 (*Deutschrechtliche Beiträge*, XIV, 2).

YVER (J.), *L'Interdiction de la guerre privée dans le très ancien droit normand* (*Extrait des travaux de la semaine d'histoire du droit normand* . . . May, 1927), 1928.

XIV. THE INSTITUTION OF MONARCHY

BECKER (Franz), *Das Königtum des Nachfolgers im deutschen Reich des Mittelalters*, 1913 (*Quellen und Studien zur Verfassung des deutschen Reiches*, V, 3).

BLOCH (Marc), 'L'Empire et l'idée de l'Empire sous les Hohenstaufen', *Revue des Cours et Conférences*, XXX, 2, 1928–9.

—— *Les Rois thaumaturges: étude sur le caractère surnaturel attribué à la puissance royale, particulièrement en France et en Angleterre*, Strasbourg, 1924 (*Bibliothèque de la Faculté des Lettres de l'Université de Strasbourg*, XIX).

EULER (A.), *Das Königtum im altfranzösischen Karls-Epos*, Marburg, 1886 (*Ausgaben und Abhandlungen aus dem Gebiete der roman. Philologie*, 65).

KAMPERS (F.), 'Rex und sacerdos', *Historisches Jahrbuch*, 1925.

—— *Vom Werdegang der abendländischen Kaisermystik*, Leipzig, 1924.

HALPHEN (Louis), 'La Place de la royauté dans le système féodal', *Revue historique*, CLXXII, 1933.

KERN (Fritz), *Gottesgnadentum und Widerstandsrecht im früheren Mittelalter*, Leipzig, 1914.

MITTEIS (Heinrich), *Die deutsche Königswahl: ihre Rechtsgrundlagen bis zur Goldenen Bulle*, Baden bei Wien, [1938].

NAUMANN (Hans), 'Die magische Seite des altgermanischen Königtums und ihr Fortwirken', *Wirtschaft und Kultur. Festschrift zum 70. Geburtstag von A. Dopsch*, Vienna, 1938.

PERELS (Ernst), *Der Erbreichsplan Heinrichs VI.*, Berlin, 1927.

ROSENSTOCK (Eugen), *Königshaus und Stämme in Deutschland zwischen 911 und 950*, Leipzig, 1914.

SCHRAMM (Percy E.), *Die deutschen Kaiser und Könige in Bildern ihrer Zeit, I, 751–1152*, 2 vols., Leipzig, 1928 (*Veröffentlichungen der Forschungsinstitute an der Universität Leipzig, Institut für Kultur- und Universalgeschichte*, I).

—— *Geschichte des englischen Königtums im Lichte der Krönung*, Weimar, 1937 (English trans.: *A History of the English Coronation* (with general bibliography relating to the royal consecration, in Europe).

—— *Kaiser, Rom, und Renovatio*, 2 vols., Leipzig, 1929 (*Studien der Bibliothek Warburg*, XVII).

SCHULTE (Aloys), 'Anläufe zu einer festen Residenz der deutschen Könige im Mittelalter', *Historisches Jahrbuch*, 1935.

SCHULTZE (Albert), *Kaiserpolitik und Einheitsgedanken in den Karolingischen Nachfolgestaaten* (*876–962*), Berlin, 1926.

VIOLLET (Paul), 'La Question de la legitimité à l'avènement de Hugues Capet', *Mémoires de l'Académie des Inscriptions*, XXXIV, 1, 1892.

BIBLIOGRAPHY

XV. THE TERRITORIAL POWERS

ARBOIS DE JUBAINVILLE (D'), *Histoire des ducs et comtes de Champagne*, 7 vols., 1859–66.

AUZIAS (Léonce), *L'Aquitaine carolingienne (778–897)*, 1937.

BARTHÉLEMY (Anatole de), 'Les Origines de la maison de France', *Revue des questions historiques*, XIII, 1873.

BOUSSARD (J.), *Le Comté d'Anjou sous Henri Plantagenet et ses fils (1151–1204)*, 1938 (*Bibliothèque de l'École des Hautes Études, Sc. Histor.*, 271).

CHARTROU (Josèphe), *L'Anjou de 1109 à 1151*, 1928.

CHAUME (M.), *Les Origines du duché de Bourgogne*, 2 vols., Dijon, 1925–31.

FAZY (M.), *Les Origines du Bourbonnais*, 2 vols., Moulins, 1924.

FICKER (J.) and PUNTSCHART (P.), *Vom Reichsfürstenstande*, 4 vols., Innsbruck, Graz and Leipzig, 1861–1923.

GRIMALDI (Natale), *La contessa Matilde e la sua stirpe feudale*, Florence, [1928].

GROSDIDIER DE MATONS (M.), *Le Comté de Bar des origines au traité de Bruges (vers 750–1031)*, Bar-le-Duc, 1922.

HALBEDEL (A.), *Die Pfalzgrafen und ihr Amt: ein Überblick.* in HALBEDEL, *Fränkische Studien*, Berlin, 1915 (*Ebering's Historische Studien*, 132).

HALPHEN (Louis), *Le Comté d'Anjou au XIᵉ siècle*, 1906.

HOFMEISTER (Adolf), 'Markgrafen und Markgrafschaften im italienischen Königreich in der Zeit von Karl dem Grossen bis auf Otto den Grossen (774–962)', *Mitteilungen des Instituts für österreichische Geschichtsforschung*, VII. Ergänzungsband, 1906.

JAURGAIN (J. de), *La Vasconie*, 2 vols., Pau, 1898.

JEULIN (Paul), 'L'Hommage de la Bretagne en droit et dans les faits', *Annales de Bretagne*, 1934.

KIENER (Fritz), *Verfassungsgeschichte der Provence seit der Ostgothenherrschaft bis zur Errichtung der Konsulate (510–1200)*, Leipzig, 1900.

LA BORDERIE (A. le Moyne de), *Histoire de Bretagne*, vols. II and III, 1898–9.

LAPSLEY (G. T.), *The County Palatine of Durham*, Cambridge (Mass.), 1924 (*Harvard Historical Studies*, VIII).

LATOUCHE (Robert), *Histoire du comté de Maine*, 1910 (*Bibliothèque de l'École des Hautes Études, Sc. histor.*, 183).

LÄWEN (Gerhard), *Stammesherzog und Stammesherzogtum*, Berlin, 1935.

Les Bouches du Rhône, Encyclopédie départementale, part I, vol. II. *Antiquité et moyen âge*, 1924.

LEX (Léonce), *Eudes, comte de Blois . . . (995–1007) et Thibaud, son frère (995–1004)*, Troyes, 1892.

LINTZEL (Martin), 'Der Ursprung der deutschen Pfalzgrafschaften', *Zeitschrift der Savigny Stiftung, G.A.*, 1929.

LOT (Ferdinand), *Fidèles ou vassaux?*, 1904,

MANTEYER (G.), *La Provence du Iᵉʳ au XIIᵉ siècle*, 1908.

PARISOT (Robert), *Les Origines de la Haute-Lorraine et sa première maison ducale*, 1908.

POWICKE (F. M.), *The Loss of Normandy (1189–1204)*, 1913 (*Publications of the University of Manchester, Historical Series*, XVI).

PREVITÉ-ORTON (C. W.), *The Early History of the House of Savoy (1000–1223)*, Cambridge, 1912.

ROSENSTOCK (Eugen), *Herzogsgewalt und Friedensschutz: deutsche Provinzialversammlungen des 9.–12. Jahrhunderts*, Breslau, 1910 (*Untersuchungen zur deutschen Staats- und Rechtsgeschichte*, H. 104).

SCHMIDT (Günther), *Das würzburgische Herzogtum und die Grafen und Herren von Ostfranken vom 11. bis zum 17. Jahrhundert*, Weimar, 1913 (*Quellen und Studien zur Verfassungsgeschichte des deutschen Reiches*, V, 2).

SPROEMBERG (Heinrich), *Die Entstehung der Grafschaft Flandern*. Part I: *Die ursprüngliche Grafschaft Flandern (864–892)*, Berlin, 1935. Cf. F. L. GANSHOF, 'Les Origines du comté de Flandre', *Revue belge de philologie*, 1937.

TOURNADRE (Guy de), *Histoire du comté de Forcalquier (12th century)*, [1930].

VACCARI (Pietro), *Dall' unità romana al particolarismo giuridico del medio evo*, Pavia, 1936.

BIBLIOGRAPHY

VALIN (L.), *Le Duc de Normandie et sa cour*, 1909.
VALLS-TABERNER (F.), 'La Cour comtale barcelonaise', *Revue historique de droit*, 1935.
WERNEBURG (Rudolf), *Gau, Grafschaft und Herrschaft im Sachsen bis zum Übergang in das Landesfürstentum Hannover*, 1910 (*Forschungen zur Geschichte Niedersachsens*, III, 1).

XVI. NATIONALISM

CHAUME (M.), 'Le Sentiment national bourguignon de Gondebaud à Charles le Téméraire', *Mémoires de l'Académie des Sciences de Dijon*, 1922.
COULTON (G. G.), 'Nationalism in the Middle Ages', *Cambridge Historical Journal*, 1935.
HUGELMANN (K. G.), 'Die deutsche Nation und der deutsche Nationalstaat im Mittelalter', *Historisches Jahrbuch*, 1931.
KURTH (G.), 'Francia et Francus', *Études franques*, 1919, vol. I.
MONOD (G.), 'Du rôle de l'opposition des races et des nationalités dans la dissolution de l'Empire carolingien', *Annuaire de l'École des Hautes-Études*, 1896.
REMPPIS (Max), *Die Vorstellungen von Deutschland im altfranzösischen Heldenepos und Roman und ihre Quellen*, Halle, 1911 (*Beihefte zur Zeitschrift für roman. Philologie*, 234).
SCHULTHEISS (Franz Guntram), *Geschichte des deutschen Nationalgefühls*, I, Munich, 1893.
VIGENER (Fritz), *Bezeichnungen für Volk und Land der Deutschen vom 10. bis zum 13. Jahrhundert*, Heidelberg, 1901.
ZIMMERMAN (K. L.), 'Die Beurteilung der Deutschen in der französischen Literatur des Mittelalters mit besonderer Berücksichtigung der Chansons de geste', *Romanische Forschungen*, XIX, 1911.

XVII. FEUDALISM IN COMPARATIVE HISTORY

ASAKAWA (K.), 'The Origin of Feudal Land Tenure in Japan', *American Historical Review*, XXX, 1915.
—— *The Documents of Iriki Illustrative of the Development of the Feudal Institutions of Japan*, New Haven, 1929 (*Yale Historical Publications, Manuscripts and edited texts*, X). With an important introduction.
—— 'The Early Sho and the Early Manor: a Comparative Study', *Journal of Economic and Business History*, I, 1929.
BECKER (C. H.), 'Steuerpacht und Lehnwesen: eine historische Studie über die Entstehung des islamischen Lehnwesens', *Islam*, V, 1914.
BELIN, 'Du régime des fiefs militaires dans l'Islamisme et principalement en Turquie', *Journal Asiatique*, 6th series, XV, 1870.
DÖLGER (F.), 'Die Frage des Grundeigentums in Byzanz', *Bulletin of the International Commission of Historical Sciences*, V, 1933.
ECK (A.), *Le Moyen Âge russe*, 1933.
ERSLEV (K.), 'Europäisk Feudalisme og dansk Lensvaesen', *Historisk Tidsskrift*, Copenhagen, 7th series, II, 1899.
FRANKE (O.), 'Feudalism: Chinese', *Encyclopaedia of the Social Sciences*, VI, 1931.
—— 'Zur Beurteilung des chinesischen Lehnwesens', *Sitzungsberichte der preussischen Akademie, Phil.-hist. Kl.*, 1927.
FUKUDA (Tokusa), 'Die gesellschaftliche und wirtschaftliche Entwickelung in Japan', Stuttgart, 1900 (*Münchner volkswirtschaftliche Studien*, 42).
HINTZE (O.), 'Wesen und Verbreitung des Feudalismus', *Sitzungsberichte der preussischen Akademie, Phil.-Hist. Kl.*, 1929.
HÖTZCH (C. V.), 'Adel und Lehnwesen in Russland und Polen', *Historische Zeitschrift*, 1912.
LÉVI (Sylvain), *Le Nepal*, 2 vols., 1905 (*Annales du Musée Guimet, Bibliothèque*, XVII, XVIII).
LYBYER (A. H.), 'Feudalism: Saracen and Ottoman', *Encyclopaedia of the Social Sciences*, VI, 1931.

477

BIBLIOGRAPHY

OSTROGORSKY (Georg), 'Die wirtschaftlichen und sozialen Entwicklungsgrundlagen des byzantinischen Reiches', *Vierteljahrschrift für Sozial- und Wirtschaftsgeschichte*, 1929.

RUFFINI AVONDO (E.), 'Il feudalismo giapponese visto da un giurista europeo', *Rivista di storia del diritto italiano*, III, 1939.

SANSOM (J. B.), *Japan: A Short Cultural History*, 1938.

STEIN (Ernst), 'Untersuchungen zur spätbyzantinischen Verfassungs- und Wirtschaftsgeschichte', *Mitteilungen zur osmanischen Geschichte*, II, 1923–5.

THURNEYSSEN (R.), 'Das unfreie Lehen', *Zeitschrift für keltische Philologie*, 1923; 'Das freie Leben', *ibid.*, 1924.

UYEHARA (Senroku), 'Gefolgschaft und Vasallität im frankischen Reiche und in Japan' *Wirtschaft und Kultur: Festschrift zum 70. Geburtstag von A. Dopsch*, Vienna, 1938.

WOJCIECHOWSKI (Z.), 'La Condition des nobles et le problème de la féodalité en Pologne au moyen âge', *Revue historique de droit*, 1936 and 1937 (with bibliography).

SUPPLEMENT
TO THE BIBLIOGRAPHY

The following is a list of books and articles on feudal subjects published since 1939. Most of the works listed are concerned with feudalism and feudal institutions in the stricter sense, and this supplement is therefore narrower in scope than the original bibliography. But even within these limits it makes no claim to be exhaustive, and the omission of a publication implies no judgment as to its value.

L.A.M.

BALON (J.), *L'Organisation judiciaire des marches féodales*, 1951.

BARROW (G. W. S.), 'The Beginnings of Feudalism in Scotland' in *Bulletin of the Institute of Historical Research*, XXIX, 1956.

BERGENGRUEN (A.), *Adel und Grundherrschaft im Merowingerreich*, Wiesbaden, 1958.

BLOCH (Marc), *Les Caractères originaux de l'histoire rurale française*, 2nd edn., 2 vols., Paris, 1952 and 1956. (Vol. I is a reprint of the original edition of this fundamental work; Vol. II, *Supplément établi par Robert Dauvergne d'après les travaux de l'auteur*, is based on Bloch's later writings and the notes he had made in preparation for a new edition.)

BONENFANT (P.) and DESPY (G.), 'La noblesse en Brabant aux XIIᵉ et XIIIᵉ siècles. Quelques sondages' in *Le Moyen Age*, 1958.

BONGERT (Y.), *Recherches sur les cours laïques du Xᵉ au XIIIᵉ siècle*, Paris, 1949.

BORST (A.), 'Das Rittertum im Hochmittelalter. Idee und Wirklichkeit' in *Saeculum*, X, 1959.

BOSL (K.), *Die Reichsministerialität der Salier und Staufer*, 2 vols., Stuttgart, 1950–1. (Vol. X of *Schriften der Monumenta Germaniae Historica*.)

—— 'Vorstufen der deutschen Königsdienstmannschaft', *Vierteljahrschrift für Sozial- und Wirtschaftsgeschichte*, XXXIX, 1952, pp. 193–214; 289–315.

—— 'Der Wettinische Ständestaat im Rahmen der mittelalterlichen Verfassungsgeschichte' in *Historische Zeitschrift*, Vol. CXCI (1960).

BOUSSARD (J.), 'L'Enquête de 1172 sur les fiefs de chevalier en Normandie', *Mélanges Brunel*, Paris, 1955, I, pp. 193–208.

—— *Le Gouvernement d'Henri Plantagenet*, 1956.

—— 'Les mercenaires au XIIᵉ siècle. Henri II Plantagenet et les origines de l'armée de métier' in *Bibliotheque de l'École des Chartes*, 1945–46, pp. 189–224.

BOUTROUCHE (R.), *Seigneurie et féodalité*, I: *Le premier âge des liens d'homme à homme*, Paris, 1959.

BRUNEL (C.), 'Les Juges de la paix en Gévaudan au milieu du XIᵉ siècle' in *Bibliotheque de l'École des Chartes*, CIX, 1951, pp. 3–12.

BIBLIOGRAPHY

CAHEN (C.), *Le Régime féodal de l'Italie normande*, Paris, 1940.

CAM (H. M.), 'The Evolution of the Mediaeval English Franchise' in *Speculum*, XXXIII, no. 3, July, 1957.

Cambridge Economic History of Europe (ed. J. H. Clapham and Eileen Power), I, *The Agrarian Life of the Middle Ages*, 2nd edn., 1942. (Ch. VI, 'The Rise of Dependent Cultivation', is by Marc Bloch.)

CARABIE (R.), *La Propriété foncière dans le très ancien droit normand*, I, *La propriété domaniale*, Caen, 1943.

COHEN (G.), *Histoire de la chevalerie en France au moyen âge*, Paris, 1949.

COULBORN (R.) (ed.), *Feudalism in History* (studies in the comparative history of feudalism by various authors), Princeton, N.J., 1956.

CRONNE (H. A.), 'Historical Revisions, XCI. The Origins of Feudalism' in *History*, XXIV (1939–40), pp. 251–9.

DANNENBAUER (H.), 'Königsfreie und Ministerialen' in *Grundlagen der mittelalterlichen Welt*, Stuttgart, 1958.

DAVID (M.), *Le Serment du sacre de IXᵉ au XVᵉ siècle*, Strasbourg, 1951.

DHONDT (J.), *Études sur la naissance des principautés territoriales en France*, Bruges, 1948.

—— 'Les "solidarités" médiévales. Une société en transition: La Flandre en 1127–1128' (*Annales, E.S.C.*, 1957, pp. 529–60).

DIDIER (N.), *Le Droit des fiefs dans la coutume de Hainaut au moyen âge*, Lille-Paris, 1945.

DILLAY (M.), 'Le "Service" annuel en deniers des fiefs de la région angevine' in *Mélanges Paul Fournier*, Paris, 1949.

DOUGLAS (D. C.), 'The Norman Conquest and English Feudalism' in *Economic History Review*, IX, 1939, pp. 128–43.

DUBY (G.), *La Société aux XIᵉ et XIIᵉ siècles dans la région mâconnaise*, Paris, 1953.

—— 'La noblesse dans la France Medievale' in *Revue historique*, CCXXVI (1961), pp. 1–22.

ESLEY (F. N.), 'The *Fideles* in the County of Mâcon' in *Speculum*, XXX, no. 1, 1955, pp. 82–9.

FEUCHERE (P.), 'Essai sur l'évolution territoriale des principautés françaises (Xᵉ–XIIIᵉ siècles)' in *Le Moyen Age*, IV, 7 (1952), pp. 85–117.

GANSHOF (F. L.), *Qu'est-ce que la féodalité* (3rd edn. revised and enlarged), Brussels, 1957.

—— *Feudalism* (translation of 2nd edn. of above by Philip Grierson, with foreword by F. M. Stenton), London, 1952.

—— 'Benefice and Vassalage in the Age of Charlemagne' in *Cambridge Historical Journal*, VI, 1939, pp. 149–75.

—— 'Le Roi de France en Flandre en 1127 et 1128' in *Revue historique de droit français et étranger*, 4th series, XXVII, 1949, pp. 204–28.

—— 'Note sur le rattachement féodal du comté de Hainaut à l'église de Liége' in *Miscellanea Gessleriana*, Antwerp, 1948, pp. 508–21.

—— 'Manorial Organization in the Low Countries in the Seventh, Eighth and Ninth Centuries' in *Transactions of the Royal Historical Society*, 4th series, XXXI, 1949, pp. 29–59.

—— 'A propos de la cavalerie dans les armées de Charlemagne' in *C. R. Acad. Inscript.*, 1952–3, pp. 531–7.

—— 'L'Origine des rapports féodo-vassaliques. Les rapports féodo-vassaliques dans la monarchie franque au nord des Alpes a l'époque carolingienne' in *I Problemi della civiltà Carolingia*, Spoleto, 1954. (Settimane di Studi del Centro Italiano di Studi sull'Alto Medioevo, I, 1953).

—— 'Les Relations féodo-vassaliques aux temps post-carolingiens' in *I Problemi communi dell'Europa post-Carolingia*, Spoleto, 1955 (Settimane di Studi del Centro Italiano di Studi sull'Alto Medioevo, II, 1954).

—— 'Note sur l'apparition du nom de "hommage", particulièrement en France'. *Aus Mittelalter und Neuzeit. Festschrift für Gerhard Kallen*, Bonn, 1957.

—— 'Charlemagne et le serment' in *Mélanges Louis Halphen*, Paris, 1951.

479

BIBLIOGRAPHY

GAUSEIN (Roger), 'De la seigneurie rurale à la baronnie: l'abbaye de Savigny en Lyonnais', *Le Moyen Age*, vol. LXI, 1955, nos. 1–2, pp. 139–76.

GENICOT (L.), 'Le Destin d'une famille noble du Namurois. Les Noville aux XIIᵉ et XIIIᵉ siècles' in *Annales de la Société Archéologique de Namur*, XLVI (1953), pp. 157–232.

—— 'De la noblesse au lignage. Le cas des Boneffe' in *Revue belge de philologie et d'histoire*, XXXI (1953), pp. 39–53.

—— *Les Lignes de faîte du moyen âge*, Tournai and Paris, 2nd edn., 1952.

—— *L'Économie rurale namuroise au bas moyen âge. I. La seigneurie foncière*, Namur, 1943; *Les hommes, la noblesse*, Louvain, 1960.

HAGEMANN (A.), 'Die Stände der Sachsen' in *Zeitschrift der Savigny-Stiftung, Germ. Abt.*, 1959.

HIGOUNET (C.), 'Les Alaman, seigneurs bastidors et péagers du XIIIᵉ siècle' in *Annales du Midi*, 1956, pp. 227–53.

—— *Le Comté de Comminges de ses origines à son annexion à la couronne*, 2 vols., Toulouse and Paris, 1949.

—— 'Observations sur la seigneurie rurale et l'habitat en Rouergue du IXᵉ au XIVᵉ siècle' in *Annales du Midi*, 1950, pp. 121–34.

HOLLINGS (M.), 'The Survival of the Five Hide Unit in the Western Midlands' in *English Historical Review*, LXIII (1948), pp. 453–87.

HOLLISTER (W.), 'The Significance of Scutage Rates in Eleventh and Twelfth Century England' in *English Historical Review*, LXXV (1960), pp. 577–88.

—— 'The Annual Term of Military Service in Medieval England' in *Medievalia et Humanistica*, XIII (1960), pp. 40–47.

—— 'The Five Hide Unit and Military Obligation' in *Speculum*, XXXVI (1961), pp. 61–74.

—— 'The Norman Conquest and the Genesis of English Feudalism' in *American Historical Review*, LXVI (1961), pp. 641–63.

HOLLYMAN (M. K. J.), *Le Développement du vocabulaire féodal en France pendant le haut moyen âge, Étude sémantique*, Geneva and Paris, 1957.

JOHN (E.), *Land Tenure in Early England*, Leicester, 1960.

KEENEY (B. C.), 'Military Service and the Development of Nationalism in England' in *Speculum*, XXII, 1947, pp. 534–49.

—— *Judgement by Peers*, Cambridge, Mass., 1949.

KIENAST (W.), 'Untertaneneid und Treuvorbehalt', *Zeitschrift der Savigny-Stiftung für Rechtsgeschichte, Germ. Abt.*, LXVI, 1948, pp. 111–47.

—— *Untertaneneid und Treuvorbehalt in Frankreich und England*, Weimar, 1952.

KOCH (A. C. F.), 'L'Origine de la haute et de la moyenne justices dans l'ouest et le nord de la France' in *Revue d'histoire du droit*, 1953, pp. 420–58.

KOSMINSKY (E. A.), *Studies in the Agrarian History of England in the Thirteenth Century*, Oxford, 1956.

LEICHT (P. S.), 'L'introduzione del feudo nell'Italia franca e normanna' in *Rivista di storia del diritto italiano*, XII, 1939.

—— 'Il feudo in Italia nell'età Carolingia' in *I Problemi della civiltà Carolingia*, Spoleto, 1954 (Settimane di Studi del Centro Italiano di Studi sull'Alto Medioevo, I, 1953).

—— 'L'Organisation des grands domains en Italie du Nord pendant les Xᵉ–XIIᵉ siècles', *Société Jean Bodin, Recueil IV: Le Domaine*, 1949, pp. 165–76.

LEMARIGNIER (J. F.), *Recherches sur l'hommage en marche et les frontières féodales*, Lille, 1945.

—— 'Les Fidèles du roi de France (936–987)' in *Mélanges Brunel*, Paris, 1955, II, pp. 138–92.

LENNARD (R.), *Rural England, 1086–1135*, Oxford, 1959.

LLOYD (L. C.), *The Origins of Some Anglo-Norman Families* (Harleian Society, vol. CIII), London, 1951.

LOT (F.), *L'Art militaire et les armées au moyen âge en Europe et dans le Proche Orient*, 2 vols., Paris, 1946.

BIBLIOGRAPHY

LOT (F.) and FAWTIER (R.) (eds.), *Histoire des institutions françaises au moyen âge, I: Institutions seigneuriales*, Paris, 1957.

LOUSSE (E.), *La Société d'Ancien Régime*, I, Louvain, 1943.

LYON (B. D.), *From Fief to Indenture*, Cambridge, Mass., 1957.

—— 'The Money Fief under the English Kings, 1066–1485' in *English Historical Review*, LXVI, 1951, pp. 161–93.

—— 'Le Fief-rente aux Pays-Bas: sa terminologie et son aspect financier' in *Revue du Nord*, XXXV, 1953.

—— 'The fief-rente in the Low Countries. An Evaluation' in *Revue Belge de Philologie et d'Histoire*, XXXII, 1954.

MAYER (T.), *Fürsten und Staat*, Weimar, 1950.

MEYER (B.), 'Das Lehen in Recht und Staat des Mittelalters' in *Zeitschrift für schweizerische Geschichte*, XXVI, 1946, pp. 161–78.

MITTEIS (H.), *Die Rechtsidee in der Geschichte, gesammelte Abhandlungen und Vorträge*, Weimar, 1957.

MOR (C. G.), *L'età feudale*, 2 vols., Milan, 1952.

NAVEL (H.), *Recherches sur les institutions féodales en Normandie, région de Caen*. (Bulletin de la Société des Antiquaires de Normandie, Vol. LI; also published separately, Caen, 1951.)

ODEGAARD (C. E.), 'Carolingian Oaths of Fidelity' in *Speculum*, XVI, 1941, pp. 284–96.

—— *Vassi and Fideles in the Carolingian Empire*, Cambridge, Mass., 1945.

OLIVIER-MARTIN (F.), *Histoire du droit français des origines à la Révolution*, Paris, 1948.

PAINTER (S.), *Studies in the History of English Feudal Barony* (Johns Hopkins University Studies in Historical and Political Science, series LXI, no. 3), Baltimore, 1943.

—— 'Castellans of the Plain of Poitou in the Eleventh and Twelfth Centuries' in *Speculum*, XXXI, no. 2, 1956, pp. 243–57.

—— *French Chivalry: Chivalric Ideas and Practices in Mediaeval France*, Baltimore, 1940.

—— 'The Lords of Lusignan in the Eleventh and Twelfth Centuries' in *Speculum*, XXXVII, no. 1, 1957, pp. 27–47.

—— 'The Houses of Lusignan and Châterrault, 1150–1250' in *Speculum*, XXX, no. 3, 1955, pp. 374–84.

PERRIN (C. E.), 'Chartes de franchise et rapports de droit en Lorraine' in *Le Moyen Age*, 1946, pp. 11–42.

—— 'Le Servage en France et en Allemagne' in *X Congr. Internaz. di Scienze Stor. Relazioni*, III, Florence, 1955, pp. 213–45.

PERROY (E.), 'La noblesse foregienne et les ligues nobiliaires de 1314–1315' in *Bulletin de la Diana*, XXXVI (1959).

PLUCKNETT (T. F. T.), *A Concise History of the Common Law*, 4th edn., London, 1948.

—— *The Mediaeval Bailiff*, London, 1954.

—— *The Legislation of Edward I*, Oxford, 1949.

POOLE (A. L.), *Obligations of Society in the Twelfth and Thirteenth Centuries*, Oxford, 1946.

—— From Domesday Book to Magna Carta (The Oxford History of England), Oxford, 1950.

POWICKE (M. R.), 'The General Obligation to Cavalry Service under Edward I' in *Speculum*, XXVIII, no. 4, 1953, pp. 814–33.

PRESTWICH (J. O.), 'War and Finance in the Anglo-Norman State' in *Trans. Royal Hist. Soc.*, 5th series, vol. 4, 1954, pp. 19–43.

RICHARD (J.), 'Châteaux, châtelains et vassaux en Bourgogne aux XIᵉ et XIIᵉ siècles' in *Cahiers de civilisation médiévale*, 1960.

RICHARDOT (H.), 'Francs-fiefs: essai sur l'exemption totale ou partielle des services de fief' in *Revue historique de droit français et étranger*, 4th series, XXVII, 1949, pp. 28–63, 229–73.

—— 'Quelques textes sur la reprise de censive en fief' in *Revue historique de droit français et étranger*, 4th series, XXVIII, 1950.

481

BIBLIOGRAPHY

SANCHEZ-ALBORNOZ (C.), *En torno a los origenes del feudalismo*, 3 vols., Mendoza (Argentina), 1942.
—— *El 'stipendium' hispano-godo y los origenes del beneficio prefeudal*, Buenos Aires, 1947.
—— 'Espana y el feudalismo Carolingio' in *I Problemi della civiltà Carolingia*, Spoleto, 1954 (Settimane di Studi del Centro Italiano di Studi sull'Alto Medioevo, I, 1953).
SANDERS (I. J.), *Feudal Military Service in England*, 1956.
SCHEIDUNG-WULKOPF (I.), *Lehnsherrliche Beziehungen der fränkisch-deutschen Könige zu anderen Staaten vom 9. bis zum Ende 12. Jahrhunderts*, Marburg, 1948 (*Marburger Studien zur älteren deutschen Geschichte*, Reihe 2, 9).
SCZANIECKI (M.), *Essai sur les fiefs-rentes*, Paris, 1946.
SESTAN (E.), 'L'Italia nell'età feudale' in E. Rota, ed., *Questioni di storia medioevale*, Como-Milan, 1946, pp. 77–127.
STENGEL (E. E.), 'Land- und lehnrechtliche Grundlagen des Reichsfürstenstandes' in *Zeitschrift der Savigny-Stiftung für Rechtsgeschichte, Germ. Abt.*, 1948, pp. 294–342.
STENTON (F. M.), *Anglo-Saxon England* (The Oxford History of England), 2nd edn., Oxford, 1947.
—— *The First Century of English Feudalism, 1066–1166*, 2nd edn., revised, Oxford, 1961.
—— 'The Scandinavian Colonies in England and Normandy' in *Transactions of the Royal Historical Society*, 4th series, XXVII, 1945.
STEPHENSON (C.), 'The Origin and Significance of Feudalism' in *American Historical Review*, XLVI, 1941, pp. 788–812.
—— 'Feudalism and Its Antecedents in England' in *American Historical Review*, XLVIII, 1943, pp. 245–65.
Studien und Vorarbeiten zur Geschichte des grossfränkischen und frühdeutschen Adels (published under the direction of G. Tellenbach), Freiburg-im-Breisgau, 1957.
TELLENBACH (G.), *Königtum und Stämme in der Werdezeit des Deutschen Reiches*, Weimar, 1939.
VALDEAVELLANO (L. G. de), 'El prestimonio, contribución al estudio de las manifestaciones de feudalismo en los reinos de León y Castilla durante la Edad Media', *Ann. Hist. Derecho espan.*, XXV, 1955, pp. 5–122.
VERRIEST (L.), *Questions d'histoire des institutions médiévales. Noblesse, chevalerie, lignage. Condition des gens et des personnes. Seigneurie, ministérialité, bourgeoisie, échevinage.* Brussels, 1959.
—— 'Le Servage en Flandre, particulièrement au pays d'Alost', *Revue historique de droit français et étranger*, 1950, pp. 35–66.
WERNER (K. F.), 'Untersuchungen zur Frühzeit des französischen Fürstentums (9–10 Jahrhundert)' in *Die Welt als Geschichte*, 1958–60.
YVER (J.), 'Les Caractères originaux du groupe de coutumes de l'ouest de la France', *Revue historique de droit français et étranger*, 1952, pp. 18–79.

INDEX

INDEX

488

INDEX

manorial system, 49f, 442; in Germany, 267ff; survival of, 448
mansus (-*i*), 243, 332
Mansurah, 124, 307
manumission, 259
Marcel, Étienne, 325
Marignano, 316
markets, 67; as fiefs, 174; Viking, 21, 22
Markward of Anweiler, 343
Marmoutier, abbey of, 267
marquises, 395
marriage, 135, 226ff; of clergy, 345; consanguineous, 139n; repeated, 136; restriction of, 328; of retainers, 341; of serfs, 263, 267; of tenants, 258; of wards, 203; *see also* remarriage
Marseilles, 6, 7
marshal, 340, 343
Martel, Charles, *see* Charles Martel; Geoffrey, *see* Geoffrey Martel
Martigny, 39
Mass, the, 82
Massif Central, 397, 418
mathematicians, 74f
mathematics, 103
Maurille, archbishop of Liège, 63
Mauvoisin, Guy de, 124
May-day festivals, 83
Meaux, 425
Mediterranean, Vikings in, 19
Meissen, 199
Melun, 233, 423
memory, and law, 114, 115
mercenaries, 290
merchant class, 71; as fighters, 290; and knighthood, 322
Mercia, 18, 22, 42, 45, 391
Méréville, 64
Merovingians, 36, 80, 101, 149, 283, 388, 394; judicial system, 363; military system, 152; society under, 148
Merseburg, 193
Messay, 20
Metz, abbey of St. Arnulf, 275
Meurthe, river, 10
Meuse, river, 179, 306, 376, 378, 382
Mexico, 243
middle classes, urban, 69
migrations: Germanic, 15; Scandinavian, 16; causes of, 36f
Milan, 198
miles, 161f
millenarianism, 84f
ministeriales, 337ff; imperial, investiture of, 200
Minnesang, 310, 317
minors, as heirs, 201f
minting, 66
missi, 62, 394
missions, Christian, to Hungary, 14; to Scandinavia, 33f
Mistral, 176
mithium, 450
Mjösen, lake, 23
Modena, 41

Molesmes, abbey of, 63
monarchies (-y): English, 272, 375; European, 375ff
monasticism, decay of, 40
money, 66–8, 70f, 174; payments, on investiture, 206; *see also* aids
Mongolia, 13
Mongols, 54, 56
monks, 345; and epics, 95f, 98; wanderings of, 42, 63
monopolies, 251
Mons, 74
Mons-en-Pevèle, battle of, 323
Montbrison, Hospitallers of, 246
Montesquieu, xvii, xviii, 190, 426, 441
Montfort, Simon de, 316; sire de, 265, 400
Montmorency, lord of, 130
Montpellier, 117
Mont-Saint-Michel, 333
morality, 308
Morava, river, 11
Moravians, 9
Morigny, abbot of, 215
Morocco, 18
Morville-sur-Nied, 275
Moselle, river, 40
motte, 301
mund, 181
mundium, 150
mundporo, 225
Muntmen, 269
Mur, river, 11
murder, 128f
myths, 82

name-giving, 137f
names: family, 140f; personal, 45, 137; place, 46f
Namur, 215
Nantes, 18, 27, 30, 397
Naples, 394
Narbonne, 413, 423; Council of, 414
nationality, 431ff
nature, 72; inadequate knowledge of, 83
nature-rites, 82f
Navarre, 376
Neustria, 19, 176, 396
Nevers, 426; count of, 323
Newfoundland, 20
Nibelungenlied, 100, 136, 295, 308
Nicholas I, Tsar, 158
Nidaros, 35
niefs, 270, 271
Nimes, 10, 12
nobility, 283ff; distinctions among, 332ff; evolution in England, 329ff; — in France, 334ff; — in Germany, 336ff; exclusivity of, 328f; letters of, 323, 331; revolt against, 325; rules of conduct, 305ff; as warriors, 289; *see also* knighthood; knights
'noble', meaning, 286ff
Nogi, Marshal, 211
Noirmoutier, 20, 21
nomads: Asiatic, 8; military superiority, 54
non-prejudice, charters of, 115

INDEX

INDEX

Tagus, river, 5
taille, 223, 421; rural, 252*f*
tallage, 278; *see also taille*
Talmont, Sire of, 340
Talvas, 127, 141
Tannhaüser, 232
Taormina, 4
taxation, development of, 421, 430
Templars, 320*f*
tenancy, burdens of, 249*f*
tenants: free, 265; status of, 257
tenant-in-chief, 333
tenements: inheritance, 250*f*; manorial, 241: servile, 279; slave and free, 243
terriers, 249
Tertullian, 113
Teutons, 435
Thames, river, 17, 38
Thanet, Isle of, 21
thegn, 182, 183, 184, 185, 289; twofold meaning, 186
Theodoric the Great, 101
Theotisci, 435
Thérouanne, bishop of, 172
Thiais, 262
Thietmar, 193
thiudans, 382
Thomas Becket, St., 346, 369
Thomasin, 317
Thrace, 9, 11
Thuringia, 398
Tiel, 31
time: end of, 84*f*; indifference to, 74; measurement of, 73*f*
Tisza, river, 8
tithe(s), 174, 252; appropriation of, 252
tithings, 271
title-deeds, 115
titles, official, 335
Tivoli, 392
Tofi, 47
tolls, 174
tombs, Scandinavian, 35
Tostig, 62
Toul, 378, 402
Toulon, 39
Toulonges, 414
Toulouse, 176, 310; counts of, 284, 394, 395, 397*n*, 418
Touraine, 39, 195
Tournai, 299, 402
tournaments, 304*f*
Tournehem, 302
Tournus, 20
Tours, 149, 211
Toury, 64
tower, wooden, 301
towns: as commercial centres, 299; effects of Scandinavian attacks, 39; internal strife in, 127*f*; and law, 118; nobles and, 299; and villages, 353
Towthorpe, 47
trade, 65*ff*, 70*ff*; balance of, 66; law and, 360
tradition, oral legal, 109
traditionalism, 91

transitoriness of world, 84
Transjurania, 377*f*
translation(s), 78, 103
transport, 62*f*
travel, speed of, 62
treason, 118
Trent, Council of, 345
Tribur, Council of, 304
Trier, 168, 378
Trondhjem, 35
Trosly, 3
troubadours, 307
trouvères, 94, 96
Troyes, 397, 425; count of, 397*n*
truce of God, 412, 414, 418, 419
trustis, 155, 156
Turkestan, 66
Turkish languages, 8
Turks, 56
Turpin, archbishop, 93
Tuscany, 248, 381, 403
Tyrrhenian sea, 70

Ukraine, 16
unchastity, sacerdotal, 107
Upland, 25
Upsala, 34, 35
Urban II, pope, 113, 413*n*
Usagre, 124
Utrecht, bishop of, 31

Vacarius, 117
Vaik, king of Hungary, 13
Valais, 6
Valence, 379
Valenciennes, 442
Valerius Maximus, 104
va(r)let, 156
Van, lake, 296
Vannes, 30
Varangian kingdom, 36
Varennes-en-Argonne, 451
vassal(s), 155*f*, 442; in Anglo-Saxon England, 181; household and beneficed, 169; in Italy, 178; landless, 169; 'of the Lord', 159; methods of rewarding, 163*ff*; private, 160; relation to lord, 158; use of word in Spain, 186
vassalage, 145*ff*; Carolingian, 157*ff*; in the Church, 348; in England, 181*ff*; in France, 176*f*; in Germany, 179*ff*; in Italy, 177*ff*; Japanese, 447; law of, 327; obligations of, 147; quasi-family character, 224*f*; in Spain, 186*f*; as warriors, 289*ff*
vassi dominici, 159, 160, 171
vavasours, 296, 332, 334; in Lombardy, 197*f*; Norman, 177
Vegetius, 104
Velluto di Buonchristiano, 125*f*
vendetta, 125*ff*, 365; extent of obligation, 138*f*
Vendôme, 304; abbey of, 197
vengeance, 225, 412; *see also* vendetta
Venice, 64, 66, 70, 377, 385, 394
Ver, 114

498